Peoples of the Sea Wind

Peoples

of the Sea Wind

The Native Americans of the Pacific Coast

VINSON BROWN

Collier Books

A Division of Macmillan Publishing Co., Inc.
New York

Collier Macmillan Publishers

London

*Macmillan Publishing Co., Inc.
866 Third Avenue, New York, N.Y. 10022
Collier Macmillan Canada, Ltd.*

Library of Congress Cataloging in Publication Data

Brown, Vinson, 1912–
   Peoples of the sea wind.

   Bibliography: p.
   Includes index.
   1. Indians of North America—Pacific coast.
I. Title.
E78.P2B76   979'.004'97   76-30677
ISBN 0-02-517300-6
ISBN 0-02-030700-4 pbk.

First Collier Books Edition 1977

Peoples of the Sea Wind *is also available in a
hardcover edition by Macmillan Publishing Co., Inc.*

Designed by Jack Meserole

Printed in the United States of America

The tables of Appendix A are reproduced from
The Social Economy of the Tlingit Indians, *by
Kalvero Oberg, with kind permission of the
publisher, the University of Washington Press.*

To the native Americans of the Pacific Coast who are working to renew and understand some of the unique and wonderful elements of their cultural heritage

Acknowledgments

To the following people I wish to extend my sincere thanks for their help with this book: *Artists:* Mrs. Gladys Fox for her many fine drawings of Indian artifacts adapted from various sources, Robin Holmes for his art work on the Makah (Nootka) people. *Anthropologists and museums:* Dr. Albert Elsasser of the Lowie Museum of Natural History at the University of California in Berkeley for his help on the charts, Dr. Fred R. Milan of the Anthropology Department of the University of Alaska, the Southwest Museum of Los Angeles, Milwaukee Public Museum, the Smithsonian Institution of Washington D.C., the Thomas Burke Museum at the University of Washington, the Santa Barbara Museum of Natural History. *Native Americans:* to all the native Americans I have met and talked with along the coast from the Kamia in southern California to the Eskimo and Tlingit in Alaska, but especially to Elsie Allen, Pomo basket-maker, for permission to use pictures of her work. *Authors of books:* to all the authors of books and papers listed in the bibliography which have helped me gain greater insight into the lives and times of the Peoples of the Sea Wind as they were in the days of their glory and independence. To those I have not mentioned, their efforts on my behalf are still appreciated.

Contents

Introduction

The North Pacific Ocean is a caldron of weather-making in the winter and spring. The Sea Wind, which blows out of the northwest, but curves around to the south as the forerunner of storm, brings with it the dark clouds of rain or snow. In the summer and fall the wind blows more gently, but even then it brings the low clouds of the fog, creeping with ghostly arms up the valleys and canyons into the interior. From Cape Mendocino northward to Alaska, the coastlands are known for their cool days and the frequent blotting out of the sun; rarely are there extremes of heat or cold. But south of Cape Mendocino the wind is generally less blustery and warmer. Just a bit inland, the valleys are bathed in sunlight and heat for much of the year. The border between these two great climatic areas is also a dividing line between two different culture clusters of remarkable human beings of prewhite times, the Alaska-Aleut and Pacific Northwest Culture Areas to the north and the Central California and the Southern California (or Southwest) culture Areas to the south. I will try to make these native Americans along the Pacific Coast live for you in the pages of this book as they did in the days of old.

Many outworn and false ideas about native Americans, bred and nurtured by the white conquerors of this continent to justify their conquest and their treatment of those they conquered, now need to be put aside if we are truly to understand and appreciate the varied and wonderful peoples who once owned this land. Instead, let us be free and curious as the wind that blows, touching and questioning the surfaces of rocks and trees, hair and feather, fur and shell and skin of everything on this magnificent Pacific Coast. Where the sea wind went in centuries past we also shall go and see and hear what used to be.

Our civilization brought some good things to the Indians,

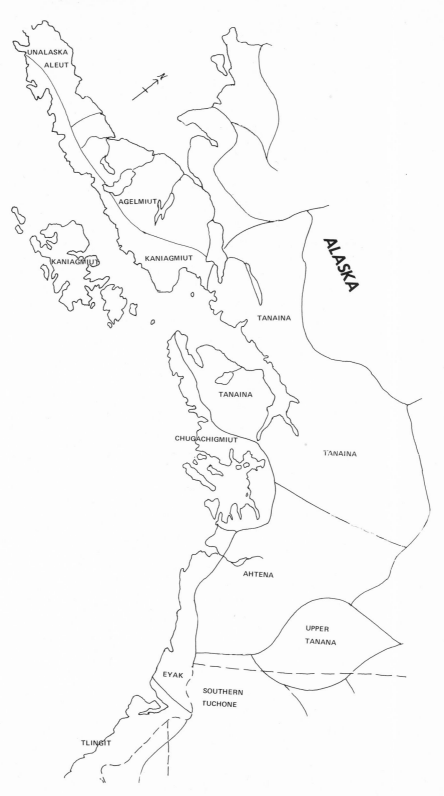

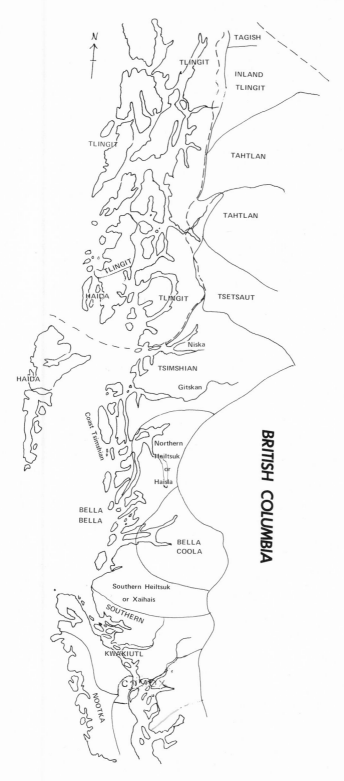

N

TAGISH

TLINGIT

INLAND
TLINGIT

TLINGIT

TAHTLAN

TAHTLAN

TLINGIT

HAIDA

TLINGIT

TSETSAUT

Niska

TSIMSHIAN

HAIDA

Gitskan

Coast Tsimshian

Northern
Heiltsuk
or
Haisla

BRITISH COLUMBIA

BELLA
BELLA

BELLA
COOLA

Southern Heiltsuk
or Xaihais

SOUTHERN

KWAKIUTL

COMOX

NOOTKA

including new and appetizing foods, more comfortable homes, useful gadgets, books, and other means of learning about the world. But it also brought many harmful things—more powerful weapons of war and more terrible wars, many new diseases, an increase in crime, harmful alcohol and drugs, and a disharmony with nature that in the end may destroy us all. At last, perhaps, we can see what they have to teach us—how to come into harmony with the earth—which in the end may be a greater gift than any we have given.

The coast is divided by anthropologists into four major culture areas: (1) the Eskimo-Aleut Culture Area of Alaska's south coast and islands, except for the southeast; (2) the vast Northwest Coast Culture Area from southeast Alaska to Cape Mendocino in northern California; (3) the Central California Culture Area from Cape Mendocino south to approximately San Luis Obispo and the Tehachapi Pass; and (4) the Southern California Culture Area south from this boundary into Baja California.

The Eskimo-Aleut Culture Area of Alaska, of which only the southwestern part is covered in this book, may be surprising to some readers. These Eskimos are quite different from the familiar Eskimos of the far northern ice with their ice-block igloos. Because of the warm Japan current, southwestern Alaska has comparatively little ice even in the depth of winter. The southwestern Alaska Eskimos and Aleuts are mainly open-sea hunters in kayaks and umiaks (skin boats), living in partly-underground houses with wooden frames and roofs. They differ from the Northwest Coast Culture Area Indians, whom they resemble in other respects, in wearing tailored skin clothing and in sometimes using sleds pulled by dogs. Their extremely pragmatic attitude toward life and their surroundings is also very Eskimo, and different from that of most Indians. They also have a terrific sense of humor!

The culture of the peoples of the Northwest Coast Area was and still is based largely on the seasonal coming of great masses of salmon, struggling upriver to the quiet gravelly spawning places in the streams above. Included in the fish catch of these people were several kinds of salmon as well as

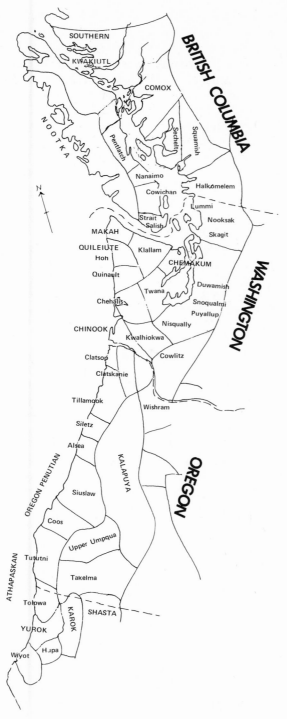

herring, trout, and the very oily eulachon or candlefish. In a few months, people in the old days could amass all the major food they needed for winter and fall. This gave them leisure time for arts and crafts, great ceremonies and dances. In addition, many sea mammals, such as sea otters, whales, and sea lions and other seals, were killed for their meat, fat, bones, and fine furs.

Two kinds of trees, the redwood tree in northwestern California and southwestern Oregon and the red cedar from northern Oregon north, were particularly important, for the wood could be split easily and was soft enough to carve. Out of this wood they built not only good weatherproof houses of wedge-split planks, some quite large (up to 500 feet long), but also sea- and river-worthy canoes, and handsomely carved boxes, dishes, and spoons, as well as the famous totem poles and other memorials to their spirit powers and ancestors.

They displayed their wealth in slaves, otter skins, dentalium money, and other luxuries to enhance their standing in their clans, and sometimes gave away vast quantities of things in their elaborate potlatches, which required the eventual giving back of a similar or greater amount. Yet this barbaric display was not without its humorous side, appreciated by both giver and taker. Its very magnificence and strangeness seemed exotic and startling to the first white men who saw it. Today the drab sameness of white culture overlays the beautiful and exciting masks, costumes, and ceremonies that have almost disappeared. Gone, too, are the savage wars, accentuated by the competition for the white man's gifts and trade, which wiped out many villages.

In the lower three-quarters of California, south of its northwest corner, were two more placid and simple areas of native culture where wealth did not take on the hectic quality of the northwest and where war was rarely heard of. Indeed California had the enviable record of having peoples of many diverse languages and backgrounds living next to each other in comparative harmony for many centuries.

The wants of these peoples were simple; yet their cultures often had beautiful complexities. In the simple-living mountain

tribes there was scarcely any specialization of work. This meant that each man and woman had to learn what in more complex societies would be the abilities of many different individuals—an impressive amount of skill and knowledge; these people survived in wilderness areas where a civilized man alone could not. However, in the great valleys, such as the Sacramento and San Joaquin, and those of southwestern California near the sea, the lowland peoples developed highly professional specialties in such areas as fishing, basketry, and medicine, little realized or understood by the white Americans who flooded upon them in the 1840s and '50s and contemptuously called them "diggers." Some of their religious ceremonies were among the most beautiful and complex in the world.

The Central California Culture Area owed none of its major culture elements to either the northwest or the southwest. It is true it had acorns as a major element of its food supply as did the south, and its clothing and housing were not markedly different either. But its major religion, the Kuksu Cult, with its fantastically beautiful feather costumes and highly original ceremonies and dances, was unique, and it lifted basketry, in the Pomo feathered baskets, to a supreme art of loveliness unequaled anywhere else.

The Southern California Culture Area was probably an extension of the vaster, and, in its center, much more complex Southwest Culture Area, whose leaders and chief innovators were found mainly among the Pueblo tribes. The southern Californians thus picked up from the Pueblos such developments as the use of pottery (in some areas), and the use of sand paintings in religious ceremonies. Yet they also developed some features uniquely their own. The Chumash of the Santa Barbara and Ventura County coasts reached a high degree of artistic development in the creation of beautifully designed steatite vessels and figures, and in cave paintings of fantastic intricacy and loveliness of design. Their maritime culture and fishing and marine-mammal hunting ability were based on a unique form of board boat or canoe, capable of very high speed and facile handling. Uniquely also, the Tongva (or Gabrieleno) people of what is now called the Los Angeles Basin developed and spread to other neighboring peoples a highly moral, one-god religion, rather astonishingly close in its strict laws and violent punishment of sins to the religion of the early Israelites.

The four culture areas listed earlier are compared in somewhat more detail in the appendix. It can be helpful to turn back to when you are reading about the different tribes. The same is true of the maps.

I have two main purposes in writing this book: first, to give the more distinctive facts about representative peoples of the four major culture areas, and second, to show through stories of individuals and families some of the spirit and essence of their people. This has not been an easy task; it has taken a tremendous amount of research, and has included talks with many native Americans from Alaska to southern California. I even had the unique experience of visiting with a tribe in Panama, the mountain Guaymi, still little touched by white civilization, and having one of them live with me on my ranch. Civilization had not yet inhibited and crushed much that was unique and creative in the past of these marvelous people.

The stories in this book are not meant to be complete life stories, but only insights into aspects of each people's culture and life that are particularly characteristic or helpful to our understanding of them. There is, of course, far more to learn if you are interested. These stories are just beginnings.

In the writings of the earlier anthropologists, such as Kroeber, Boas, and Merriam, I am able to see these peoples somewhat as they were two hundred years ago, and as I saw the Guaymi in Panama. I am indebted to all these writers, especially those who sincerely sought the truth, and to the many Indians with whom I have talked. I have not tried to equal the great anthropological works with their intimate details of the cultures of native Americans. Instead, I hope to provide a window through which to look into times different indeed from our own, a lost world with a fragrance, a quality, and a message we can all enjoy and learn from.

Note: The nine stories in this book on the old time life of different tribes can be assumed to have occurred between 1500 and 1700 A.D.

Peoples of the Sea Wind

1. The Southwest Alaskans

Along Alaska's southern border with the Pacific Ocean, for over 2,000 miles, there stretches a rugged and mountainous land. In prewhite times it was inhabited by several remarkable peoples, who were inured to storm and wave, fog and cold. But in two short centuries of conflict and economic and cultural change, their culture was all but wiped out by an encroaching and all-enveloping Western civilization. We must view them, as it were, through a glass darkly, for those who wrote about them with intelligence and sympathy often came too late to record them accurately as they were in the days of old.

Linguistically the peoples of this area are divided into two great divisions, the Eski-Aleut Language Stock, and the Athapaskan. The latter group touches the Pacific Ocean only at Cook Inlet (these people are the Tanaina), and along the clifflike and high mountain coast just west of Yakutat Bay (the Eyak), as can be seen on the map. The Eski-Aleut language is subdivided into Aleut and Eskimo, and the Eskimos themselves are divided linguistically into the Inupik (or Innuit) of the far north, stretching from Alaska to Greenland, and the Yupik, stretching from the middle of the Seward Peninsula down to the Pacific Ocean coast, where they meet the Aleuts in the Alaska Peninsula. The maps on pp. xii, xiii, xv, and xvii show the areas and names of the different tribes.

The area is divided into three biotic provinces, each with quite different flora, somewhat different land fauna, and very similar marine life. These are: (1) the Aleutian Biotic Province, (2) the Sitkan Biotic Province, and (3) the Eskimoan Biotic Province. The important marine life on which the natives strongly depended in the past included many mammals, among them the gray and the humpbacked whales, the white whale or beluga, the harbor porpoise, the bottle-nosed dolphin, the Steller's sea lion, the Alaska fur seal, the harbor seal, and the

1

sea otter. A common predator, much respected and feared, was the killer whale. For meat and eggs the people fed on puffins, auks, gulls, cormorants, guillemots, ducks, and geese. Mussels, clams, chitons, and crabs were gathered from the local rocky tide pools and mud flats by the sea.

The *Aleutian Biotic Province* covered all the Aleutian Islands, the Alaskan Peninsula, and a large part of the Kodiak Island chain, stretching for nearly 1,500 miles across the North Pacific. Precipitation is from 25 to 50 inches of rain, much dryer than the coast to the east. The ragged southern shoreline of the peninsula and Kodiak Island provides ideal habitats for marine animals in the many sheltered coves and bays. Generally this province has few trees, mostly willows and alders along the streams. Most of the area is covered by grasses, ferns, and wildflowers in summer, when days are very long and comparatively mild. But on the Aleutian Islands the conflict between cold Bering Sea and warm Japan Current (south of the islands) produces almost constant storm or fog.

Several kinds of salmon ascended the streams in great numbers, and the herring, halibut, and candlefish were also numerous and important as food fishes. Willow and rock ptarmigans were important game birds on land, while the Barren Grounds caribou, hoary marmot, moose, giant brown bear, porcupine, river otter, red fox, gray wolf, and wolverine were much hunted and trapped by the natives for their skins and meat.

The *Sitkan Biotic Province* formed a narrow strip along the southern edge of Alaska from the southeast to the Seward Peninsula and the northeast parts of the Kodiak Island chain, also continuing into the southeast of Alaska. Great mountains formed a barrier inland that kept out not only hostile people

INTERIOR OF AN UNALASKA ALEUT HOUSE. It is built for the most part underground; the ladder leads to the smoke hole; mats hide various sleeping chambers; oil lamps give fire and heat. (*New York Public Library*)

but also the cold winds and heavy snows of the north, while the Japan Current brought air warm enough to cause much more rain than snow, from 100 to 200 inches a year. Fjords and many bays and sounds stretch inland, and there are frequent islands along the indented coastline. Here great forests dominated by hemlocks, spruces, and cedars line the shores even today, while willows, cottonwoods, and rarer paper birches are found near the streams. Many forms of edible berry bushes form the undercover and are plentiful on the higher, more open slopes too. Important mammals include the mountain goat, moose, black and giant brown bear, the hoary marmot, snowshoe hare, porcupine, gray wolf, river otter, and wolverine. Important land birds for food are the willow ptarmigan and the spruce grouse.

The *Eskimoan Biotic Province* is found farther inland in colder areas and is an area generally of tundra and low plants except for willows along the streams. The Barren Grounds caribou was by far the most important animal food for the natives.

In this whole area, as well as in the vast majority of all the areas south from here to Baja California, the social foundation of human life in the old days was the village or the family camp; rarely did these peoples ever band together in larger units. There were practically no true tribes with central political control. When I use the word *tribe* I mean a linguistic or ethnic, not a political, association.

The Aleuts (Aleutian Biotic Province)

The Aleuts were an Eskimolike people, though with somewhat different customs, whose habitat was the wind-ravaged and fog-shrouded Aleutian Islands and the tip of the Alaskan Peninsula. Their houses were mainly built underground, except for a wood-board roof, to avoid the worst of the weather,

ESKIMO WEAPONS OF SOUTHWESTERN ALASKA: **A** sinew-backed bow; **B** leister spear for fish; **C** arrow; **D** bird spear; **E** blunt bird arrow; **F** harpoon with detachable point and cord line; **G** bird spear. (*Drawings by Gladys Fox after Oswalt*)

though most men bathed in the cold seawater daily. Elements of material and social culture that distinguished these people from the neighboring Eskimos were both negative and positive. For example, they did not use hot steam baths like the nearby Eskimos, and they did comparatively little hunting of large whales as did the Pacific Ocean-based Eskimos. They were noted for their hospitality to strangers, until the Russians and other white men ruined this by treating them badly. They gave presents without expecting a return, unlike the Pacific Ocean-based Eskimos and Indians like the Tanaina and the Tlingit.

They were probably the most expert of all kayak men, possibly because of their storm-beaten islands and because their main living came from the sea. They were able to break through gigantic waves in these small craft, and maneuver them through hours of vicious storm home to safety. Sealed-in air kept the waterproof sealskin kayaks afloat in heavy seas. They did not ship water, as their waterproof skin clothing was laced to the edge of the kayak's seat hole. Many sea mammals streamed through these islands in fall and spring migration and were vigorously hunted by the Aleuts, using their kayaks, spears, harpoons, and darts that were hurled by aid of a strange, boardlike instrument. They also shot seabirds with special three-pronged arrows and skillfully trapped them with nets.

There is some indication that in the old days the Aleuts had larger and better organized political units than the Eskimos whom they often captured as slaves.

Left UNALASKA MAN: wearing a visor to protect his eyes from the glare of sun on ice, from a painting by John Webber, 1778. (*Peabody Museum, Harvard University*)

Right CHUGACHIGMIUT ESKIMO MAN OF PRINCE WILLIAM SOUND: from a painting by John Webber, 1778. The bone nose ornament and three lip labrets of shells are commonly worn by southwestern Alaska Eskimos. (*Peabody Museum, Harvard University*)

The Agelmiut

The ending "miut" of the Eskimo tribal names usually means "people." Very little is known about the Agelmiut. They came into the Alaskan Peninsula just west of the Kaniagmiut and east of the Aleuts at the beginning of the exploration and colonization of Alaska by the Russians. They apparently were so quickly adulterated by Russian contact that most of their old culture was soon lost.

The Chugachigmiut or Chugach (Sitkan Biotic Province)

These people were far removed in appearance and social life from what we think of as typical Eskimo. In their home around Prince William Sound they were much influenced by the neighboring Tlingit and the Athapaskan Eyak, with whom they were often at war. Their houses, which were closely similar to the Tlingit slab houses and mainly above ground, were different from the usual semisubterranean houses of other Alaskan Eskimos, though they did often use giant whale bones to form their roofs. They also had borrowed from the Tlingit a full type of potlatch, a ceremony and dance at which numerous gifts were bestowed and expected to be returned in equal or greater amounts. And they in turn had passed on knowledge of whale hunting with aconite-poisoned, slate-tipped harpoons or lances to the nearest colony of Tlingit at Yakutat Bay.

The Chugachigmiut hunted bear and other animals while dressed like a bear; tattooed the backs and breasts of their women; allowed their slaves to marry free people (though the Kaniagmiut did this, too); used wooden slats for armor (like the Tlingit); and had no communal building for ceremonies and dances. They shared with the Kaniagmiut a culture item apparently borrowed from the inland Athapaskan tribes—sweathouses or sweat rooms. These rooms, in larger dwellings, contained hot rocks over which water was thrown to produce steam. In other respects, their culture and life was much like the Kaniagmiut, as may be seen in the story on p. 7.

A

B

C

D

E

The Kaniagmiut or Koniag (part Sitkan and part Aleutian Biotic Province)

These people were probably the wealthiest and most numerous of all the Eskimo tribes, at least on their main living area, Kodiak Island. This huge island off the coast of southern Alaska and its associated islets were rich in natural resources. There were deer, caribou, grouse, sea mammals, salmon and other large fish, clams, chitons, and other rocky shore life, as well as a plentiful supply of wood for carving and building from the spruce and hemlock forests on its northeast end. Consequently, the Kaniagmiut, unlike most other Eskimos, were rarely in danger of periods of starvation. That they generally built their villages on high points of land and often fortified them showed, however, that they did suffer from occasional invading war parties of Aleuts, Tanaina Athapaskans, Chugachigmiuts, and even Tlingits. However, their position 20 miles out in an often stormy ocean probably prevented such attacks from becoming very intensive.

They shared with the Chugachigmiut a highly developed whale-hunting technique, strangely similar in certain ways to that of the Nootka whale hunters far to the south (see chapter 5). They also shared with the Chugachigmiut the habit of mummifying their more noble dead, and the distinction of three classes of people: nobles, commoners, and slaves. They wore a skin parka, often with open armholes, and without pants or footwear except in very severe weather. The breasts and cheeks of their women were tattooed. They had dance leaders who also acted as a kind of priesthood, teaching morals and ceremonial conduct to the youth.

ARTIFACTS OF SOUTHWESTERN ALASKA: **A** slate-bladed knife; **B** adze with stone blade; **C** stone maul; **D** flaker for flaking rock points; **E** ulu or curved knife; **F** chisel with rock point held by wooden handle; **G** scribing knife; **H** slate adze; **I** strap twirled drill; **J** flint knife. (*Drawings by Gladys Fox after Oswalt*)

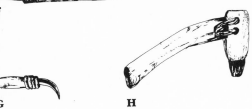

F

G

H

I

J

Hunting the Giants of the Sea

TUSERPIK lived in the large four-family house of his noble uncle, the famous whale hunter, Kahmonoshar. Here the young man was training to be a whale hunter, learning the secret esoteric and magic techniques that only a few were ever taught. He worked at long and arduous lifting and throwing of larger and larger rocks to strengthen his muscles for the plunging of the heavy killing lance into the vitals of a giant whale. He spent four days in a cave without food or water, praying and meditating beside the mummified bodies of hero ancestors who also had been famous whale hunters. But these were not the greatest difficulties in his training and initiation. Rather, it was the presence in the home of a slender teen-aged girl slave, Tiviat. She was no ordinary slave but a princess, daughter of a Yakutat Tlingit chief, who had been captured on a war expedition a few years before.

She was a lovely but secretive girl. She had dug her own room in the earth wall of the semisubterranean house, lined it with spruce boards, and waterproofed it with pitch, so she could have her own privacy. She had even insisted sweetly that

ESKIMO VILLAGE ON ALASKA'S SOUTHWEST COAST. Note partially underground dwellings, large nets for fishing, seaweed drying on rack, and kayak boat with double-bladed paddle. (*Diorama by Elizabeth Mason, Southwest Museum, Los Angeles*)

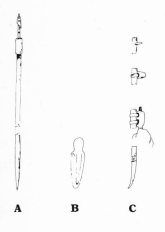

A   B   C

D

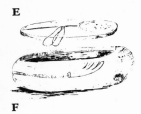

E

F

all the pits in the house, used for the disposal of body waste, be covered over with dirt after each use. (The Tlingits dug holes in the woods behind their homes for use as outdoor privies.) She claimed that otherwise the smell made her sick; and she had enough force of character to convince Kahmonoshar that this was a better method for his whole household. Kahmonoshar's first wife, Thala, had grumbled at first, but Tiviat had shown her a better way to weave mats out of grasses and cedar bark and won her approval.

"That girl," Thala grudgingly admitted to Tuserpik, "is going to make somebody a wonderful wife, but your uncle, who is as fond of her as if she were his own daughter, says he is going to free her and send her back to her family unless some young man of our tribe can win her love fairly." She glanced slyly at Tuserpik as he turned his face away to hide his emotions.

Tuserpik knew he had to win the help of a guardian spirit, preferably one of the spirits who represented one of the great whales, before his uncle would let him try to kill a whale on a trip with him. But his first try at fasting had been a failure; he had been thinking too much about Tiviat. Now he swore to himself that next time he would concentrate his mind on the ghost of his mighty ancestor, and find the spirit help he needed. So now he turned his head away resolutely every time Tiviat entered the cooking room, until she was curious about his actions; while Thala jokingly asked: "Are you playing hard to get?" and laughed uproariously, as the Eskimo love to do, when his face turned crimson.

The following night in the cave high on the hillside with the mummies of the dead all about him, he kept his eyes on the body of his hero ancestor, and sang:

ESKIMO WEAPONS AND ARTIFACTS OF SOUTHWESTERN ALASKA: **A** typical harpoon and parts; **B** different kind of harpoon blade; **C** connections for attaching sealskin floats to harpoon head or cord; **D** decorated wooden storage box; **E** wooden box top; **F** wooden foot box; **G** paint box; **H** wooden toolbox; **I** carved turtle dish. (*Drawings by Gladys Fox after Oswalt*)

G

H

I

My eyes are on you, son of the waters,
You who followed the great whale to his den in the seas.
The Spirit of all the Whales was inside you, singing his power
Come to me also, Master of Whales, spirit who helped my
    grandfathers.
Show me the way to sing the whales in from the sea,
To do honor to them that we may eat them, giving their bones
    back to the sea,
Honoring them in death that they may live again and follow the
    dark pathways of the waters.

Over and over he sang this new song, and always he kept his
eyes fastened on the mummy, his thoughts on the whale spirit,
his body growing weak from lack of food and water, but his
spirit remaining strong. At last, on the fourth night, his body
and mind had been cleansed of all material things by the fasting, praying, and singing. Into that crystal clarity a great form
swam in his dreams, the flukes churning white waves of foam,
an immense eye looking at him with fathomless wisdom, as a
deep voice said: "We hear you grandson; we will help you!"
And he saw the dark gray body, marked with white barnacles,
and knew it was the spirit of the gray whale that spoke to him.

When his uncle, Kahmonoshar, found him in the morning,
he told the famous hunter of his dream. The older man laughed
in delight and beat him on the shoulder with a powerful hand.
"Now you are a man!" he exclaimed. "Now I can show you the
sacred ceremony, and give you the amulets, the secret things of
power. We will do this now in the cave of our ancestors, with
their bones about us, and their souls watching us."

He had Tuserpik kneel with him before the mummy of the
hero, and he took from a skin bag he was carrying certain
sacred things, amulets, that no other man can be told about,
because these are the secrets of the Kaniagmiut whale hunters
alone, and he asked that the whale spirit bless them. Then he
took a great skull of a whale from the back of the cave, a skull
it took all the strength of both of them to move, and turned it
so it could hear the sound of the sea, the far off rumbling of the
waves. Then he took a knife and cut a small cut in his finger

and in Tuserpik's, so the blood flowed. He mingled the two bloods together in a thimble of whale skin and painted the side of the whale's skull with it. Then he sang:

"Now we be of one blood with the whale people. Their flesh we ask from them, but we give their bones back to the sea that they may live again."

When Tuserpik followed Kahmonoshar back to the village, he walked as a true man must walk, a whale hunter, his back arched with pride despite his weakness from fasting. That night he slept deeply, dreaming of whales and of the feast the people would have in his honor when he brought back one of the noble lords from the singing sea. But Tiviat was in his dreams also.

From the age of ten, when he had been given his first small kayak, Tuserpik had learned to paddle with the two-bladed paddle, and to find his way on the waters. Now, when they put the large, two-man, two-hole kayak into the waves in the early dawn, he was doing what he had already done for several years. He helped his uncle push the boat out with considerable expertise, and they both leaped into the holes that would hold them. Quickly he fastened the skin flaps about his parka-clad body with a line of rawhide, tight enough to keep out water from his lower body even if they were turned turtle with a wave. And about his neck also the waterproof sealskin parka with its hood was tied tightly to keep out the sea.

Tuserpik was in the hole in front of the kayak for the first time in his life, with Kahmonoshar behind him as steersman and main paddler. The younger man would be the thrower of the razor-sharp, slate-pointed, poison-tipped spear. The secret formula for that poison, made of aconite poison from the monkshood flower, poison also from the backs of toads, and probably other things, was known only to Kahmonoshar, but would be taught to Tuserpik when the younger man proved himself as a whale hunter. Two of the poisoned spears, their points hidden and protected by skin sleeves, were fastened to the thwart beside the younger man, ready for use when the time came. But whether his heart and muscles were ready, he was not sure, though he had watched and helped the older hunter many a time and knew what to do.

Kahmonoshar let Tuserpik take full command of the expedition, signaling by hand which way to turn the kayak as they cruised out into the great bay. Steadily they paddled farther and farther from the little village on the hill, the waves gradually getting a little stronger and higher as they approached the open ocean. The kayak rode the seas like a duck and the feeling of being master of the waters was glorious. Tuserpik always enjoyed the adventure of these trips, the singing of the wind in his hair, the touch of the spray on his dark cheeks, the cries of gulls and terns and kittiwakes against the sky, the black form of a cormorant skimming the waves, then diving beneath them to fly-swim after the fish. But this time his nerves were taut and under his breath he was singing his new sacred song, his spirit seeking beneath the heaving seas the coming of the noble whale, his eyes scanning the waters constantly for the sign of a spout, the breath of the whale after it surfaced forming a pear-shaped cloud of moisturized air against the sky.

All day they cruised and hunted without seeing the great whales, though they saw a few belugas or white whales and, in the distance, the great black dorsal fins of killer whales. By late afternoon Tuserpik was growing discouraged, when suddenly he held up his hand and pointed toward the open ocean. A spout broke upward into the air out there, spread out and gracefully faded into the sky, then another and another!

"A herd!" he called excitedly, above the splashing sounds of the waves on the kayak's hull. The two drove the kayak swiftly forward till it seemed to skim the wave tops, as silently as a swimming seal. When they drew near the herd they could tell they were gray whales by the short and narrow pearlike spouts, given quickly one after another. They knew the whales were feeding on amphipods at the shallow bottom of the bay, one by one diving down into the depths, then surfacing to suck in great gasps of air after several minutes below. The water came roiling and foaming white out of their mouths, as they threw their heads up out of the sea so that gravity could help them down their food, which was trapped behind the baleen or whalebone sieve behind their lips.

Now, as the hunters approached very cautiously, Tuserpik lashed his paddle to the side of the kayak, and unloosed one of the long keen slate-pointed lances, drawing off the hood from its dark-poisoned tip. Slowly, slowly they came closer to the whales, Kahmonoshar paddling with great care so as not to make the slightest splash, the kayak going shadow-quiet over the waves. Now Tuserpik made himself ready on his knees, the lance in his right hand raising slowly. There was no need any longer to signal Kahmonoshar, as the experienced hunter eased the boat straight for the critical point right behind the left front flipper of a huge gray bull.

Tuserpik, seeing the bull's immense size and knowing the power of those great flukes to crush his kayak like a gull's egg, felt a spasm of fear. With a fierce effort of his will, he overcame this fear. Then he rose as high as he could on his knees, as the boat slipped silently up beside the bull, aimed his point at the base of that great forward fluke, and threw his whole body and arm into a movement forward and down, the lance blade burying itself deep into the whale's left side.

The lance was instantly jerked from his hands as the huge bull jumped, and he pulled himself quickly back into the kayak hole. Kahmonoshar let out a yell, dug his paddle deep, and shot the kayak forward with one mighty heave. At the same instant the body of the whale turned down, the great gray flukes tipped up and then smashed down where the boat had been a second before! Down the bull dove, almost straight down, trailing blood, the detachable back length of the lance floating on the waves where Tuserpik soon seized it.

"A good thrust of the lance," approved Khamonoshar. "Now we must wait for the poison to take effect. We can go back to the village and try to sing the whale in from there in the sacred cave with our honored ancestors, or we can stay out and sing him in from here."

"Let us stay out," replied Tuserpik. "I saw the tall black fins of killer whale bulls only a while ago. If they find this dying bull, they will tear him to pieces before we can get him ashore."

"You would fight the killer bulls of the seas!" exclaimed Kahmonoshar. "We can do nothing against them. They are the ocean chiefs!"

"I will fight them if I have to," said Tuserpik, "and I have a way to fight them that I will show you. Let us find a kelp bed, for I have an idea."

Searching over the bay waters, they soon found a floating bed of kelp with its long hollow brown stems rising out of the sea to the floats and leaves on the surface. Tuserpik found some stems that had been broken loose by storms from the bottom holdfasts, and cut them into two 30-foot lengths, which he tied to the kayak, dragging them behind like tails.

"What are you going to do with those?" asked Kahmonoshar.

"We know that sound carries farther and louder underwater than in air. We will roar our voices into one end of these pipes, keeping the other end underwater, perhaps, even on the other side of the whale when we find him and if the killers come. I hope our roaring will keep them away."

"It is worth a try!" exclaimed Kahmonoshar, looking at the younger hunter with respect, for Eskimos are very inventive and honor this ability.

Soon they were cruising back and forth over the bay waters, watching for the poisoned whale. It was summertime, so the daylight hours stretched clear through the Arctic nighttime, with the sun only just below the horizon at midnight, and plenty of light still on the waters. Each took a turn dozing and sleeping in his warm skin clothing while the other stayed on watch. When they felt hungry they dipped into stored baskets of dried salmon flesh they carried in the kayak; each also had a seal's stomach pouch filled with water by his hole in the kayak.

As sunlight came back with a new day, both began to sing

at intervals, Tuserpik singing his new whale medicine song, while his uncle sang the ancient songs passed down from the famous whale hunters of the past. At noon they again sighted the great gray bull, moving sluggishly near the entrance to the bay, the poison obviously having taken effect.

"We must get him to come as near the village as possible," said Kahmonoshar. "Let's sing him in for the feast!" And he took up the task with a lusty song of old about the welcome that waited the bull when he came home to the village.

As they came behind the great whale and began their singing, they saw that he was all alone. His great eye was dull, foam was on his mouth, and his fins moved slowly. The herd had deserted him, probably in fear at his strange actions. Behind him then and on either side of him the men moved, gradually turning him and directing him toward the village, their voices seeming to give him strength and confidence, as if somehow he felt they were friends. Perhaps with his herd gone out to sea, he felt the need for companionship, even if it were human, and their voices were soothing with no alarm in the songs, only a merging with the sea wind and the waves like a lullaby of the great sea. So they began singing him back to the village with little need to drive him, but only to direct his movements and encourage it by their voices.

Come, oh sea lord, chief of the waters. We are your friends!
We wish you well. We bring you to a place to do you great honor.
You are dying, but your death will not be forgotten.
We will strip your bones of flesh, but we will send them back
   to the sea that you may live again, so fear not.
Let us lead you to the Kaniagmiut, people who admire you,
   great lord of the ocean!

Dazed and dopey from the poison, the great whale kept swimming slowly toward the land, as if obeying their commands, as if realizing they would bring an end to his pain and confusion. A mile from the village, they saw the lookout on the hill signaling their coming with the whale. But they also saw, suddenly approaching them, the great black fins of bull killer whales, leading in a pack to the kill. The black and white death-bringers had sensed with their underwater sonar the presence of the dying bull.

Now it was Tuserpik who took command, asking Kahmonoshar to help him throw the ends of the long tubes of the giant kelp over the back of the great bull, so their ends rested in the water on the farther side. Then he told the older hunter:

"We will sing and shout into the tubes so the bull is surrounded on all sides by sound. Our voices will sound under the water and they will disturb the attacking killers. They will hesitate and wait before they try to bite the bull. We must work hard to save him so the people will have time to get out and help us."

So they began to fiercely send out screams and roars and songs against the encircling herd, the sounds carrying both above and below water. The killers were rushing the great gray bull, but suddenly they swerved away, the five-foot-high, black dorsal fins of the bulls cutting the waves like huge dark knives. Suspiciously they circled the big whale, watching, wondering, alarmed by the sounds and yet anxious for all that meat that was awaiting them. Somehow the gray bull sensed that he was not only surrounded by enemies, but protected by friends, and he struggled feebly but steadily to drive himself toward the nearing shore. And then Kahmonoshar shouted:

"They are closing in on the tail!"

The men reversed the direction of the kayak, whipped one of the tubes of kelp over to the back end of the whale, and started shouting loudly. At the last possible instant the black dorsal fins sheared to one side, as the men saw a huge mouth open and gleaming white teeth, each as large as a man's whole foot, snap together like an immense trap with a sound like a thunderclap!

But now there were shouts coming from over the sea, and a whole swarm of kayaks descended upon them, the men shouting and waving clubs and spears, while in one of the single-hole kayaks was a lone woman paddling as hard as a man! When Tuserpik saw the face of Tiviat flashing him a smile and heard her happy cheer, he realized suddenly and joyfully who the young man was who had won a Tlingit princess!

The Athapaskans of the Northwest

Over a vast area of northwestern Canada and interior Alaska are many Athapaskan tribes, also called the Dineh People. They are distantly related to the Navajos and Apaches of the southwest and to a number of small Oregon and California tribes discussed elsewhere in this book. The northwestern Athapaskans impinge on the Pacific Ocean only where the Eyak come down through the high Mount Saint Elias Range to the ocean between Prince William Sound and Yakutat Bay. Farther west the Tanaina Athapaskan people pushed between Eskimo tribes to touch the sea around Cook Inlet, the base of the Alaska Peninsula, and the Kenai Peninsula (see map on p. xii).

Most Athapaskan tribes of the northwest were what we might call outer-fringe people, living primitively in wild forest areas where life was very hard, especially in winter when the long cold nights, deep snow, and storms kept them pinned to their semiunderground bark and earth huts. If enough dried and smoked meat or other preserved food had not been put away for the times of the "short white days," starvation became a reality. Both the Eyak and the Tanaina, had picked up elements of culture from both the Eskimos and the Tlingit that gave them greater comforts and complexity in their lives. Thus the Tanaina built wooden-slab houses like their more sophisticated Athapaskan-speaking relatives, the Tlingit, and had even begun to develop three classes similar to those of the Tlingit—nobles, commoners, and slaves.

Like the more interior tribes they still hunted caribou for their main meat and hide supplies, often driving the caribou into "pounds" or large fenced corrals where they could be more easily killed. They also hunted and trapped, mainly with snares and deadfalls, foxes, martens, lynx, and other fur-bearers. They used the skins for trade and for the fine tailor-made skin clothing their women sewed together; also for blankets and bedding. To travel they had abandoned the toboggan of the northern Canadian woods Indians and borrowed the Eskimo sled with its husky dogs pulling it, usually in tandem. They had even changed their birchbark canoes from the more slim and graceful form found to the east to a kind that looked like an Eskimo skin umiak, with wide sloping sides and a flat bottom. Though they still used the forest Indian birchbark dishes for eating, these were in the process of being replaced by the more lasting and practical Eskimo wooden food trays. But they still cooked their food with hot stones put into tightly woven baskets full of water, the baskets made from tamarack or spruce roots, done with the twining method.

Men were decorated more colorfully than the Eskimo. They wore bright-colored headbands, colorful pendants and necklaces, and painted their faces with stripes or designs of black lead and red ochre, using many brilliant feathers in their hair, which was usually plastered down with grease. These warriors walked nobly and with pride of bearing, like true masters of the woods. Their wives tattooed lower lip and chin, but never dressed brilliantly like the men. Their lives were also harder, as they were the burden bearers and the wood gatherers, the cooks and the housekeepers, while the men had the fun of fishing and hunting. Still, people of both sexes were happy, often singing and dancing and loving good jokes.

The domed sweathouse, which the neighboring Eskimos used much more sparingly, was a place for men only, for conferences and steam baths, from which they could run out and dive into the nearest stream. The roof in winter was often banked with snow except for the smoke hole, and the floor covered with fragrant branches of fir.

The Tanaina had begun to pick up from the Tlingit distinctions of rank and the use of potlatches for gift-giving, with returns expected, and they had begun to use slaves by the time of white contact. But their religion still remained the simple one of each youth going into the wilderness to seek a guardian spirit. The shamans had great power over the people. However, they led a dangerous life, as failure to cure might cause a family to waylay and kill them, and other shamans often tried to poison them or steal their power. The dead were either burned immediately or after several months, following the placing of the wooden coffins in trees.

About the Eyak we know very little, though they probably had kept the more primitive ways. One of these was the three moieties, or tribal divisions; people could not marry others of the same moiety. This was unlike the Tanaina, who had developed two moieties. The Eyak were warlike, noted for once severely defeating the Chugachigmiut Eskimos and splitting them into two divisions.

2. The Tlingit

The three great northern tribes—the Tlingit, the Tsimshian, and the Haida—had developed the most complex and interesting culture on the Pacific Coast, and their ideas radiated in all directions. In chapter 3, on the Tsimshian, this northern division of the Northwest Culture Area is discussed as a unit.

In the following story of a Tlingit couple I have taken one day or so of each month and dramatized its major activities. It should be realized that several other activities may be going on during the same month. A graphic view of these activities is shown in Appendix A. I have visited the Tlingit at Klukwan in southern Alaska where this story is supposed to have taken place.

The Year of the Tlingit

KASAKA (MARCH)

IT WAS DAWN, and the last clouds of a severe storm were fleeing like wild geese into the southeast. Even thirty miles up the Chilkat River at Klukwan the smell of the sea was strong in the air, and gulls swept by on fast-beating wings, going from their hiding places against the storm down to the sea.

"It is a good sign," said Storm Dodger to his wife, Half-Man Woman, looking at her with love. "We should have at least three days of good weather for our fishing. You have been dancing about for days, eager to go, my sweet. Now you shall have your chance!"

"You have been dancing, too!" she laughed. "As have all the fishermen. But I am glad it is my husband who has the spirit to protect us from storms. With you I feel safe!"

Other men could not understand how Storm Dodger was so

attracted to his wife, for she was as strong of body as a man and as bold as a warrior, often antagonizing those who expect girls and women to be meek and shy and subdued. But Storm Dodger saw beneath her rough exterior to the beautiful spirit within.

For days they had been getting their hooks and lines ready for the fishing. They had drawn their twenty-foot canoe down from its brush shelter and had seared its hull smooth of slivers with a blazing torch of pine. A good-luck amulet in the shape of a dolphin was hidden in the bow, and food, blankets, and a container of water, protected by close-woven mats of cedar bark fiber, were lashed in the middle. Two air-filled seal's bladders were ready to hold sinkers and lines.

As she shoved off the canoe into the river and leaped in to seize her paddle, Half-Man Woman heard a voice thick with ugliness spit at her from the shore.

"There goes Half-Man Woman. Make sure, Storm Dodger, that your wife is not half-witch, too!"

As the two looked back in surprise, they saw a shaman of the Kaklawedi Clan, of the Wolf Phratry, standing on the sand and pointing a finger at them. His name was Whale Spirit Singer, a shaman noted for his magic tricks and his supposed

OUTSIDE OF TLINGIT HOUSE. Note small fishing and pleasure canoe, vertical planks on wall of house, large carved totem pole, and man wearing hat whose piled cylinders denotes great wealth, as does the Chilkat blanket or cape he is wearing made of goat's hair and cedar-bark twine. (*Diorama by Elizabeth Mason, Southwest Museum, Los Angeles*)

power over sea life. But the eyes that blazed from under his black tangled hair were full of menace.

Half-Man Woman laughed aloud, and shouted back at him:

"Go back to your dark forests and caves where witches live. We are dwellers in the light and singers of the waves and mountaintops."

The shaman shook his fist at her and turned back toward the great houses of the village.

"Be careful, my wife," murmured Storm Dodger, with worry in his face. "That one hates you for the time at the potlatch when you showed up one of his tricks. If he can make the people believe you are a witch, they will kill you."

Again she laughed defiantly.

"We are of the great clans, you from the Ganaxtedi, and I from the Kagwantan. Our chiefs know us and will protect us."

"Unfortunately, there are too many men and women in both clans who envy your skill at fishing, hunting, and weaving. They say only men should act as you do."

"As long as you love me, I shall have no fear!" She smiled at him so sweetly as she said this that he forgot his worries and bent to his paddle, but somewhere in the back of his mind, he knew that before this year was out the enmity between his wife and Whale Spirit Singer would come full circle.

But meanwhile down the river there was laughter and fun for the young couple as they put out their hooks and lines, at first trolling for trout. At the first solid tug on her line, Half-Man Woman joyfully sang a magic fishing song, calling the fish from the waters. Soon more were being pulled out, the water splashing from their silver scales as they struggled. One by one they were killed with a blow from a club, then tossed into one of the two big fish baskets in the canoe.

That night they camped on the river shore on a sandy beach and together watched their fire and showers of bright sparks leap into darkness, singing songs of the wilderness. In the

---

TLINGIT BARK SCRAPER AND BARK BEATER (beating bark into shreds used in twine). (*Niblack*, The Coast Indians of Southern Alaska and Northern British Columbia)

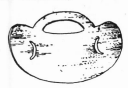

dawn they were paddling rapidly down the river to where it rolled its glacier-fed waters into an inlet of the sea. In the sea they paddled out to a shallow water area over a sandbank, changing their fishing methods. Using their two seal-bladder floats to hold out lines, they allowed the sinkers of stone holding the hooks to drop about a meter below the surface, each baited with clam meat they had garnered from a muddy beach.

Here were cod and halibut, big fish, some weighing ten to thirty pounds, and good fighters on the hooks, though, pound for pound, the trout beat them for fighting ability. They left the lines in the water for half-hour periods at different places, then drew them up to throw the fish into the canoe, clubbing each one as it came.

On the morning of the third day they headed for home, with a full load of fish in their canoe, and heeding the warning that tingled through Storm Dodger's body, telling him of a new storm coming. Up the river they paddled, fighting the current, but hugging the eddies where the current wasn't so strong whenever possible, their powerful muscles seemingly tireless. Just south of Klukwan that evening the first squall struck them with driving rain and wind, cutting visibility to zero, but Storm Dodger seemed to feel his way with his breath, and Half-Man Woman listened confidently to his every command, dipping the paddle to right or left as needed, till they struck shore and heard the shouts of the people.

TSINKADA (APRIL)

Half-Man Woman had come home from a week on the inlet beaches with other women and some older men, collecting seaweed. It had been a busy time close to the sea and the voice of the inlet waves and the wind, gathering the slimy green and yellow leaves from the rocks, piling them in large baskets in the canoes, and paddling them up the Chilkat River to Klukwan. Here they would be dried in the sun on the river beach, and then packed closely in airtight boxes to be used during the winter to come.

Her husband had gone hunting while she was away, and had returned home with plenty of blue and willow grouse from the forested hillsides, shot with bow and arrow in the trees, or clubbed when the males were drumming on logs to lure the females, oblivious of man. Now she lay in bed listening to the drums beating and the stamp and thunder of many strong feet in a hunter's dance. This time they were preparing for far bigger game. It was to be one of the great Alaskan brown bears, largest land canivores in the world, coming out of its winter den soon into the first warmth of spring, but weaker and more lethargic than it would be when it had a few full meals.

That night Half-Man Woman had a nightmare in which she saw the great bear rushing at her husband from its cave, eyes like red fire, gigantic claws reaching out, and the terrible teeth gnashing. So in the morning she told Storm Dodger she was going with him on the hunt.

"I have to go," she said simply. "I saw you in great danger and no one else loves you as I do. Only I can save you, and you know I can handle a spear!"

Over the objections of the other men she went to the chief and explained about her dream. She showed him and the others how she used a spear, her body plunging and supple as a wildcat. The chief said:

"Let it be as the woman wishes. She can hunt with the best of men."

So the five men, some grumbling, went with her up the banks of the swift-flowing river to the place on the edge of the great coniferous forest where, six months before, in the rocks, one of the men had seen a huge bear making its den. They approached this cave very slowly and cautiously. Soon they saw the great claw marks in the melting snow and the thick droppings where the bear had come out that very morning to look around and then gone back into its den.

Two of the hunters took Half-Man Woman with them up into the rocks above the den where they could roll small boulders down onto the bear when it came out and spear it, too, while the other three, including Storm Dodger, approached in front, shouting and yelling, depending on agility to get out of the way of the bear once it was speared. Rocks were thrown into the den, and suddenly there was a vast coughing roar that seemed to shake the very earth. Out of the cave rushed the monster. Two rocks came rolling down from above, but missed as the bear was too quickly in the open. Two spears sang through the air and pierced its side; Storm Dodger kept his spear in reserve. Furiously roaring, the bear charged, exactly as Half-Man Woman had seen in her dream, directly at Storm Dodger. Trying to scramble out of the way he tripped and fell on a rock and dropped his spear. A man who leaped to spear it from the side was swept away like a crushed egg, and Half-Man Woman, without thinking and in the supreme terror of the moment, seized a rock as big as her head and threw it with tremendous strength directly at the bear's head. The blow knocked the giant sideways, stunning it, just as its claws and teeth were closing on Storm Dodger. The two men above came down quickly and a spear was driven in under the shoulder and into the heart. The great bear reared up ten feet high, swaying and roaring, then collapsed, as the blood gushed from its mouth.

One man was dead, but the rest, uninjured, came and lifted the rock Half-Man Woman had thrown. Hefting it, each knew he could not have thrown it half as far. One man looked at Half-Man Woman darkly, spat on the ground, and growled. "Only a witch woman could do this!"

Storm Dodger leaped like a flame of fire and knocked him down, but the man rose with blood on his face and hate in his eyes.

A brother of Storm Dodger's whispered in his ear:
"That one will tell Whale Spirit Singer what he has seen!"

TSINKADUNAXA (MAY)

Now what glorious days came. The snow was still thick on the mountains, the river water icy cold, but grass and ferns and flowers and mushrooms were rising in the meadows and glens, and willow and birch bark was turgid beneath with the sap of spring rising in the under layers. Half-Man Woman danced on the beaches and in the meadows like a thirteen-year-old, her man laughing at her and loving her. Like others they stuffed their mouths and bellies with the young green leaves and ate the roots and tubers as fast as they could find them, their bodies winter-starved for fresh plant foods. They scraped the cambium layers under the bark of the hemlock trees into large boxes, cooked it in water heated by red-hot stones, then pressed it into cakes and put it in other boxes to store for winter.

One day soon the great job of fish-oil gathering occupied their full attention. Almost the whole village went down the river, camping near its opening into the sea, for here in May the eulachon or candlefish were gathering. These were mostly only about four inches long, but so fat and full of oil that it almost dripped from them. Again Storm Dodger and Half-Man Woman formed an efficient team, going out into the waters with dip-nets about three feet wide, dipping and dipping into the roiling river waters where the eulachon swarmed so thick they seemed to fill every cubic foot! Each time the net was dipped up, filled with fish, one of them would untie a thong at the bottom, opening it up so the fish would fall into the canoe. Then quickly the net would be tied again and dipped once more into those swarming fish. Each time, as they came ashore with the canoe almost loaded to the gunwales with squirming fish, the women and old men on the beach would set up a great shout. They gathered around, dipping the fish out with nets, then throwing them into a grounded canoe filled with boiling water, kept boiling by red-hot rocks from a fire.

The young couple were tired, disheveled, and happy after bringing many canoe loads to shore. They came onto the beach to watch and help a bit with the final scraping and skimming of the eulachon oil or grease from the cooled water; this was done with a large horn and wooden spoons. Everybody was delighted with the large amount of oil later to be fashioned into cakes and preserved; it was the favorite food dip and flavorer of all the northwest tribes. And there, even as they laughed and joked with others, they both felt a strange feeling. They looked up to see the dark topknot of uncouth, uncared-for black hair, and the dark, glowing, malevolent eyes of Whale Spirit Singer. He was watching Half-Man Woman as a wolf watches a doe he is planning to kill!

Half-Man Women laughed at him, but Storm Dodger felt the hairs on the back of his neck crawl.

TSINKADUNAXIDIXA (JUNE)

This was the month of house building. One phratry (related people who could not marry each other), the Wolves, was putting up a new dwelling for the opposite phratry, the Ravens. It was a time also to go egg hunting on the little islands and big rocks in the inlets of the sea. And it was a time just to be lazy and lie in the sand on the beach when all the world seemed to be bright with sunlight and full of new life.

"But most of all," sang Storm Dodger into the ear of Half-Man Woman, "it is the time for you and me to leave our enemies behind and cross the mountains to see the other side of the world, taking some good things to trade."

"Wonderful!" she cried, and gave him a big bear hug that nearly cracked his ribs!

So they joined a party of traders under the leadership of a wise old yitsati, a keeper of the wealth in one of the great houses on the beach. They started up the valley of the Chilkat River to cross the snow-covered, massive mountains to the north. On their backs they carried wide-woven snowshoes, for there would be no way across the deep-snowed passes without them. They also wore mittens, fur caps, sewn caribou-skin clothing, and fur-lined moccasins for the journey through the icy wastes. Two weeks later they came out of the stillness of the vast wilderness into a wild and lovely valley, filled with the new green leaves of the quaking aspen like a thousand mirrors in the breeze, tranquil in a sunlight that lasted for more than twenty-two hours of the mid-June day.

On a knoll at the edge of the valley they stopped and made

a fire, from which they soon induced smoke signals with wet fir branches; the smoke rose in uniform puffs toward the sky. Soon a group of Tagish Athapaskan warriors appeared to the north, approaching cautiously until they say the great packs loaded with trade goods that told them the Tlingit came in friendship to trade. They were still more reassured when they saw a woman among the men, and came running and leaping over the grass and rocks, shouting and laughing.

These men had faces painted with red and black stripes, color-dyed feathers in their black hair, and they held themselves proudly. The Tlingit made the outheld flat-palm sign of peace and passed to each of the Tagish a small packet of salt, enclosed in seal gut. This each solemnly tasted and then smiled in delight, for salt was a rare treasure in this interior country. The Tlingit leader or yitsati asked them in Tagish to lead them to their village, and off they went like boys bringing some new friends home.

Two hours later the Tlingit were resting their packs and backs against the fir trees in a Tagish village of round and domed huts made of skins, while a noble-looking chief greeted them and invited them to a welcome feast. All the women and children peered curiously and shyly at Half-Man Woman until she smiled. Then they smiled, too.

After roast venison and boiled tubers mixed with greens, the long speeches began, each tribe praising the other, and Half-Man Woman grew sleepy and bored. Then the Tagish started the first dance of welcome. The sinuous brown bodies of the men formed a circle about the fire, their figures leaping to the beat of a drum and their feathers waving in the twilight of the Alaskan summer midnight. After the Tlingit had given a return dance, the visitors were invited into the huts to sleep.

Half-Man Woman awoke from a sound sleep to the brilliant light of near midday. She saw the other Tlingits gathering outside her hut in the center of the village to display their items of trade on the grass. Yawning, she came out to sit with them and take from her own pack the things she had elected to trade on the first day. To her the bolder women came, as if to a magnet, smiling shyly and showing her baskets, skin clothing, and fur blankets they had made. The tailored clothing of deer, mountain goat, caribou, and elk skin was finer than anything made by the Tlingit and she knew her own people would be eager to buy it. For her own trading she laid out on the grass little bags of salt, dried seaweed, dried meat of the seashells and octopus, and many pretty seashells she knew these women would like for ornaments. The Tlingit men had brought much dried and smoked salmon, larger seashells to be used in tools, large round teeth taken from stranded pilot whales, mats made of cedar bark, and carved cedarwood spoons.

Now the long haggling began, each side trying to convince the other that it had items of extreme value. In this bargaining the Tlingits had most of the advantage, first, because they were a more sophisticated and cultured people and clever talkers, and second, because they had items of greater value because they came from the sea. In two hours Half-Man Woman had traded most of her seaweed for a beautiful dress of caribou skin that she knew would be delightfully warm to wear in midwinter. But she knew the Tagish would bring out their most valuable items later in the evening, so she was careful to hold back her most valuable things also, keeping them hidden in the bottom of her pack sack. And it was fortunate she did, for about the time the sun set, very late indeed in the night, and after a second feast, she saw exactly what she wanted. A Tagish man was displaying a thick sheet of beaten copper, probably from White River to the north where native copper was found in veins in the rock. It was about three feet long and two feet wide, but capable of being rolled into a large tube for carrying. The lustrous copper color shone richly in the dying sunlight. But when she started to bargain for it, Storm Dodger spoke disparagingly of it, saying:

TLINGIT BASKETS: woven from split spruce roots and artificially colored grasses; the Tlingit baskets were of a finer quality than those of surrounding tribes. (*American Museum of Natural History, New York*)

"That stuff is good only for temporary knives. It is too soft and does not keep its sharpness as long as horn, bone, or rock."

"It is beautiful!" she said. "And I want it."

She unrolled a lovely decorated mat of soft woven cedar bark, and placed on it some of her most prized shell necklaces. Then, while the eyes of the Tagish man grew suddenly greedy, she placed on the mat four enormous teeth, taken from the great brown bear she had helped kill.

"Will you trade?" she asked haltingly in Tagish. She saw him hesitate, as if to do some more bargaining, but his greed for immediate possession of these treasures, some of which his wife would like, while the huge teeth would be perfect for a warrior's dance costume, overcame him and he nodded his head.

Half-Man Woman carefully rolled up the heavy and crudely beaten sheet of glowing metal and stored it in her pack sack. Inwardly she planned to keep it hidden until it became ready for its destiny. As far as the trading was concerned, she was finished. She went off to a hut to sleep.

TLEXA (JULY)

The Tlingit enjoyed the calm, warm days of summer, so different from the cold ice, snow, and rain of winter. Many just lay on the beaches and sunned themselves. Half-Man Woman was relaxed, watching her husband prepare his fishing gear for the running of the salmon up the river, the main food event of the year. After a day of picking berries, she went with him, prepared to help. They went down to the place where the platform of sticks he had built stretched out over the shimmering waters. The sound of the rapids was loud in their ears. She had forgotten all about her danger, until he said:

"I have seen Whale Spirit Singer watching you, but there is no danger now. He is waiting for the long dark nights when the people are bored and restless and the stored food is getting stale. Then he will give them the excitement they crave, and you will be in the center!"

"Don't worry," she laughingly called to him. "I have a surprise for that man when the time comes!"

"He will be gone soon with one of the big slave-hunting expeditions in the great canoes far to the south," her husband replied. "They rely on him to make magic against our enemies and find the best time to attack. But he will be back in the fall with a new black magic to use on you!"

But she tossed her head in derision, and settled back comfortably to watch the beginning of his fishing. When he caught his first salmon she would need to club it and then start smoking it on the willow stick racks she had prepared. Soon he was expertly wielding a long dip net to catch some of the first salmon coming upriver to spawn. She admired the gleam of his bronze skin in the sunlight and the roll of his supple muscles as he dipped the net again and again into the fast-swimming silvery bodies below, tossing the caught fish up to her to be killed with the club and then tossed into a large basket.

ESKUDISI (AUGUST)

Now the people were thinking more and more of storing food for the time of the short white days and the long cold nights. With her hard wood digging stick, Half-Man Woman helped other women gather herbs and roots to make plenty of food for the first big summer potlatch. Later she helped them fill large boxes with the delicious blueberries, salmon berries, huckleberries, and others, though they ate the small sweet black caps as they found them. As she ladled eulachon fish oil from a sealskin bag to cover and protect the top of the berries for winter storage, she whispered to her best friend, Silver Salmon Woman, "The sign has come that I will have a child and it will come in the time of the new green leaves. It will be a child of the sunlight!"

But Silver Salmon Woman whispered back: "I hope you will live to see the child!"

Half-Man Woman laughed and laughed. "Don't listen to the rumors of the old women!" she exclaimed. "I shall be alive and playing with my baby when he who threatens me is gone beyond the mountains." And she left the berry preserving to help her husband prepare, with sharp knives of horn, the bodies of the salmon he had been catching, cleaning out the guts, and spreading the two gleaming pink-fleshed halves of each fish on racks over the fire to be smoked and dried for winter storage.

NUSKEAH (SEPTEMBER)

It was early in Nuskeah when the slave-hunters came back from the south in the great war canoes, their high prows adorned with the cruel faces of killer whales and wolves. They were just in time for the slaves to be put to work in the month when salmon fishing and preserving was the overwhelming need of the village of Klukwan. But first the warriors must have their victory dance and their selling of the extra slaves they did not keep for themselves. So they leaped high with bent bodies that evening on the beach, shaking their rattles, showing their fierce black and red painted faces, some of them covered with the savage-toothed masks of wolves and bears, fiercely whooping their yells to the sky. In their midst danced the shaman, Whale Spirit Singer, howling like a wolf, his tangled hair shaken out like black snakes in the wind, waving a killer whale-toothed club in the savage rites of war.

Most of the newly-captured slaves were women and teenagers or older children, all with the sloping flattened heads of the Coast Salish, people so far away from the Tlingit that it would be hopeless for them to try to escape their new masters. Half-Man Woman took pity on a middle-aged woman with a face ravaged by despair and tears, and asked Storm Dodger to buy her for her, but Whale Spirit Singer, watching the purchase, sneered:

"You will not live long to enjoy your slave!"

Right TLINGIT STONE DAGGERS. (*Niblack*, The Coast Indians of Southern Alaska and Northern British Columbia)
Below DETAIL OF WEAVING ARMOR. (*Niblack*, The Coast Indians of Southern Alaska and Northern British Columbia)

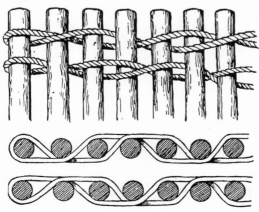

Half-Man Woman almost lost her calm, but she smiled instead and spoke sweetly: "The eagle steals the fish from the osprey. In the same way I shall steal my life from you."

The shaman snarled at her, but she turned her back on him and led her slave away with her hand touching gently the woman's shoulder and telling better than words could do that somehow in this strange cold northern land she had a friend.

TAKUNA (OCTOBER)

Although the bulk of the salmon had been caught, dried, smoked, and either hung or stored in boxes for winter use, some were still being driven into the shallows to be clubbed, and others struck by the barbed spear and harpoon in deeper water. Most of the people had come home to the village after their summer and early fall months of free camps along the beaches, in the mountains, or visiting friends and relatives on the islands. It was time now for the great fall hunts before the winter snows filled the woods and the passes too deeply with the white and the cold.

Half-Man Woman felt the first stir of her baby within her, but she climbed up to near timberline in the mountains with her husband to help him and his brothers and cousins drive a herd of mountain goats into a great net trap set up by the men in one of the narrow canyons. Thus did they intend to gather both the meat and the fine soft warm goat's wool for the making of the famous Chilkat blankets.

Beating box drums, shaking horn rattles, and yelling loudly, they formed a vast half-circle behind the herd when it was located, and drove it remorselessly toward the canyon, away from the safety of the higher rocks, until the goats smashed into the net walls and there were clubbed and speared by the hunters. Still, Half-Man Woman was happy to see a great moun-

A

CHILKAT BLANKETS: **A** Chilkat blanket suspended from the frame of a loom; **B** blanket pattern done on a board by a man to direct woman weaver; **C** typical Chilkat blanket pattern. (*Drawings by Gladys Fox, A and B after Goddard*)

B

C

tain billygoat crash with splendid power through the nets in one place and then leap away to safety, dodging the spears that were thrown at him, up and up the rocks into the heights, with his long white beard streaming in the wind.

"Go, go!" she called to him in her secret heart. "So shall I escape when Whale Spirit Singer spins his net of lies and death for me!"

But the end of the month saw a great uncertainty fall upon her. The old Chief Heron of the Ganaxtedi Clan and of the village, who had always been a strong friend, died from a fall among the rocks, and the new chief-to-be, his nephew, was untried and untested.

(Among the Tlingit, Haida, and Tsimshian, the descent is matrilineal—goes through the mother instead of the father. The chief's son would belong to the clan of the chief's wife and not be entitled to be leader of his father's clan. The son of the chief's sister, though, belongs to the chief's clan and so inherits the chieftainship.)

KISINA (NOVEMBER)

Kisina was like the ripe wild plum falling from the tree, an end before a new beginning. Before it even began the widows of Chief Heron had blackened their faces and cut their hair short in mourning, hiding themselves in a small room while the people outside sang the dirges of the Ganaxtedi Clan. The chief's body had been placed in a seat of honor, dressed in his regal robes and his sacred Chilkat blanket of bright colors and clan spirits design, while his tall basket hat with its clan crests rose above his head. Here he was left for a few days for the mourners to sing his praises. Then he was taken away for cremation, and his ashes put in a grave box high on cedarwood posts carved with his clan crests, in the woods behind the village.

But long before this the young men of the clan had been

TLINGIT METHODS OF HOUSE BURIAL. House on right is open to show placement of corpse. (*American Museum of Natural History, New York*)

sent forth to call the opposite clan, the Kagwantan (of the opposite moiety, the Eagles), the clan the chiefs always married into, to come to a great fall potlatch at Klukwan to honor and name the new chief-to-be of the Ganaxtedi (of the Raven moiety). The two branches of the Kagwantan, one from Sitka, and the other from Klukwan, actually came to the potlatch in rivalry. It was up to the new chief of the Ganaxtedi, still not officially named, to keep the two branches from changing rivalry into physical conflict, a difficult task with these highly charged and warlike people.

In June the Kagwantan of Klukwan had built a new great house for the old Chief Heron. It was in this brand-new house, strong with its huge posts of cedar, its forty-foot, three-inch-thick boards on sides and roof, and its center hall, big enough to hold over two hundred people, that the potlatch in memory of the old chief and in honor of the new chief was to be held. The new chief's head wife, Dawn Woman, had been sent to Sitka with the young men to call her relatives and father and mother to the great feast, also asking them to give some property to her husband to help with the great expense of such an important potlatch. There he would establish his name and rank in Tlingit society by how much he could give. They sent 25 sea otter skins, 12 slaves, 40 blankets, 10 boxes of eulachon oil, and 20 strings of dentalium shell money.

Half-Man Woman and Storm Dodger were down at the beach on Chilkat River by Klukwan when the great canoes from Sitka came riding up the river through the cold mist of evening, with the house chiefs standing in the prows as the canoes nosed toward land with their clan crests, masks, and symbolic rods of the wolf, murrelet, eagle, grizzly bear, and killer whale held high in their hands. A great shout of welcome went up from the people on the shore, and the house chiefs of the Ganaxtedi also displayed their crests of the woodworm, the frog, the black-skinned heron, and the sacred Mother Basket that marked their ancient heritage. Soon Half-Man Woman was hugging her mother and father and a young sister and brother, as they stepped ashore from a canoe.

She and her new slave, Kaksi, had been working for days

getting food ready for the potlatch, and the two women were part of the welcoming committee that gave 20 boxes of berries and 18 boxes of eulachon grease plus plenty of dried salmon and meat to help feed the incoming clan when it landed. Soon they were also helping set up temporary beds near the fire in one of the great houses.

In the morning, after breakfast of goat's meat and seaweed, came the display of crests again, and then the two branches, the Sitka and the local, of the Kagwantan Clan began their rivalry with lines of masked or painted dancers each chanting in perfect unison its songs of clan greatness. Soon also came songs of mockery and jibing at each other, the voices getting loud and a little angry. But the new young chief showed his wisdom, calming them down by personally throwing eagle down on all the singers, a symbol of peace among the Tlingit, and, in this case, a warning to observe the rules.

After the dinner there were more songs and dances, and the Kagwantan clansmen of both groups sang to the new chief: "We your opposites, and the kinsmen of your wife, are going to dance and sing to drive your sorrows away!"

Night and day for four days and nights the feasts and the potlatch continued, with both clans displaying their crests and most valuable property. At last the new chief began to give away great quantities of food, blankets, and other presents to give prestige to his name, putting his young son (who was of the opposite clan, the Kagwantan, because of inheritance from his mother) on top of the great pile to give him honor. Then all the guests began dancing together, singing the old, old words of peaceful harmony: "I am holding your daughter's hand" to families of the opposite groups and clan. This peaceful dance showed respect for the host.

Toward the end of the potlatch feats of strength, eating,

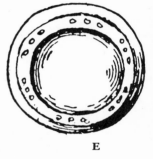

E

TLINGIT WOODEN HOUSEHOLD UTENSILS: **A** treasure or trinket box (some as large as 2 feet by 3 feet), with ornamental top and handle of cord; **B** small food dish with totemic carvings; **C** Food dish ornamented with opercula; **D** ladle; **E** large bowl. (*Niblack*, The Coast Indians of Southern Alaska and Northen British Columbia)

A

B

C

D

and magic power were performed. Two young men tried to outeat each other, gobbling from their carved wooden plates as fast as they could, to the laughter and mocking cries of the audience. Strong men tried to wrestle their opponents to the ground, and the famous shaman, Whale Spirit Singer, demonstrated some of his magic powers. He caused flames of fire to come out of his mouth, walked on red-hot coals, and (seemingly) cut a woman in two with a knife only to bring her back alive again; his feats had the young men and women fawning on him and clapping their hands. Toward Half-Man Woman he turned a savage glare at times, which some of his friends among the clans, slavishly following their hero, also took up.

Half-Man Woman returned his glare with a sweet smile that only made him angrier, and some heard him saying: "That witch has poison in her smile!"

As the guests left on the fifth day for their journey back to Sitka, the new Chief Heron was so happy over the honor given him, that he announced that three months later he would give a great prize to whoever produced the most beautiful tribute to the crests of his clan.

TLEDUSA (DECEMBER)

In the month of heavy snow and damp cold, the people of Klukwan spent most of their time inside the great houses with lesser ceremonies or storytelling to pass the time, or working at the manufacture of baskets, Chilkat blankets of goat wool, beautifully carved wooden boxes, or other decorative objects and materials, and the many implements needed for the hunt or for fishing. It was strange that, though they had spent so much effort gathering, preserving, and storing food for winter, they had neglected to gather dry wood. So each day in winter the poor slaves and many of the young men had to go out into the chill, wet forest to bring in the wet wood for the fires. No wonder the great houses became so smoky and dirty during the winter!

Half-Man Woman was glad to turn over most of the cooking to her willing and adoring slave, Kaksi. She herself retired into a special little room she had made with cedar bark mats; here she worked on the copper she had obtained during the trading trip to the Tagish. With a little hammer she had made especially for the purpose and some grooving tools of stone, she spent long hours hammering away, learning to work the copper into forms of beauty. The sound was so light, however, that it hardly penetrated through the thick cedar bark fiber mats that surrounded her. But it was a secret work that planted seeds for her undoing.

"They are saying," said her husband worriedly, "that you are making magic and witchcraft behind your screens that you will soon be using to bewitch people who are your enemies and make them sick or die."

"Who is saying this?"

"Whale Spirit Singer, and the many even among our own clans, who believe in him. I think it is time we find another shaman to counteract his power, a good shaman, like the one they call Good Thunder, he who is of the Thunder and Eagle People Crest, the Sinkukedi."

"No!" she said angrily, and for the first time in years the words sounded loud and harsh between the man and wife, so that Kaksi ran to close her ears and hide her head in a corner of the great house. But finally Storm Dodger calmed his temper and spoke gently, convincing his wife that they needed help from Good Thunder.

The new shaman was a quiet man, totally different from the domineering Whale Spirit Singer, and Half-Man Woman immediately liked him. He listened quietly, named his price, an otter skin and four of Half-Man Woman's beautiful baskets, and left to begin his countermagic. But before he did, Half-Man Woman whispered something in his ear that caused him to smile and nod his head.

"What was that about?" demanded Storm Dodger, like a true husband. But she only gave him a smile that was like the wild strawberries in springtime, and whispered, "It is a secret to help his magic. To tell you would spoil it!"

DAGADUSA (JANUARY)

The short white days continued now, but also the days of the greatest storms, the winds roaring out of the south and west in great gusts that shook the heavy timbers of the great house's roof, the snow lying thick all about the village. The poor slaves and young men who gathered wood fought to keep their hands from freezing when they dug under the wet snow for logs and branches or traveled far to find a dead tree. Close to the fires the children gathered to listen to the old men and women storytellers. They heard stories of spirits and demons and of the great heroes from the half-animal days of the world's beginnings, when they fought with giants and monsters or traveled to the far seas or the sun and stars seeking power to help the people. The eyes of the little ones were wide, and how often they sucked in their breath or reached in fear for their mothers! Other days and nights were spent watching the winter ceremonials. The masked dancers danced, the high, shrill singing sounded, and the pounding of drums and shaking of rattles echoed from the smoke-blackened rafters of the great house in rhythmic cadences that soon had children and adults alike swaying to the sounds.

But all about Half-Man Woman and Storm Dodger in those days of the long, long darknesses they felt the whispers traveling, and they could see by the dark looks cast upon her that the poison of Whale Spirit Singer was working deeper. Ostentatiously Storm Dodger sharpened the blades of his knives and his spear until they could cut a hair, swearing in his heart there would be plenty of blood flowing if anyone touched his wife. But Half-Man Woman shook her head at him and frowned. She knew that she could not be saved by violence.

NESKADUSA (FEBRUARY)

This was the month of boredom. This was the month of longing for the coming of spring and first good weather, for long fishing trips down to the inlets and sounds. The men were busy preparing their fishhooks, their lines, and their many nets for the good days to come. The women were busy with their tongues with gossip about Half-Man Woman and her secret room, while the long-stored food of winter began to taste stale. All were ready for something to happen to relieve the boredom, to make them forget the food, for something exciting, wild, and dangerous to take the edge off the short white days and long nights of snow and rain and cold that seemed to be lasting forever.

The shaman's storm broke not on a dark snowy or rainy day of high winds, but on the first good day of the month of Neskadusa, when some weak sunlight appeared from the south end of the sky and the clouds began to open and show the blue. Out of the houses the people poured, to walk along the beach, to talk in the open air, and even to laugh a little. And it was in this time of seeming relaxation when Half-Man Woman and her husband were away from the protection of the great house and, lulled by the comparatively good weather, had almost forgotten her danger, that Whale Spirit Singer struck.

Suddenly he was there on the beach with many of his followers from all the clans shouting: "Half-Man Woman is half-witch, and soon she will be a whole witch. She has been making black magic in her room to destroy us." He lifted his powerful arms in a gesture strong with menace. "Torture her!" he roared, his eyes blazing like hot coals, his hands clenched. "She will soon confess that she is a witch!"

Storm Dodger drew his knife and turned, but as he did so the man he had once knocked down up on the mountainside sneaked up behind him and struck a blow with a club that knocked him to the ground unconscious. Immediately there was an uproar, Storm Dodger's brothers and friends rushing up to protect him. But meanwhile his wife had been seized

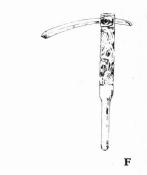

NORTHWEST PACIFIC COAST WEAPONS: **A** halibut clubs (Kwakiutl); **B** trailing hook for salmon (Kwakiutl); **C** bird spear (Nootka), bird arrow (Kwakiutl), sea otter arrow (Kwakiutl); **D** double-bladed whalebone knife (Tlingit); **E** whale rib war club (Tlingit); **F** slave killer axe with jade blade (Tlingit); **G** sinew-backed bows (Kwakiutl). (*Drawings by Gladys Fox after Goddard*)

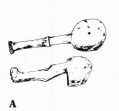

A **B** **C** **D**

by a dozen pairs of clawing hands and dragged down to the river, where she was shoved under the icy water and held. When she came up gasping for air, they screamed at her:

"Admit that you are a witch! Admit that you are a witch or we will drown you!"

"Never!" She spoke firmly, but she could not help a despairing cry as she struggled.

"Storm Dodger, Good Thunder, where are you? Help!" Then she was viciously shoved under again. She was saved momentarily by Kaksi. The slave woman, overlooked by her mistress's enemies, was suddenly among them, scratching and tearing like a wildcat defending her kitten. So astonishing was her attack that, for an instant, she managed to thrust half the mob aside and dragged her beloved mistress partly from the river. In the next instant a club smashed down on her skull, and she lay lifeless and bloody by the water.

"Hold it!" suddenly roared a voice with great authority. "I who am chief of the Ganaxtedi, the mother clan of Klukwan, call on my clan and all the other clans who are our friends to stop this fighting. Any clansman of mine who disobeys shall be killed! I have proof here that Half-Man Woman is not a witch, but has done our clan a great honor!"

Facing each other in the middle of the crowd were Whale Spirit Singer and Good Thunder, the unkempt hair of the two shamans almost standing on end with the electric power of their emotions, rage from the darker and bigger of the two, outrage and courage from the lighter and smaller. Like a striking snake Whale Spirit Singer hurled a dark poisoned dart at his opponent, but the other moved ever so lightly and quickly, seeming to turn the dart around his hand so it fell to the ground harmlessly. Again a dart was hurled, and again it fell harmlessly, while the watching crowd hardly dared to breathe.

Suddenly the brothers of Storm Dodger, seeing that the mood of the crowd had changed, rushed like a single man to seize Whale Spirit Singer from behind in their powerful hands. They held him while Chief Heron, lord of the Ganaxtedi, lifted up before the amazed eyes of the on-lookers a marvelously wrought shield of copper. It glittered in the light like a hundred tiny fires, and the animals and humans shown on its surface were so natural they almost seemed to be alive.

"This is a work of love!" he exclaimed. "This is what Half-Man Woman has been doing all these months in her secret room, instead of the witchcraft you believed she was practicing. This great copper has all the crests of our clan on it. It may be the first of its kind in the world, but not the last. Bring her here and we will honor her. She shall have a new name, Beautiful Heart, and she shall be sung about in the days to come!"

3. The Tsimshian and Their Neighbors

The Tsimshian, the Haida, and the Tlingit apparently form the center from which most of the distinctive features of the Northwest Culture Area spread to other peoples. These three tribes constitute the Northern Province of the area. Some of the culture elements that distinguish them as a whole are described in the appendix. Below are some elements that help distinguish them from each other. It appears that the material culture as well as the social and religious culture of the Tsimshian were, on the whole, more complex and inventive than that of the Haida and Tlingit.

MATERIAL CULTURE

Tsimshian	Haida	Tlingit
Grid fish trap with a barrier of logs and stones and inverted-V entry	Grid fish trap with fixed and floating screens for entry	Stone weirs for salmon
		Grid fish trap with V wings
Small rectangular saltwater fish traps	Black cod oil developed	Copper fish-cutting knife
Bent U-shaped halibut hook		Whole salmon frozen for winter
Fishline of cedar bark cord	Fishline of gut	Fishline of gut
Harpoon line free or tied to canoe thwart	Springpole-type snare for geese	Mountain sheep hunted
	Basketry quiver	Skin-covered canoes (among Yakutat Bay Tlingit)
Lure for porpoise	Urine used as detergent	Urine used as detergent
Waterfowl hunted by torchlight		
Bark dishes	Single chair die game	Single chair die game
Earth floor for house	Tobacco grown	Tobacco grown
Fire on floor level	Board floor for house	Board floor for house
Stone chisel	Fire in pit with sand	Fire in pit with sand
Goat horn arrow points	Fire bow drill	Fire bow drill

Tsimshian	Haida	Tlingit
Shredded bark apron for women		
Leggings of furs		
Yarn spun with spindle	Yarn spun on thigh	
Woven fur robes		
Tobacco imported		

SOCIAL AND RELIGIOUS CULTURE

Tsimshian	Haida	Tlingit
Descriptive moon count	Descriptive moon count (each month named)	Numerical moon count (each month also numbered)
Eclipse means a chief will die		
Offerings burned at eclipse		
Dogs used in hunting		Dogs used in hunting
Wooden cradle	Wooden cradle	
Feast for infant	Special burial for shaman	Special burial for shaman
Name given at birth	Shaman has several spirits	Shaman has several spirits
Potlatch after first puberty seclusion of girl	Contagious magic from a revelation	Contagious magic from a revelation
	Souls take animal form	Shamans fight with each other with magic
Formal proposal party for girl		
Bride price given	Bride price given	
Food offerings to dead	Food offerings to dead	
Territorial rights on hunting grounds		
Shaman captures soul in bone tube		
Special land of the dead	Special land of the dead	
Ghosts dangerous to the living	Ghosts dangerous to the living	
Secret societies		

Tsimshian	Haida	Tlingit
Ranked dances	Grizzly bear dancer	
Cannibal dancer	Cannibal dancer	
Dog-eating dancer	Dog-eating dancer	
Potlatch at birth		
Marmot skins as wealth		Marmot skins as wealth

Upper Northwest Coast Art

Northwest coast native art reaches its most complex, technically perfect, and interesting forms from the Kwakiutl in the south to the Tlingit in the north. Though the Nootka and the Coast Salish sometimes approached this degree of excellence, they did not equal it.

This area is known for its distinctive totem poles (actually clan crests), masks, carved and painted boxes, carved and painted house poles and grave markers, elaborate raven rattles and spoons, and other artifacts and art. A part of the incredibly long history of artistic development in the area is reflected by the years of training and apprenticeship of the painters, sculptors, and weavers, and the highly sophisticated and complex culture that produced them. No one book can do true justice to this area. Despite their slave trade and really ferocious warfare (both common to our own culture in the recent past!), these people were very far from meriting the term "savage" so often applied to them by their white neighbors and conquerors.

A plentiful supply of food animals, particularly fish, and sophisticated methods of food gathering, provided these people with months of leisure, especially in winter, when they could devote themselves to creativity. The most obvious feature of this we see today is the totem pole, actually a visual symbol of a family or clan crest rather than a "totem." Its extensive development was very recent in the history of these peoples, mainly after the white people brought the steel for tools that made such elaborate carvings on huge posts so much easier to do. The basic skill and knowledge, however, were there long before; beautiful and intricate work was done for centuries with tools of bone, horn, beaver teeth, and stone.

Cedar, because of its soft, easily carved wood and its even grain, was the primary material used for carved and painted boxes, house posts, poles, and grave markers. Bone, horn, ivory, and soft stone were also carved, though with greater difficulty until steel tools appeared. Common motifs were the animals, monsters, human beings, and spirits of the tribal legends, particularly those about the historical or mythical foundations of ancestral families and clans, and parts of the legends were often shown in the art. Certain animals and birds that had a great deal to do with the life of the people entered into these legends and were shown much more often, such as the bear, the mountain goat, the beaver, the frog, the killer whale, the sea otter, and the sea lion among animals, and the raven, the eagle, the cormorant, the gull, the owl, and the heron among birds.

Emphasis in art was achieved by bold lines and sharp colors, deep incisions in the wood, and other visual effects designed to catch and hold the eye. There was meticulous attention to detail. Eyes were often done in such a way that they seemed to be staring at you no matter where you stood. Sculptures and paintings were painted in several colors, with yellows, reds, blue-green, blue, white, and black the most common. The paint, which had a base of fish-egg oil, was applied without an undercoat so that it looked flat.

There were three artistic approaches: realism, adaptive realism (in which the realism was gradually adapted to symbolic meanings), and nonrealistic conventionalization (in which real creatures are indicated by symbols). Three-dimensional techniques were used, both high and low relief, as well as linear designs done on the surface, and combinations of these

---

Left TSIMSHIAN (KUNG) INDIAN VILLAGE: Virago, British Columbia. (*National Museums of Canada, Ottawa*)
Right RIGHT QUARTER VIEWS OF TSIMSHIAN TOTEM POLES: at Gitsegyloca, British Columbia. (*National Museums of Canada, Ottawa*)

techniques. Carvings usually expressed the original shape of the material carved, such as a log, and were generally divided into a number of sharply separated and articulated parts. Contrasting large and small elements in layers, as for example a layer of small human figures between two layers of large animal figures, gave a monumentlike quality to some of the sculpture.

Despite some natural overlapping and borrowing of traits and ideas among the tribes, the major linguistic groups had certain distinctive characteristics:

Haida Art: Haida art shows the most dramatic development of mammal, fish, and bird figures by spectacularly exaggerating and sharply accentuating special attributes for each type, usually in stylized form. For example the tail of the beaver, its principal tool for work, would be emphasized, or the great dorsal fin and sharp teeth of a killer whale. In Haida totem poles a continual vertical development of interwoven motifs often takes up every square inch of space. There is intricate development in depth as well, often much of it in nonrealistic conventionalized figures to indicate large numbers or the importance of a particular clan symbol, all done with a high quality of control on the part of the artist. Human figures are generally small and are a minor part of the design. Haida art could be described as baroque (highly ornamented, with many curved lines) or classical (in the sense of being typical of old northwest culture as it was before the Tsimshian and the Tlingit began to deviate from it with more imaginative and revolutionary designs).

Tlingit Art: In Tlingit territory, the easily carved cedar trees are less numerous and smaller than they are to the south. Consequently, perhaps, Tlingit totem poles tend to be more slender than those of the more southern Haida, Tsimshian, and Kwakiutl, and also more complicated in appearance. They have often been visually enlarged by adding wings, fins, and tails to

HAIDA MASK, "KELORA'S WIFE": used in film *Loon's Necklace,* from Massett, Queen Charlotte Islands, British Columbia. (*National Museums of Canada, Ottawa*)

their outer edges, making them appear less like poles and more like a series of separate carvings attached one on top of the other. Parts of the pole usually appear in smaller scale and with more common use of color than among the southern tribes, apparently to make better or more spectacular use of the narrow limits in which they have to work. Sometimes, however, Tlingit art conveys a feeling of greater freedom than does Haida or Tsimshian art; in this it is more like the free-flowing, natural art of the Kwakiutl. It can be called adventuristic and perhaps rococo if you can think of it in the sense of showing many small side additions to the main art of the pole.

Tsimshian Art: The bulk of Tsimshian art is probably the most classical of northwest tribal art, though some Tsimshian have deviated into new fields more than the Haida. Tsimshian art is generally dignified, with great rhythm and balance. It often appears on a totem pole as a series of horizontal groupings, with small figures interspersed between and dramatizing the size of much larger figures. This emphasizes the convex nature of the pole, and the eye is carried upward in a series of steps to the point of greatest dramatic importance. Most of the figures are more realistic than in Haida or Tlingit art and are done in a simpler, more severe style, but in some carvings, nonrealistic conventionalized figures are also used. Carving, done with much cleverness and clearness, is more important than line work; it is done without the dramatic exaggeration usually found in Haida and Tlingit art.

Kwakiutl and Nootkan Art: The art of these two tribes could be called Wakashan art, as they are related linguistically in the Wakashan language family. It differs from the "northern style" of the above three tribes by not being an applied art. It is not decorated or modified by any applied design, except in rather rare instances; a statue is a statue, not a carved house post

---

Left KWAKIUTL TOTEM POLE: from Fort Rupert, British Columbia. (*National Museums of Canada, Ottawa*)
Below EAGLE HEAD MASK: open to show inner face (Bella Coola). (*National Museums of Canada, Ottawa*)

with interwoven figures. Thus, Wakashan art is more realistic. There is also a frequent feeling of exuberant movement in the sculptures of a bird in flight or an animal springing or running.

Another distinctive feature of most Wakashan art is its lack of unimportant detail. It can be called dramatically centered and, unlike Haida and Tsimshian art, is not bothered by having large spaces between figures. Although less disciplined than the more northern art, Wakashan art is bolder and more majestic. The Raven or chief's rattle is stylistic in the north, while in Wakashan art it is realistic; both are beautiful. It is likely that the Wakashan style was an earlier one, and that the northern style was a later, more elaborate development of Wakashan's originally free and simple way.

Two Who Honored the Nass

IN THE OLD DAYS, the Nass River of northern British Columbia was a large stream of clear water all the way down to its entrance into the sea near Cape Fox. It was a river noted for the vast quantities of eulachon or candlefish that gathered there in summer, a fish so concentrated with fat that nearly half its body could be rendered into an oil. Natives far up and down this rugged coast considered this rich oil delicious to mix with other food. It was largely the harvest of the oil by the Tsimshian, particularly by their Nisquan branch, that gave these populous and powerful people a wealth that other tribes could only dream of. In order to guard that wealth, the four Nisqua villages of the lower Nass, a well as some other Tsimshian villages along the Skeena River, formed into organized chieftainships in the early 1700s. The village chiefs and later true tribal chiefs had such concentrated wealth and organized fighting power in warrior strength that the Tsimshian as a whole were

HAIDA TOTEM POLE: from Massett, Queen Charlotte Islands, British Columbia. (*National Museums of Canada, Ottawa*)

able most of the time to fend off the attacks of Haida and Tlingit war parties. Thus these warlike peoples were driven to make war journeys far to the south for easier sources of slaves and booty. The Nisqua were probably among the first to turn their villages into fortifications, building them on bluffs overlooking the sea, with high rock and timber walls that were generally impenetrable to bow and arrow or spear- and club-wielding invaders.

The three main divisions of the Tsimshian—the Nisqua, the Coast Tsimshian, and the Gitskan of the Upper Skeena River—were not bound by their rivers. Instead they often traveled far over the sea in their great canoes and far inland on the natural canals. The Douglas Channel and the Portland Canal formed deep fjordlike arms of the sea that extended many miles inland, while the Nass itself was navigable without rapids for nearly eighty miles, and the Skeena could be traveled a tremendous 250 miles inland. The Tsimshian escaped up these channels, behind the almost impenetrable forests of firs, hemlocks, and cedars in the rain forest along the coast, to a drier climate and more open forests behind the coastal ranges, with numerous lakes and waterways over which canoes could travel. Here the hunting for deer, elk, marmot, and mountain goat was excellent, and the otter, mink, marten, fox, and wolverine they trapped furnished them with beautiful furs. No wonder the Tsimshian, in this marvelous area, lush with life, were a rich and many-sided, well-traveled people! Their unique language must have developed over many centuries in their fortresslike river systems and mountains. Their strong sense of unity and cultural cohesion nourished a magnificent barbaric civilization, probably the main cultural diffusion point of all northwest America.

Into these proud people, in a village on the lower Nass, among the Nisqua, were born a boy and a girl who later became a gifted couple, destined to lead the way into new artistic achievements and adventures for their dynamic society. We shall call them Cedar Man and Goat Woman, for the life of one was tied to the magnificent coastal tree whose fine long-lasting red wood made such excellent houses and canoes, while the other came to create artistic magic out of the long and lustrous white wool of the Lord of the Peaks, the snowy-white wild goat.

At the beginning of their marriage, the future did not look very bright, for Cedar Man was the youngest son of the youngest son of the youngest wife of a chief, and by the time you got to the tail end of two such big families there was little honor and little wealth left to be shared. Indeed, since inheritance was through the mother instead of through the father, Cedar Man's position was little higher than that of a slave. So he had to marry Goat Woman, whose wedding price was very small, since she was the youngest daughter of the youngest son of a youngest son also.

Yet the two realized they had good blood and, in their quiet way, they had pride. They also had a love and respect for each other. It was manifested in the silent, unassuming way they helped each other in their work and in the way their voices and actions taught their children to obey, not by harsh words, but by firmness, love, and the fine example they set. In the great house where they lived with other families, their humble quarters were always neat and tidy and their dinner always on time, their children merry and yet mannerly. Goat Woman sang softly in a voice that her children and her husband adored, and her fingers were clever at making beautiful baskets and preparing delicious foods, at healing cuts and bruises and infections with natural plant medicines.

Cedar Man was always busy making boxes out of cedar wood, carving them, and painting them. He used fine, beaver-tooth chisels, woodworking knives, and knives of sharp obsidian. He made the boxes out of cedar boards that had been split from large logs, then scraped down until they were thin enough. He scribed the boards deeply with his knives to form the places where they could be bent, then lashed them together with cedar bark cord or sinew from the back of a deer. The four sides of the box next had to be drilled all around the edges with small holes so that a bottom could be lashed neatly to the whole and a top fitted with side flanges to make it complete. He carved the boxes with semirealistic designs of human and animal life, in scenes from the great legends of the people. To paint the boxes he used clam shells filled with the bright salmon-egg-based paints of many colors. When the boxes were complete, they were sold for dentalium shell money to various chiefs and subchiefs and other nobility of the Nisqua and Coast Tsimshian.

One day Cedar Man looked at his gentle-faced wife and gave a long sigh, and as many a husband in a poor family down through the centuries, he said:

"We struggle to make ends meet, but we never seem to get ahead. When I married you I promised that I would work hard so we could have our own house and enough wealth to give the children a good start in life. But it seems that no matter how hard I work at these boxes they never sell for enough to really help us. I have a feeling that there is something I can do that will one day make us known and honored and give us at least a little wealth."

"My dear husband," said the wife, touching him lovingly on the face. "I know how hard you have struggled and I know your work has quality. I feel strongly that not only can you do something better and more spectacular but that I also have a hidden talent that must flower. I think you must work with something larger and taller than these boxes to give full scope to your art, and I look with longing myself at those noble women who weave blankets out of cedar bark and the brilliant white wool of the mountain goats. I think I could enhance their quality with a trimming of marten or mink fur, or that you could lay out a striking design for me that I could weave into a blanket. The blankets now done by these women have little design in them at all, and you know I have learned to put nice designs into the baskets I make."

"Yes! Yes!" cried the husband. "You have a wonderful idea for a new kind of blanket, a blanket that, if well done and beautiful in color and texture, might be worth the price of one of the great coppers the chiefs show with pride at the potlatches. And you have given me an idea. I will put a post in front of one of the great houses and carve the lineage and legends of the chief on it as is done now in a small way on the interior house posts. If I carved a design on its front, it would tell the world of his noble lineage just as a great potlatch does!"

Then they both looked at each other and laughed at the same moment.

"But I need the wool of the white goat!" she cried. "And you know all the goat-hunting areas are now controlled by the rich people of the Nisqua and the Gitskan. You cannot hunt and kill goats for me."

"And I need a better carving tool than these obsidian and beaver-tooth knives and chisels to do such a big job!" sighed her husband.

Goat Woman suddenly looked alert.

"I heard there is a Haida chief coming from the outer islands next fall to trade for eulachon grease. He is the owner of a piece of metal like the copper we value so highly, but of a strange whitish color and far harder than copper or horn. They say it comes from some land far to the northwest. If you could get this metal and make it into a chisel or knife, you could carve much faster and better than you do now!"

Her husband seized her hand.

"We know that the chief will ask a small fortune for such a metal. But there is one chance. I will go alone into the hills to fast and pray, and you must pray too. If the spirits of our ancestors are kind, they will answer my prayer and tell us what to do to get both the white goal wool and the strange hard metal!"

Cedar Man washed himself four times in the cold water of the river Nass, letting the waters chill him. Then he took willow withes and vigorously switched himself to bring the blood and heat flowing back into the skin, as his ancestors had done long ago when seeking purity. Putting on the warm clothes of the mountain people, the Gitskan, of sewn white goat skin, and carrying a blanket of brain-softened elk hide, all loaned to him by a good friend, he started for the high peaks. His feet followed trails learned in his youth, his eyes read the story of the wind and the rain from the vegetation of the rain forest through which he first passed. A day later, when he had crossed the pass over the coastal mountains, he knew he was entering the land of lesser rain and more open forest. Before him the great ridges lifted to the peaks of ice and snow like steps carved by the magic power of the thunderbird. That evening he came to rocky country where he knew the herds of the great white goats ranged. This was land where he was not supposed to hunt without permission, but he had brought no weapns for killing. He came only with the desire to seek an answer to his problems in the loneliness of the wilderness below the peaks.

In a secluded vale he heard an eagle screaming far above him and the waters of a streamlet whispering over mossy rocks and down into a bright flowering meadow. Here he found an indentation in the wall of a cliff, protected in front by the low sweeping boughs of a noble fir. He made a bed of fir needles and boughs, piling more fir needles high about himself for protection against the cold, and rolled in his warm skin blanket, listening to the last cries of the marmots whistling among the rocks as the early summer darkness fell. He sang his prayer songs to the spirits and, when he grew tired, turned to sleep under the blanket and the needles.

In the dawn, too chilled to stay warm even under his blanket and piled needles, he rose, beating arms and legs to arouse the inner heat. Quickly he produced two sticks of wood, one long and round and hard, and the other flat and soft, with hollows along one edge. In his pocket he had an old mouse nest and a pile of chips for tinder in emergency, which he laid out beside the wood sticks. Then he put the round stick's point into one of the hollows on the flat stick and began to twirl the first stick between his hands at high speed. He worked with desperate vigor, for he knew that his life depended on getting a few sparks flying from the wood to make fire as soon as possible. He twirled the stick for some minutes. Finally a little smoke rose from where wood met wood, and he put on a last burst of speed that ran a little trickle of sparks down into the dry tinder. Suddenly it burst into flame—but such a tiny flame!

He put little chips and twigs on it, careful not to smother it, until at last it flamed higher and ate hungrily at each bit of wood he fed it. Only then did he let out a little cry of joy, for death had been very near. He needed to warm his hands and then his whole body as quickly as possible because both feet and hands had been near to freezing.

He had a knife and small hand ax of sharp obsidian to get more wood, so the fire grew and grew until a delightful warmth spread over him. Now he built a rock wall along one side to keep out the wind and another one behind the fire to reflect its heat into his shallow cave, and cut more wood and fir branches until he had it more comfortable. Now he was ready for the four days and nights of fasting and praying and singing to the spirits. His chief song was:

Lord of the Thunder, help me!
From the peaks send me your spirit.
My ancestors won their strength from you,
But now I need a new strength, a new dream.
By their purity and courage they broke the wall of silence.
Humbly I call to you to tell me what to do,
With my mind wholly upon you, I seek your guidance.
Listen, listen to me, and tell me your answer in the song of
    the wind!

He knew that few of his people sought spirit power in this way. It was mainly those who chose to be shamans who fasted until they fainted and they were carried off to the cave of the spirits where they got their power. But he had spent much time in the wilderness or on the edge of the sea, drawing and drawing with charcoal on cedar bark or board, the shapes of fishes and bears and eagles, beavers and mountain lions and mountain goats, to learn to carve them in turn on the boxes of his trade. In the heart of the wilderness he hoped to find his answer near the animals he loved to draw but not to kill. Here among the high peaks and in this beautiful meadow he would watch the life soaring on wings in the blue, or leaping gracefully through the meadow and up the rocks, and somehow from it the spirit would come.

On the fourth night a chill rain fell and gradually turned to sleet and then to snow. His heart sank, for it would be a long night. But in the meantime he had added a lean-to to the shelter provided by the shallow cave, lacing it with fir boughs. On this the rain fell and hissed, and later the snow came softly. He had a warm fire going and plenty of wood, but he was weak now from lack of food; if he fell asleep the fire might go out and he could freeze to death without even knowing what had happened. Somehow he stayed awake, singing on and on through the long hours until he saw light coming in the east. It was as if the wind was speaking to him, for it seemed to be telling him a new song to sing, a song to call the goat people, to make friends with them, and ask them for their wool. So he sang:

Come, come from the mountains, you who are my brothers!
Down the rocks I hear your hoof-steps, my brothers, my brothers!
You who ride the winds of the peaks shall come to my meadow,
To the good green grass, and I shall protect you and sing to you.
Give to me your wool when you are too warm and the flies swarm.
Come to me to be scratched, for I will stop your itching.
Come, come from the mountains, my brothers, my brothers,
And no man save me, your friend, shall touch you!

In the new dawn the clouds passed over the peaks and disappeared. The sun came with the first warmth of beginning summer, the heat growing to replace the cold till the goats came to eat in the meadow, a herd of fifteen led by a wise old nanny. So he rubbed his body with the sweet-smelling herbs of the meadow, the clovers and sages and violets, until all man smell was gone; this was helped also by his fasting. Then he crawled toward the goats in his white skin clothing, skin of the white goat, and sang his song to them, making goat noises between the verses. He saw the heat was bothering them so he called them until the old nanny came and let him scratch her. Then the others came to be scratched and he knew they trusted him because they felt his love for them, that in his heart he had no wish to kill. So it became a very natural thing for him to take his sharp obsidian knife and softly, gently begin to shear them of their outer wool, until he had made a great pile of it in one place, and they were grateful because it took so long to get used to the warmth of summer when the cold time ended.

He filled his elkskin blanket with all the wool he could gather, tied it together with some sinew cord he had and made it into a back pack that he could carry. But he was so weak that he had to stagger until he found some edible roots and bulbs in the meadow that gave him strength again. Still lower he caught a rabbit in a snare and cooked it over a little fire. Thus by degrees he built the strength to get down from the mountains, back to the Nass River, and in another day to his home.

Singing, he came into the village and to the great house where he lived. His wife, crying, clung to him and hugged him, for she had been afraid he was lost. He told his story to his clansmen and showed them the sheared goat's wool as proof that he had brought it without a killing, for there was no blood anywhere upon it. The chief came to see what all the noise was about. Cedar Man was filled with the power of his dream song and spoke boldly, saying:

"Lord of the Beaver Clan and of our village, Great Chief, listen to me. The spirit taught me a song to sing to the goat people and I called them to me like my children, and here is the proof of their coming. Now I was also given the dream that I would make a great pole for you to stand in front of your house and carve on it the story of the great legends of your ancestors for all to see, and to give glory to you and our clan. It will be the first of its kind in the world and I will draw it for you with charcoal on a cedar board so you can see what I mean to do."

The chief smiled then and said, using the first words of rank that Cedar Man had ever heard applied to him: "Noble nephew and artist, we will be glad to see your plan. How soon can you submit it?"

"In thirty days."

The most delighted person of all was Goat Woman when she

saw all the fine wool, white as snow, that her husband had brought for her. Throwing her arms around him, she startled him with a sudden kiss and the words:

"Lord of my heart, no man in the world has been so kind to his wife as you. This is enough to make the most beautiful blanket on my loom. I shall mix the goat's wool with red cedar bark twine, and you will draw for me on a cedar board a colorful design that I shall mix into the wool with the aid of dyes. How wonderful also that I have a friend who has done some of this work before and will show me what I do not know."

But Cedar Man wondered what in the world he could do to earn the wealth necessary to buy the strange white metal that could cut so much better than any obsidian or beaver-tooth chisel or knife he had now. He worried for a while and then realized he had plenty of work to do without spending time moping. He rushed down to a house that had just been built to find some pieces of cedar boards that had been cut off. He found one 3- x 12-foot piece and another 3 x 4½ feet that were just what he needed. First he worked to smooth them with pieces of sandstone rubbed over the wood, and then with some pieces of dog shark skin. With some thin pieces of fairly hard charcoal he started to draw his designs, one for the goat-wool-and-cedar-fiber blanket his wife was starting to make and then the much larger design for what would be the first of all totem poles.

Instantly he had an idea about the blanket; he began to see it in his mind. It would be generally rectangular in shape, but with the lower part coming out to a shallow V from which the cords would hang in a graceful bottom fringe. There would be a solid black rim around the outer edge with a light-tan band inside of that, and then would appear the designs, showing the eyes, teeth, and tails of crest animals and the beaks and eyes of crest birds, but with only a stylistic hint of their bodies. Thus the whole blanket could tell in symbolic form the legendary history of a clan. Quickly but carefully he proceeded to work out the pattern on the smaller of the two cedar boards.

When finished he took it all to his wife. She was already

setting up the simple three-sided Tsimshian loom; the cedar-bark strings were carefully wrapped with goat's wool hanging down evenly and close together from the top bar. She was ready to put the warp and weft together and had her blue, yellow, and black dyes ready in little basket cups for working up the designs, but she looked up and exclaimed, "How wonderful!" when he held out his pattern for her to look at.

"Use the colors as you want to," he urged her, "but remember, you need to make the more important parts of the design stand out with dramatic effect."

She nodded her head vigorously and turned eagerly to get started with her work, knowing that it would be several months before it was finished.

Immediately Cedar Man was busy on the new design for a carved pole. He laid out his large 3- x 12-foot board and started to trace in the outlines of the design. This all took a long time, for there was much detail and thought involved, but in twenty-five days he had it finished. When Goat Woman saw what he had done, she laughed like a delighted girl and cried:

"This is really tremendous!"

"I know, but you always like what I do."

"My husband, I am serious. This is by far the best work you have ever done, and it is so because you have room to really expand your talents, not like the crowded covers of those boxes!" Now all the children rushed up to see what their father had done, with many an "Ooh!" and "Ah!" For a minute the father basked grandly in their adulation. Then a frown of worry crossed his face.

"But I have to get that piece of white metal to make into a chisel to do that much carving. Without such a tool, it may take me more than two years to do the job, and the chief will become impatient!"

"My darling," said his wife fondly, "you won the power of the spirit on the mountaintop because your heart was good. It will help you again. And I will help you too! When my beautiful blanket is finished, it will be yours to use to help buy the new metal blade!"

Cedar Man's eyes turned wet as he grabbed his wife and hugged her, hiding his face in her hair, for a Tsimshian man must not show tears.

When Cedar Man showed his charcoal drawing of the design for the carved pole he would put in front of the great house to the village chief, Sea Eagle, the chief, as befitted a man of great authority and dignity, looked at it impassively. But gradually, though he tried to hide it, he could not prevent an eager trembling of his lips and a staring of his eyes, as he began to drink in every detail, reliving the ancient legends of his ancestors and the animal spirits that were supposed to have helped them. Then he touched Cedar Man on the shoulder and said:

"Your art has greatly improved over what you have done with the boxes, for it is as if the pole gives you the sweep of power you needed. If you can do this in wood, it will be the finest work of carving in our world! How long will it take?"

"If I work with bone or tooth chisels, it may take two years or more, but if I can get a piece of the new metal I hear is coming down the coast from the west for trade, I can do it in a few months."

"But what do you have to trade for such rare metal? I also would like some of that metal to make myself a dagger, but I have expected to pay as much as a dozen otter skins for it, or even ten slaves, or a great copper, beaten with the sacred signs."

"If you will come with me, I will show you what my wife is making as a gift for me, to be used to pay for the metal."

Cedar Man took him to his house and led him to where Goat Woman was working on her loom. Only the upper third of it was done, but this was enough to give the feeling that was emerging. The light parts of the blanket were ethereal designs of pulsing sun's rays. The whole great motif of the art was alive, the eyes seeming to stare at the watcher, the black and red markings adding grandeur and majesty.

Chief Sea Eagle's eyes gleamed, but he controlled himself proudly.

"Your wife has woven magic!" he said simply. "I have never

seen a blanket to equal this. But it is too valuable to give to a stranger; it should stay in our village to enhance the greatness of our people. Give it to me and I will buy for you the metal you need for carving. Truly it is greater that this metal should be used for peace than for war!"

Cedar Man and Goat Woman went to bed that night in a daze of happiness. Held in his arms, she murmured: "Our sons and daughters shall walk the way of honor and greatness because of what we have done today!"

"Perhaps," he said cautiously, "but remember, my dear one, that even our chief may not be able to buy the strange metal that comes from the east."

She snorted in exasperation: "You are always too pessimistic! Remember what happened on the mountain!"

It was two months later when the great day came and ten huge trading (or war) canoes of the Haida came out of the west, cutting the water into lines of light, their great carved prows reaching to the sky, and a proud chief in each one with his mantle of otter fur flowing from his shoulders and his high basket hat topped with the clan crests. Down to meet them at the beach came the Tsimshian chiefs and the heads of noble families, equally finely dressed. The greetings were dignified, even stilted at first, but later they would grow more friendly.

Along the beach, large canoes had been dragged up some days before. These, filled partly with water, served as enormous pots into which fat from the eulachon or candlefish had been thrown; the whole was brought to a boil with red-hot stones. Already quantities of the highly valuable and much sought after eulachon grease had been scraped and put into seal-stomach bags or into watertight boxes to be used in the trading.

On the beach each tribe put on a dance for the other, the men trying to outleap each other, to play their rattles better, to beat the board drums louder. Feet pounded the ground until

---

HAIDA STONE BLADED KNIVES. The handles are of deer horn, the blades of jade, and the lashings of buckskin. (*Niblack*, The Coast Indians of Southern Alaska and Northern British Columbia)

the earth seemed to tremble. Feathers waved wildly, and the masks of some dancers were meant to frighten by their terrible looks. But the spectators laughed with delight and made ribald comments, echoed by the opposing tribe. Though there was no war motive in the dancing, these were still virile, warlike people, and violence lurked behind every move in the dances. The chiefs had to be very careful to honor their guests and to offer rich foods and gifts. They had also to handle the trading with honor and dignity and justice, or disagreement and raised voices could easily flare into open war. The greatness of Chief Sea Eagle was that he knew exactly how to use his immense wealth and prestige, his words of wisdom and warning, to keep the other chiefs and their warriors from the dark edge of the precipice where hate and revenge lurked.

After the dances the minor trading of the first two days started. It was on the third day that the great and valuable things began to appear, and the talk of the people took on an edge of excitement and suspense.

Finally a Haida chief, muscles rolling on his mighty arms, stepped out before all the people with such impressive dignity that all knew a surprise was coming. From under his magnificent otter-skin robe he drew forth two pieces of metal attached to wooden handles, one a knife and the other a chisel. The strange white metal was far less beautiful than copper, but it was hard and strong. The chief drove the knife blade into a hardwood board with a swift thrust, and the people gasped to see it dig into the wood—wood that would have bent a copper blade, and against which a horn blade or even a beaver tooth would only have bounced!

"One of these treasures," he said, "I offer for sale, the other I keep for war!" and his fierce eyes glittered as he held up the knife. Then he placed the blade to be used as a chisel against a piece of cedar wood and chipped away with such quickness and ease that again a great gasp ran through the ranks of the watchers.

"This I sell!" he said.

A chief from higher up the river Nass offered a large canoe

for it, but the Haida chief laughed scornfully. "So great is the value of this metal," he said, "that I doubt if there is a Tsimshian who has the wealth to buy it."

"Three canoes and a slave!" shouted another chief, this one from the Skeena River Tsimshian.

So the bidding went up and up. Cedar Man anxiously watched his uncle, Chief Sea Eagle, but the great man's face was impassive. He was watching and waiting. Finally there was a pause, as the bidding chiefs seemed to have reached the limit of what they cared to bid, and still the Haida chief scornfully shook his head. At last Chief Sea Eagle spoke with great dignity:

"I offer a dozen sealskin bags of eulachon grease, six canoes, six stalwart slave women, three of them good cooks, two well-muscled slave men, and this dance rattle that is carved out of a fine hardwood from the far south." He held up an extraordinary rattle of great beauty, and all knew that it was an heirloom worthy of the greatest of families.

But a large canoe filled with warriors from the southern Tsimshian had just landed on the beach, and out of it strode a chief with a beautiful silver fox-skin cape across his mighty shoulders, holding in his hands an equally beautiful blanket of glistening white goat wool, interwoven with cedar bark, its edges bordered with mother-of-pearl shells.

"I will offer for the strange metal chisel what Chief Sea Eagle has offered, plus this beautiful goat's-wool blanket," said the new chief from the south.

The faces of all the followers of Chief Sea Eagle's village grew dark and sad, as all felt that the new chief had offered as high as any chief could possibly offer for such a piece of hard metal. But Cedar Man strode with an uncharacteristic purposefulness to his chief's side and whispered in his ear earnestly:

"Listen, my lord," he whispered. "The blanket my wife made for you from the wool of my sacred dream is far more beautiful than this one. Offer her blanket for the metal and she will make you another one even better and showing your crest upon it!"

The chief's face widened into a broad smile and he tossed a command to a willing slave who ran off and soon returned with Goat Woman's creation, the first blanket any of the people had seen that was decorated with the sacred eyes of the sea-animal people. A long sigh hissed through the crowd when they saw its luminous beauty glistening in the sunlight.

"Here," he said proudly, turning to the Haida chief, "choose which blanket is the most valuable, mine from the north or his from the south. And let this decide the matter."

The Haida was impassive of face, but there was a gleam in his eyes. "Be it so!" he said, and strode swiftly over to take Chief Sea Eagle's blanket, presenting the new metal chisel to him in exchange for the blanket and the other items already offered.

The face of the huge chief from the south was a mixture at first of surprise and then of anger. But he mastered his anger, bent his head in agreement to his defeat, and smiled.

"We of the Tsimshian must know how to lose as well as win," he said with dignity. "I congratulate my brother from the north, Chief Sea Eagle. But I will ask where he got such a blanket, for I would like to have one like it."

Thus did Goat Woman soon get an order for a third blanket of goat wool, paid for in advance by eulachon grease, dried salmon, goat skins, and dentalium money, and thus did Cedar Man receive the new iron-bladed chisel that was his heart's desire, to be paid for in full by half his work on what was probably to be the first true totem pole of the northwest! Proudly he started on his work, his oldest son, Straight Arrow, coming to watch him and learn.

He selected a pole that, when cut, was 2 feet thick and 20 feet high, of fine-grained cedar wood, which, with the help of the chief's slaves, he laid on two large wooden blocks about 2 feet high so that he could do his carving standing up. Almost immediately he found the iron chisel a delightful instrument to work with. It could take off flakes of wood with great ease and little pushing; it also stayed sharp much longer and could be quickly sharpened by working it back and forth over a piece of granular sandstone.

"Now, my son," said Cedar Man to the watching Straight Arrow, "watch how all my observing and studying of the wild animals and birds of the woods and seas and rivers, and the bodies and faces of people, will help me reproduce them in this great post. I will have to cut very carefully so that I do not cut too deep and so ruin my story. But everything must be marked out first on the wood with a light touch of the charcoal. The chief's hero ancestors of long ago were saved from the monsters of the sea by a sea eagle. The eagle signifies his crest and my crest, for I am of the same eagle clan. But one day we will have our own special crest for our family. It will be the mountain goat, because she helped me when I needed help badly."

"Will we have our own pole someday?" asked the boy. "And maybe live in our own great house too?"

"We shall if our hearts are good and our spirit helpers continue to help us. If many hear of this pole and after it is carved ask me to do others like it, we will become wealthy. Then we can pay for our own great house, for which I can carve a pole. Thus do noble families start, and you, as my first-born son, will marry into a noble family and spread our honor."

As the boy became more and more interested in the carving, the father continued to teach him the art of the carver.

"The chief's ancestor was also helped by the killer whale, and by the little people of the woods, so I shall show all these as they play the story on the pole. I will make groups of big figures, and then little figures above and below them, to give contrast, but most of all I must make every living thing on the pole seem to be alive. Watch this face that I am starting to carve and see how with little touches here and there with the chisel I put flesh over the bone, and light into the eyes to make them seem to stare at you. My fingers touch the wood and I feel what is in it so I can draw forth with my art the character of man and beast. I close my eyes and see with my mind's eye what I want to carve and then I carve it. What I see comes from a thousand experiences. You must have these also; then you can translate with the feeling of your fingers your experiences and dreams into carvings that seem to live and breathe."

The boy was equally intrigued with the work of his mother on the loom, as were the other children, for hers were the first of what later came to be called the famous Chilkat blankets, first done by the Tsimshian, but later spread to the north among the Tlingit and done to this day along the Chilkat River. But it was Cedar Man and Goat Woman who started all this and gave honor to the river Nass and to their people, the Tsimshian!

4. Kwakiutl and Their Neighbors

The Kwakiutl-speaking peoples occupied northwestern Vancouver Island and the opposite mainland of the British Columbia coast as far north as the area called Ocean Falls, which borders on the lands of the Tsimshian. In the south were the South Kwakiutl; to the north were the southern Heiltsuk, called the Xaihais, and then the northern Heiltsuk, called the Haisla, both often lumped together under the name Bella Bella, and both cutting off the Salishan-speaking Bella Coola of Burke Channel and the Bella Coola River from the sea. The whole area is one of rugged mountainous coasts, covered with a thick coniferous forest of spruce, hemlock, Douglas fir, and cedar, though long fjordlike inlets of the ocean often extend dozens of miles inland, and there are some flat areas near the coast with grass and bushes. In the old days no cultivation of edible plants was known in this area; most of the food used was obtained from the sea and the rivers, mainly in the form of fish or other water food, of which the salmon was the premier item.

The basis of the political structure was the extended family or clan, ruled by a clan chief. Parts of several clans together often formed a village in which one clan chief had some control over the others due to higher rank in the form of inherited honors and privileges or greater ability as a leader. How strong his control was depended on his personality and drive, with some village chiefs acting as virtual tyrants, others as revered leaders who were obeyed through respect, and others having only nominal control. Sometimes, for mutual defense against enemy tribes, several villages banded together in a loose confederacy, again directed by a dominant chief with the greatest prestige.

Each clan chief, in cooperation with his clan, had certain inherited spiritual powers, as well as control over certain hunting and fishing areas and special ceremonial rights and cus-

toms. He was usually very jealous of these, though in practice
he often gave other clans the right to fish or hunt in his clan's
territories, if they asked permission in the correct way, or, if
required, paid for the privilege.

The Kwakiutl-speaking peoples belong to a larger language
group called the Wakashan, which also includes the Nootka
and the Makah. Legends hint that all of these people came up
into this area long ago out of the southwest.

The basic material culture items for this area are mentioned
in the charts in the appendix. The large board-covered houses
and the large seagoing canoes carved out of cedar logs were the
dominant items. Generally the Kwakiutl-speaking peoples
seemed to prefer the larger canoes of the Haida and Tlingit to
the north, with their uplifted and outcurved bows and sterns,
to the probably equally seaworthy Nootka canoe to the south,
which had a blunter lower stern, but a similar outcurving high

G

F

E

D

C

Opposite, top KWAKIUTL VILLAGE SCENE. Alert Bay, Vancouver Island. The
skirts worn by these women are very similar to those worn up and down
most of the coast in the old days. The woman on the left has a carrying
basket. Note the high and pointed head of the woman in the middle.
This was done by shaping the head with boards when the child is little
and is a sign of high rank. The canoes are northern type, sharply pointed
at both ends with high prows for ocean travel. (*Milwaukee Public
Museum*)

Opposite, center VIEW OF ANOTHER KWAKIUTL VILLAGE: on Vancouver
Island, showing somewhat different house structures. This warns us not
to always expect the same kind of houses for any one tribe. The totem
pole shows the usual well-spaced and naturalistic figures, quite different
from the crowded figures and symbolic designs of the more northern
tribes. (*American Museum of Natural History, New York*)

Opposite, bottom PAGAN BELLA COOLA VILLAGE: looking eastward up Bella
Coola River. Though this is a Salish-speaking tribe, their art and culture
is much closer to that of the Kwakiutl than it is to the Coast Salish
farther south. (*American Museum of Natural History, New York*)

Below CANOE AND FISHING GEAR: **A** northern type Haida canoe with decorated and separately attached bow and stern; **B** three Kwakiutl canoe-
bailers of wood; **C** steering paddle; **D** Kwakiutl sealskin float; **E** typical North Pacific coast harpoon, pitch coated, with one bone point and
two horn barbs; **F** codfish hooks; **G** various other hooks. (*Drawings by
Gladys Fox; A to D after Goddard, E to G after Drucker*)

A

B

A

prow. The higher structures were put on as separate items but so carefully fashioned to fit and sewed so securely and tightly to the main part of the canoe with cedar cord lashings that the line between the parts was hard to see. Farther north the Northern Heiltsuk or Haisla, for example, copied more the ways of the Haida and Tsimshian, building their houses with vertical boards on the side instead of the horizontal boards to the south.

The contrast in artwork among the various northwest tribes is discussed in chapter 3.

Most of the major items of religious culture are listed in the charts in the appendix. The Kwakiutl had developed religious ceremonialism probably to the most complicated degree of any of the peoples of the Pacific Coast, so complicated indeed that Dr. Franz Boas and others of the great early-day anthropologists who took notes on these ceremonies were under considerable strain trying to understand them and explain them. Boas's book on the subject was enormous. What I say in this book, because of limited space, can only be considered a partial outline. Boas grew bored after a time with the constant repetition, but he acknowledged that, although a white man finds it hard to understand, to the Kwakiutl the ceremonies were rich in meaning.

B

In the two stories that go with this chapter, one of a girl seeing the ceremonies from the standpoint of the completely uninitiated, and the other a story told from the viewpoint of the actual planners and actors in the ceremonies, you will see the curious combination of the sacred and the profane in this ceremonialism, some of it deadly serious, and a lot of the rest in great good humor. The seriousness stems from the origin of

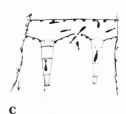

C

FISH TRAPS AND NETS FROM THE PACIFIC NORTHWEST CULTURE AREA: **A** Kwakiutl fish basket and dam for salmon; **B** North Pacific coast tidal trap for fish in cove at ebb tide; **C** North Pacific coast double stream trap, trapping upstream-swimming salmon that try to escape by turning downstream again; **D** North Pacific coast fishing gear: eulachon funnel-shaped tubular net, dip net, herring rake for spiking herring. (*Drawings by Gladys Fox; A after Goddard, B to D after Drucker*)

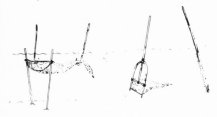

D

the ceremonials in deeply believed ancestral spiritual experiences or vision quests. During the ceremonies the actors appear to relive the experiences of their ancestors, though without doubt there has been much elaboration of each original story down through the centuries. Some seek to recapture or parallel the ancestral experiences by having vision quests themselves before the ceremonies. They then may sing of these visions and act them out as a part of a ceremony.

The serious parts of the ceremonies are countered at different times by humorous clowning and practical jokes plus a good deal of deliberate fakery, which may make some observers believe after a while that the whole thing is a "big lie put on to scare and dominate the women and children!" But this can be a superficial view, for even the fakery can have deep meaning to those who act it out or direct it, as will become evident in the second story.

Most of the more primitive native Americans sought spirit power by going on vigils alone into the wilderness. The Kwakiutl did this less frequently, preferring to seek power or luck for the most part by the performance of ritual acts. Their rituals were supposed to bring help from the ancestral spirits as the vigil might do, and special ritual secrets were passed from generation to generation, particularly in the richer, more successful, or dominant families. Poorer families might pick up some of this power by special help given to the richer and more powerful. They also gained honor by assisting a chief or clan head in the ceremonials.

The main social classes on the surface appeared to be the slave and the free because, theoretically, all the free people were members of the clans and as such shared in the hunting and fishing grounds and other special privileges of each clan. So it appeared that there was only a graded series of clan members and each member had his unique place in the series. Such

KWAKIUTL HOUSE: showing frame supports for roof. (*American Museum of Natural History, New York*)

A

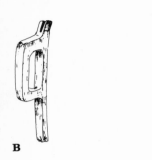

B

C

D

E

F

a system was found from the Nootka and Kwakiutl north to the Tlingit, while the Coast Salish had more sharply separated classes of the poor and the rich (see chapter 6). But in practice even the Northern Province peoples, as well as the Kwakiutl, had a feeling in their relationship with each other that divided off the noble or rich from the commoners or poorer people. Thus we can think of there being actually three classes: slaves, common people, and nobles.

The main difference in the clan inheritance system between the Northern Province (including the Haisla or northernmost Kwakiutl-speakers) and the Wakashan Province is the matrilineal inheritance of powers and privileges in the Northern, and the mainly patrilineal, sometimes bilateral inheritance in the Wakashan. In both cases the clan system differed from the Scottish clans in their lack of cohesion except in a specific village. Thus there were often clan members scattered among several villages, but there was rarely a way (except in the rare instance when villages formed a confederacy) for a clan to get together for a concerted effort, as happened often with Scottish clans. It was the village, under a dominant chief, that got the several different clans of the village to work together for unified ends.

Two Widely Different Viewpoints

1. THE GIRL WHO HATED VIOLENCE

SHE WAS a chief's daughter, and her nickname was Rainbow Girl, which we can shorten to Rainbow. As a twelve-year-old chief's daughter she would soon go into a long period of seclusion around the time of the onset of puberty. During this se-

NORTHWEST COAST ARTIFACTS: **A** wooden shredder for cedar bark; **B** beater for cedar bark; **C** spindle whorls; **D** anklet; **E** tongs for handling hot rocks; **F** digging stick; **G** woman's apron of shredded cedar bark; **H** cradel with cedar bark bedding (Kwakiutl). (*Drawings by Gladys Fox after Goddard*)

G

H

clusion she would be watched constantly and advised how to act by an old, wise woman of the clan. This was to prepare her spiritually for a proper marriage (the groom would be selected by her father and mother), and to protect her so she would come to her marriage with the honor of a virgin.

Rainbow did not look forward to this trial. She had heard from her older sister, Dentalium Girl, how long and boring it was, particularly because she would be allowed to do no work and little play for the many months of its duration. However, being a girl of considerable inventiveness, she had already figured out some games she could play with herself and a way to do some artwork. But before she began her lonely vigil, she knew she had an even worse ordeal ahead, the winter ceremonials.

"Mother," she asked Cedar Tree Woman, "Why do I have to watch the ceremonials? You know how I hate all the gory details and I don't understand why they are needed at all!"

The mother clenched her fist and raised it as if to strike, but the girl looked at her calmly, refusing to flinch.

Cedar Woman lowered her fist, still looking sternly at her daughter.

"Don't ever let your father hear you say such a thing! You know what happened to Chief Killer Whale's daughter. She peeked at her father when he was making a sacred mask and he had to have her killed. The same thing could happen to you if you are not careful."

"I will try to be careful, Mother, but can't you give me a better explanation of the meaning of these ceremonials?" Rainbow stood so tall and straight, her beautiful face so serious and sincere, framed in its long, black, lustrous hair, that the mother looked at her in surprise.

"I thought I had told you enough before, but I will tell you

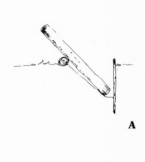

A

B

C

D

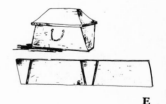

E

ARTIFACTS AND BOXES OF THE NORTHWEST COAST: **A** erecting house post; **B** raising beam for house; **C** chisels; **D** hand adze; **E** box with unfolded box below; **F** dish that was dug out of an alder; **G** large box; **H** method of joining boards with twine to make boxes. (*Drawings by Gladys Fox*)

H

G

F

more now. There are, of course, secrets you cannot be told at present; when you are an older woman and purified, you will be told some. But you must understand that your life and your future depend upon these winter ceremonials. That is why in winter we take new names, names given us by the spirits, and why we must strive during the winter to be spiritually clean so that none of the harmful effects that appear in the ceremonials will touch and harm us. The ceremonials are a great test to all the people, but particularly to the older children and youth like yourself. As a chief's daughter you must learn to hold yourself in control, to be calm and collected, your heart purified, so that all the evil will be blown away from you and not hurt you. To learn to watch these ceremonials with a calm and brave spirit is a lesson in courage."

"But Mother, why is there so much blood?"

"Be patient and I will try to explain. Long ago our ancestors lived in the interior mountains, where the snow is deeper and the cold greater than here and where there is much less food. Like the animals and birds they had to learn to stay alive during the winter. The winter was the time of great testing when the weak died, but the strong and clever survived. In those difficult times our ancestors sought spirit power to help them face and overcome these great difficulties, some much worse and more dangerous than those we face now. They met spirit monsters who were like the fierce winds of the north that bring the cold rain and snow of winter. From these monsters, such as the Cannibal Spirit, they were given certain spirit powers, but they had to learn to control the wilder parts of them and to use them in a purified way or otherwise the humans would all have been destroyed. To keep our powers over the animals, birds, and fishes, now we have the winter ceremonials. In them we see again how our ancestors were given these powers, but some so dangerous that they needed to be tamed, and we see how the taming is done through special songs and by the special powers of the shamans so that sometimes even the dead can be brought back to life. By looking death bravely in the face, we also can overcome it. The blood we see spilled in the ceremonials is the blood of life. Though taken away, we can restore it by our magic powers. Then death has no fear for us. You will grow strong and brave if you control your fears during the ceremonials. You are someday to be the wife of a great chief, and he will need your love, your courage, and especially your strength of spirit to help him in his great task of leading the people and preserving us from our enemies."

"I will try to be strong of heart," promised Rainbow.

Soon she was outside, down by the beach where the waves curled in from the sound, and the wind blew wet and cold from the north. She drew her otter-skin robe more tightly about her and pulled her basket cap closer over her black mass of hair. Here was the beauty of earth and sky and sea, clouds scudding dark across the sound, the shore forests stretching in great dark weaving masses to the north, a nearby tiny island silvered into glory by the mist-filtered light of the setting sun.

"Ah," she thought, stretching our her arms to the last bit of blue above her, "in the midst of such beauty why must man do such ugly things?" We do not know if many of her people ever had such a thought, for she lived in a culture often given

KWAKIUTL SEA MONSTER MASK: made of wood with obsidian eyes; painted white, red, black, and green; had moveable jaw; height, 21 inches. Its name, Numxilexiu, means "one who throws a big wave before him." This monster was supposed to bring storms and big waves that sunk canoes. (*Milwaukee Public Museum*)

to war and violence and the conquest of the weak by the strong.

When a young, flat-headed slave girl, probably captured from one of the Coast Salish tribes to the south, came to bid her come to dinner, even Rainbow did not realize that this was another sign of man's ugliness to man! The Salish considered the flat head a sign of their superiority to the more round-headed people to the south and east. The Kwakiutl, on the other hand, considered a head that was high-pointed in the rear to be superior; Rainbow's head had been so fashioned by board pressure when she was a baby.

A week later Rainbow heard the strange whistles sounding outside the great house of split cedar boards where her father and mother and all her next of kin and the twenty slaves lived. She knew instantly when the weird calls came that it was the beginning of the Winter Ceremonials, serious ceremonies and dances combined with alternative periods of horseplay and humor, even mock ceremonies, and satirical skits, that might, altogether, last for ten, twenty, or even more days. They were

---

Opposite KWAKIUTL THUNDERBIRD MASK AND LIFE-SIZED COSTUME: made of wood, feathers, and cloth; painted green, red, white, and black; beak is moveable. (*Milwaukee Public Museum*)

Below LOON MASK AS SEEN IN FIRELIGHT. This gives some idea of how mysterious and terrifying, especially to the children, some of the Kwakiutl dramatic performances must have been. (*Milwaukee Public Museum*)

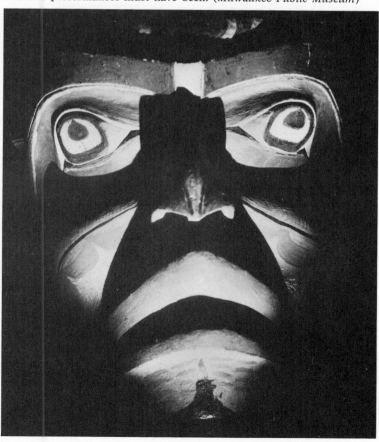

meant to break the tedium of the long winter nights, though they sometimes scared the women and children badly. These were to be the greatest winter ceremonials of Rainbow's life. We will relate only those things that most strongly impressed themselves on a sensitive twelve-year-old, and not the long horrible hours of constant repetitions and minor happenings that sometimes stretched before her to be endured stoically, though she cringed inwardly.

The whistles she heard that first night of the most complicated ceremonials on the Pacific Coast were those of the Hamatsa or cannibal dancers, young men of high lineage and nobility, two of them her own brothers, who were being initiated into the most dreaded secret society on the coast. One dark night a month before, they had been spirited away from the great house. The rest of the family was told that they had been carried off by the original Cannibal Dancer to a strange place beyond the sea, and that there, if they were strong enough, they would be given some of the magical powers that their ancestors had over the life of the sky and sea, river and land.

The whistles warned the people that the Hamatsa were filled with the spirit powers of the cannibal monster, some of which was good and some bad, and the wild and savage parts of the spirit had to be tamed before the young initiates into the Hamatsa secrets could be accepted back into human society. To do this the people were called on to dance the sacred dances that acted as pacifiers upon the Hamatsa.

So Rainbow and her younger sisters and brothers went with their mother and father to the great house that had been set aside for the dances and ceremonies. The house, about 120 feet long and 40 feet wide, was dark within on the winter day except for the blazing fire. The moving flames caused shadows and waves of light to dance on the smoke-darkened walls, and lit up eerily the figures of bears, killer whales, frogs, monsters, and men carved on the massive house posts. The dancers and singers came in from the back through a hole in the great screen that cut off a rear section of the house. Rainbow saw that their heads and bodies were ringed with cedar bark and their heads sprinkled with white eagle-down feathers, their faces painted so they were hardly recognizable. They brought with them a big box from which a strange squawking was heard; it signified that a magic spirit was speaking. Each singer and dancer, as he entered the large room, walked first to the left of the door and then to the right, in an age-old ritual movement that balanced the two halves of the world, symbolized by the house's interior.

The singers carried split sticks with which they began to beat the box in rhythm, the noise growing louder and louder, and then they began to sing. All their movements and their voices were in perfect harmony, every person's movement synchronized exactly with every other person's and with the beating on the box. They sang songs almost as old as the tribe itself, about the great days of the heroes, about their battles with monsters and cold and starvation, when the tribe was wandering over distant mountain passes and valleys and canyons. But there were new songs, too, of the new comings of spirit power, of the powers to kill enemies, of the powers to bring food and create wealth and prestige.

> I was alone in the forest.
> I heard the thunders talking to me;
> In the deep roll and boom I heard voices.
> "Listen, listen!" they roared and I listened.
> "Bow your head and listen," they warned me,
> And I bowed my head and listened.
> "We give you powers of the thunder!" they cried to me.
> "Feel them with your bones," they said.
> "Feel them with your blood when you cut your forehead."
> I cut my forehead, but it did not hurt me.
> O, I felt the power like a feather stroking me.
> Like the blood trickling down my face, oh!
> "Sing then, the thunder's song!" they roared,
> And I roared with them, like the mountain in avalanche.
> I felt the powers within me, like my heartbeat, oh!
> "You shall be a killer of enemies," they said,
> "A hunter of the great goats of the mountains."
> "You shall have no fear," they said,
> "And you shall be an honor to your people, oh!"

Rainbow liked this part of the ceremonials best. The beating of the sticks and the singing began to get inside her after a while and to be in tune with the beat of her own heart. At such times she felt as one with her people, with all their history, their great deeds, and their struggles to stay alive in the mountains. She knew that the dances and songs were trying to reach the hearts of the Hamatsa also, the cannibal dancers, who were outside listening. The songs must draw them in and tame them. But she dreaded the coming of the Hamatsa. So she watched the swaying bodies and the prancing feet and listened to the crashing of the sticks and the high thin or deep booming songs almost entranced, with a dread in her heart of what was coming.

The day came at last. The Hamatsa were shouting "Hap, hap, hap!" outside in the cold darkness; inside, the flames of the great fire leaped toward the smoke-blackened rafters. Suddenly the Hamatsa came in through the door, turning first left and then right in the sacred way, then turning and whirling again and again. Rainbow could not recognize her two brothers who were among them, for the cannibal dancers were streaked with black and red paints, and their painted faces were partly

KWAKIUTL HAMATSA (CANNIBAL DANCER) INITIATION CEREMONY: held inside of chief's large house. To achieve a dramatic entrance an actor comes through a hole in screen at back. Singers and drummers are on the right side of the room. (*Milwaukee Public Museum*)

hidden by their long tangled hair. Completely naked they came into the great house, dancing and crying "Hap, hap, hap!" Other dancers and the singers were soon among them, trying to pacify them, to calm their wild natures, to make them human again. But the savagery within them seemed to rise and fall in great waves.

For a few minutes they appeared fairly calm. Then suddenly they were dashing among the spectators, and one seized the arm of a woman near Rainbow. The woman screamed as teeth closed on her arm and tore at it; blood jetted from the arm and the woman moaned. The Hamatsa jumped away triumphantly, blood streaming from his mouth as he chewed at what he had bitten. The woman was crying hysterically, and a man rushed to her side to quickly bind her bloody wound.

A few minutes later, there were shouts outside the great house, and the people inside began calling to one another in dread.

"They must be killing a slave!"

A voice from the door shouted: "They are killing a slave to be eaten by the Hamatsa!"

Soon a body was brought in, the eyes protruding and staring, blood running from the neck and side. It was laid on a slightly raised platform. Immediately the four Hamatsa dancers rushed to the body, crouched before it, and began eating.

Rainbow screamed, hid her eyes, and leaned weakly against her mother. Then anger seized her and she spoke harshly:

"What have they done to my brothers to make them do such a terrible thing? I can't stand this any more!" And she rose, determined to rush from the building in which such things were happening. But her mother seized her in powerful hands and held her as she wept hysterically.

"Shhhh! Darling!" she hissed in her daughter's ear. "If you ran from this building, it would disgrace your father and he would have to order your death! Now calm down, and show your courage. A daughter of a chief must conquer her emotions or she will become less than a slave!"

Gradually the girl calmed and grew stronger, but for a long time she kept her eyes on the floor.

It was fortunate for Rainbow that the main dance on the next day was that of the Ghost Dancers, the Lasquenox, though when the hollow ghostly voices came out of the fire, booming with distance as if from the other end of the world, she shivered. She forced herself to sit straight and not throw herself into her mother's arms. She knew from the legends that occasionally the ghosts of the ancestors came up from the underworld to speak to the people, and that the dancer was showing what it was like to go down and visit the ghosts beneath the earth. Watching the dancer, with his two rings of skulls, one around his neck and one around his head mask of cedar bark, she could almost feel his desire to find his ancestral ghosts, particularly when he sang:

Down to the ghost world I come seeking, calling on the ghost
    chief to help me.
Down to the underworld I go singing, filled with the
    supernatural power he gives me.
The power is hidden in the beautiful stone he has put upon
    my forehead;
With it I have power over light and darkness, with it
    I can swim to the underworld through the river of darkness.
Soon I will see the ghosts of my ancestors and talk to the old ones
    I have longed so much to find.

And at this he began sinking down into the trodden earth of the floor of the great house, his attendant frantically trying to pull him back with a long rope that was attached to his body. Others rushed out to grab the rope and pull, but it was as if a great hand were pulling him down to the underworld, and the people had to let go of the rope or they would have

"MAN UNDER THE SEA" MASK: made of wood and cedar bark; painted red, green, white, and black; 12¾ inches high. This was a harmless spirit with long coarse hair and very strong teeth. Used in Luwulaxa dance. (*Milwaukee Public Museum*)

been pulled in after him. Rainbow stared and stared. She could hardly believe her eyes!

On the tenth day of the dances Rainbow had another dreaded ordeal. This was the day of the women dancers, the Toxuit, women who wore necklaces and neck and head rings of hemlock bark, and who called on the people to do terrible things to them. Rainbow watched with dread, for she knew something awful would happen. She felt her mother's fingers grip her arm, saying by their pressure: "Keep your head up! Watch what is happening. Be brave, you are a chief's daughter, a princess!"

As she watched, the first woman limped around the fire in a queer manner, lifting her hands every second step, while she held the palms upward at her sides, as if reaching for some power. Four attendant women followed her closely, watching her every move. When she had danced around the fire four times, she stretched her arms toward a distant corner of the great house. Out of an opening in the earth suddenly began to rise a Sisiul, a great and fantastic monster whose many eyes and tongues and horns were moving in the firelight. All through the house cries of fear came from the women and children, and Rainbow, too, shrank against her mother. At the very instant the Sisiul seemed about to leap forward and seize some shrieking children, shouting and crashing sounds came from another part of the house, and when the people turned back to look, the monster had disappeared under the earth again.

But then they saw the woman dancer suddenly being dragged down under the earth herself, apparently by the Sisiul. A strong man rushed forward to seize her, but he, too, was dragged partly under the earth. Here a fantastic struggle seemed to be going on, the man struggling to free the woman from the monster, while the monster dragged both of them along. As the man fought, it looked as if his whole body was being dragged along, partly under the ground, partly above, sometimes with only the top of his head in sight. People were standing, straining to see what was happening. In her excitement Rainbow jumped up and stood on her bench, while her mother held her, shouting with terror when she saw the man disappear underground.

The next woman dancer danced limping in circles, facing the people. By signs she asked them in various ways to kill her. A hand stroking across her throat meant "cut off my head"; motions to her middle meant "spear me through my stomach" or "cut me open with a knife." At first the people refused, shaking their heads, but at last one agreed to kill her. She disappeared for a minute, then came out again, walking on her knees, her body covered with a long bulky costume of cedar bark. She sat on a stool, and the long shadows and the wavering light from the flickering flames played over her till she seemed a being from another world. The giant man who had offered to kill her came forward with a large knife made from a giant clam shell. Suddenly, with all his force, he struck at her neck and her head fell off. The blood gushed up from the neck in a foot-high fountain, while the head rolled over the ground and into the bright firelight, the eyelids opening and shutting to show the glazing eyes, still seemingly alive, while the mouth opened and shut spasmodically, blood running from the severed neck in streams.

Rainbow was a rigid as a stone statue, her face chalk white

KWAKIUTL THUNDERBIRD MASK: made of wood; painted red, white, green, and black. Bird opens bill to reveal supposedly dangerous Sisiul or serpent man (as seen in photograph). Length is approximately 19 inches. The Sisiul's look was believed to bring death. (*Milwaukee Public Museum*)

as a clam shell, her fists clenched till the nails cut her hands. Then she heaved a great sigh and fainted. Anxiously her mother caught her and held her, so she did not appear to faint but was held cuddled in those loving arms. The mother's face, too, was very white.

When the girl recovered her senses, the mother whispered fiercely.

"You must control yourself, you must, you must! Your father and the other men are watching. I hope they will let you live! Don't faint again; it may be your last time!"

Frightened by the earnest words, the girl vowed she would be more brave. But how can one who hates the sight of violence with her whole being ever learn to watch such things with calmness? Violence is found in nearly every human society, but there are always those who hate it and wish it to end. And perhaps such people are the hope of the world.

2. HOW THE WINTER CEREMONIALS WERE PLANNED

The great house had been closed to the people long before the winter ceremonials. In its dark and supposedly silent interior men were planning the dances and ceremonies many weeks before they began, and then arranging everything so it would be ready. It was a vast silent rehearsal, and entirely in secret. Most people would be completely surprised by many of the things that happened.

It was a dark winter day, when the cold wind that came all the way from the Aleutian Islands was blowing down the sound and shaking all the trees above the cliffs, and snow was two feet deep outside. White Bear Kills, the chief of the village (and Rainbow's father), explained to his son, Flying Leaf, a new Hamatsa dancer-to-be, about the preparations for the ceremonials. Flying Leaf was only four years older than

NORTHWEST COAST ADORNMENTS: **A** Kwakiutl mask; **B** Bella Coola Fish Spirit mask; **C** Tlingit copper, with face carved in the copper (a sign of great wealth); **D** Kwakiutl hair ornament made of valuable dentalium shells. (*Drawings by Gladys Fox, all except C are after Goddard*)

Rainbow and was her favorite brother, as one might guess from his sensitive eyes and lips, but there was masculine strength in him, too, and he stood straight and proud before his father, as the powerful older man spoke.

"My son," said the father, "you have been alone in the wilderness, seeking the spirit and living with a corpse of our ancestors. It has been a trying experience for you, but you have stood to it manfully. Now you must be trained for the Hamatsa dancing. Are ready for the dance and are you ready to honor your ancestors even it if means eating human flesh?"

The boy quivered like a leaf in the wind, fulfilling his name, but steadied himself with a dignity befitting a chief's son. Straightening his back, he replied:

"My father, I hate even the thought of such a thing, but if I am commanded by you and by the spirits, I will do as I am commanded."

The father's stern pose relaxed and he gave an unchieftain-like sigh.

"Knowing how like your sister Rainbow you are," he said, smiling, "I expected you to refuse me. I am proud that you have had the courage to agree. We Kwakiutl abhor the idea of eating human flesh, but our reputation as cannibals drives fear into the hearts of our enemies. In our legend of the Cannibal Spirit one of our ancestors overcame this monster, who tried to turn him into a cannibal, and so the ancient one escaped from this terrible practice. By acting out this legend we renew our own control over evil powers, and also gain other powers of self-discipline and knowledge of the life of the sea, where the Cannibal Spirit dwells, that helps our food gathering. How all this happens, you will learn later, as you become more deeply a member of the Hamatsa Cannibal Society. But remember, the women and children, but particularly our enemies, must really think we eat human flesh, and then are purified by the songs, just as the original ancestor was. The women and children learn obedience through this fear; and our enemies, afraid we will eat them, leave us alone! When you do the Hamatsa dance, you will not actually eat human flesh, though many will believe you do."

Flying Leaf heaved a deep sigh.

"Now listen to me," continued the father, "and I will tell you how to act and what we will do to help you fool the people and our enemies. As you dance, you will be acting out our ancestor's struggle with the Cannibal Spirit. Sometimes you will be dancing quietly, as the music and the drum beating and the singing of the people quiets you, but whenever you feel the slightest wrong feeling among the audience, then you begin to act crazily as if the Cannibal Spirit were controlling you. You will remember carefully the names of people in the audience whom you are supposed to bite and whose flesh you are to eat. They have already been told about this and promised rich gifts and rewards for their helping with the ceremony. You will carry hidden in your hand a tiny knife of great sharpness; this you will use to cut away a piece of skin from the arm of the person whom you pretend to bite. As you do this, you squeeze a small bladder of seal's blood carried under their sleeve so that some of the blood appears to drip or squirt out of the arm. Thus it looks as if you have given a deep and painful bite, and the person bitten will act that way. You must then dance away from the person, pretending you are delighted over eating his or her flesh.

"Later we will pretend to have a slave killed outside the great house. It will appear to be a real slave, but will actually be a cleverly carved dummy. We will drag this apparent slave's body into the great house for you and the other Hamatsa to eat; but we will have substituted the body of a freshly killed seal, with the head and flippers cut off. In their place we will have cleverly attached to the body, with our own secret method, legs, arms, and head that appear as human, the face even looking as if recently alive, but smeared with blood. You do not have to eat even the raw seal meat if you do not want to, but just pretend to do so with as good an act as you can."

"I will have to be a good actor," said Flying Leaf, "I will do my best. But tell me, father, I have long wondered about the Ghost Dances and the Toxuit, the women's dances, what happens when the ghosts speak and the women appear to be killed?"

The father laughed.

"They are very cleverly and realistically done, too. For the ghosts we have long tubes of sea kelp that we plant in shallow ditches under the floor and then cover with dirt and pack down. These tubes run to private rooms in the back of the great house; some have their ends under the fireplace, others in the ceiling. People in the rooms talk into these tubes and make ghostly voices come out of the fire and from above the the audience so they think the real ghosts are talking to them.

"For the monsters that sometimes come out of the ground, we have special hidden tunnels and trenches. The monsters are made of painted skins stretched over boards, with people inside, activating their legs and moving their eyes, their tongues, and their horns. When a dancer appears to be dragged into the earth, he is taken down into one of these tunnels or trenches."

"But how," asked the youth, "do you cause the women dancers of the Toxuit to appear to be killed?"

"That is really difficult sometimes," replied his father. "When a head appears to be chopped off, the woman has not come back onto the stage at all. It is a boy with a wooden head attached above his own, cleverly carved and painted to look just like her head in the dim light of the fires. It is this head that is chopped off. At the same time, seal bladders filled with animal blood are broken and squeezed to shoot out great gouts of blood. When we appear to burn a woman to death, we put her into a box with a false bottom leading into a tunnel in the floor. She escapes by this tunnel, and we replace her body with that of a seal. Then when the box is thrown into the great fire, a body is seen burning inside of it, but, of course, it is not hers."

"Then," said the son, looking straight at his father, "most of these things we show the people are actually big lies and not true at all!"

"That is true," replied the father calmly. "But you are never to speak of this to anyone but me. For centuries we have protected ourselves from our enemies by appearing to be cannibals and powerful magicians, bringing people back from death. They think we have great magic powers and usually leave us alone. You know how the Haida, the Tlingit, and the Tsimshian go on long raiding parties far down the coast to collect slaves. Even though many of them know now that we play these tricks, our reputation is feared, and generally they leave our people alone. Is not this worth some lies?"

Slowly, reluctantly, the son nodded his head.

5. The Nootka and the Makah

The Nootka and the Makah dwelt for many centuries along one of the most storm-lashed and rain-drenched coastal areas in the entire world. They lived along the Pacific shore of Vancouver Island from Cape Cook south and around Cape Flattery on the northwest corner of Washington. From September to May vast seas, with waves sometimes sixty feet high or more and with terrifying cross-currents, hurled themselves at the rocky shores, and rains of 100 inches or more per year poured down to create the most dense and lush forests of North America. Even today few roads reach across from the more populated eastern half of Vancouver Island to reach the stormy Pacific Coast, for the mountains of the interior are rugged, some over 7,000 feet high, and very difficult to cross. Reaching deeply into the hills and mountains and between towering cliffs are wild and often narrow fjords of ocean water, through which the tide rips in sometimes frightening waves twice daily. Yet in this rugged land some 10,000 to 12,000 Nootkas and Makahs lived in barbaric splendor and prosperity for uncounted centuries, lords of the towering seas and their mighty animals perhaps more than any other native peoples. The dank and thick forests were little penetrated by them except for gathering wood for their houses and canoes, but the waters were their pathways to glory and food. The great cliffs and rough waters, and a fierce ability as warriors, helped protect them from the raids of their northern neighbors, the warlike Kwakiutl and the slave-hunting Haida.

In much of their area the Nootka and the Makah had the usual simple political unit of the extended village, with one central permanent village and one or more lesser villages in the same stream-drainage area, possibly with a premier chief for the area and a council of elders. But in the northern part of Vancouver Island, confederacies between several villages had appeared in the seventeenth century with a supreme chief to head the confederacy; this was something like a true tribe and was probably organized in defense against attacks from the north.

The basic items of material culture in this area are listed in Appendix B. Like most of the northwest tribes, the Nootkas built large houses for several families. These were made with boards split from red cedar logs; immense posts held up the board roofs, which were waterproofed against the heavy rains with two overlaps of boards and with pine resin and clay. A large pit was usually dug in the middle of the home; here fires could be built for individual families or used centrally for ceremonies and festive occasions. The so-called totem poles, which were really family crests, were done on the interior house posts. These posts, of which the early ones were smaller in size than the more recent ones, showed whole carved figures of legendary ancestors or guardian animal spirits, differing from the more symbolic bas-relief carvings of the northernmost tribes (see chapter 3). Smoke holes in the roof were created by moving boards.

Weapons for hunting and war included bone and horn-tipped clubs, strongly sinew-backed bows of yew wood, arrows with sharp stone or bone points, knives, spears, and slings.

INTERIOR OF A NOOTKA HOUSE. Woman on left is weaving tule mat on loom, the other woman on left is working on fish net baskets. Women in middle are roasting fish filets over fire. Man with bow in hand has typical high-peaked Nootka hat and dark robe of some fur, possibly seal; man on right holds typical paddle. House posts are carved and painted with huge figures, representing ancestors. (*Diorama by Elizabeth Mason, Southwest Museum, Los Angeles*)

The bulk of the hunting was of sea mammals, particularly whales and seals, which were harpooned, but fishing brought in the major part of the food, particularly salmon, sea trout, and herring. In addition, much seashell life was used, particularly mussels, clams, abalones, and barnacles. Vast quantities of salmon were captured with nets, traps, and harpoons whenever they came up the rivers, particularly the king salmon in the fall. May and September were times to hunt the gray whales when they migrated up and down the coast. Other hunters brought back elk, deer, and bear from the interior.

Money was usually made out of the long, slim dentalium shells, of which the Nootka had almost a complete monopoly for use in trading, as more of these shells were found here, on the banks of undersea rocks high in the offshore waters near Vancouver Island, than elsewhere. The shells were sorted for size and sold in strings or packed neatly into small bark baskets.

Wealth by dentalium gave the Nootka wealth by trade in many other items, such as oil and grease from the eulachon fish caught by the Tsimshian, Chilkat goat-hair blankets of exquisite design from the more distant Tlingit, and many kinds of furs from the Coast Salish, who obtained them in turn from the interior peoples. Wealth was given away in potlatches along with great feasts, but the Nootka did not believe in competitive potlatches.

Clothing was, as usual in most of the coastal tribes, worn to a minimum by the men except in very cold weather, when blankets, skin cloaks, and high basketry rain hats were common; women wore skirts of woven red cedar bark or of deerskin and sometimes of tule. A coat of lustrous otter skins was usually for the very rich. Footwear was unusual, although moccasins, probably gained by trade from the Coast Salish, were occasionally worn in the worst part of winter.

INTERIOR OF A NOOTKA HABITATION. This drawing, by John Webber, 1778, shows method of storing dried fish by hanging from ceiling; roasting fish on sticks before fire; storing of supplies; typical clothing and hat; and sleeping platforms. (*Peabody Museum, Harvard University*)

Gambling with marked sticks was a common game in winter, as it was all up and down the coast. In the flickering firelight old people made the dark days and evenings of winter rich and meaningful to the children with stories and legends of the great heroes, of the animals and birds. Dancing was mainly religious.

Like many native Americans, the Nootka used religion to attempt to influence the environment and the chances and opportunities of life by magic, prayers, and spiritual power. Solitary seeking for visions and spiritual power was used by fewer people among the Nootka and the other great northern tribes, such as the Kwakiutl and the Haida, than by the people to the south and east. Among the Nootka it was generally the leaders, such as the chiefs, shamans, and members of powerful families, who tried this way. Body and soul were purified to receive help from the spirit through prayer and fasting, continence and pure thoughts, and bathing in cold water and whipping the skin. The common people got their help from the spirits through rituals, magic charms, and helping the leaders with the ceremonies. Missionaries, who put no value on the Indian religion, sometimes calling it devil worship, failed to understand the great beauty and spiritual seeking that was often a part of it, and the wonderful feeling of harmony with earth and sky.

The Command Was Clear: "Kill!"

THE NIGHT was dark and the sea wind sang eerily when a small child, Second Boy, was kidnapped by the "wolves." They came into the great house of his father, the chief, in the night. His father was Chief Sea Wolf Lord, chief of one of the

ANOTHER NOOTKA INTERIOR: also by John Webber, 1778. This picture shows a woman weaving a tule mat on a loom, fish hanging from rafters as winter food supply, and various open-work baskets and nets used in fishing. (*Peabody Museum, Harvard University*)

large Nootka bands that had joined the Kyuquot Confederacy in northwestern Vancouver Island. When the chief was gone, they rushed into his apartment and tore the boy from his mother's arms, instantly stifling his screams with a powerful hand clamped over his mouth. Dressed in wolf skins, with wolflike heads, they seemed so like wolves that he froze in terror, his small hands clutching and tearing futilely at the fur in an attempt to get away. He was carried to a waiting canoe and saw the paddles flash and the water splash white in the moonlight as the canoe sped out across Kyuquot Sound. The great double prow, sealed so tightly by thong and pine tar that it seemed like one piece, split the lifting seas, while the long paddles, driven by experts, kept the canoe always in the right direction to dodge the grabbing waters.

Two days and nights he was kept in a secret hut somewhere down the sound. On the third day, still terrified, not knowing what was to happen, but trying manfully to hide his tears like a true chief's son, he was again bundled into a canoe, this time with other crying children, and taken back to the village. Magic songs, it is said, were calling the wolves to the winter ceremonial, that great time of fun and frolic, sometimes violent acting, sometimes serious spirit seeking, when the people danced the Wolf Dance to create the power to bring back the "lost" children.

As the wolves approached the huge ceremonial house, lit weirdly in the evening darkness by the torches dancing their light on walls and trees, Second Boy shouted with hope. Some of the people were rushing down to rescue the children, including the massive form of his own father. Then all was con-

Left NOOTKA MAN: drawing by John Webber, 1778. Notice high-peaked hat of basketry, fur-covered quiver, and short, sinew-backed bow. Robe is probably of sea otter skins (*Peabody Museum, Harvard University*)

Right WOLF MASK, WITH LIFE-SIZED BEAR-SKIN COSTUME: mask made of wood, with copper eyes and upper teeth, and haliotis-shell decorations; painted green, white, red, and black. Though this is a Kwakiutl mask and costume, it is very similar to the wolf ceremonial costume worn by the Nootka at their winter ceremonials. (*Milwaukee Public Museum*)

fusion around him. In seemingly fierce fighting, the wolves strove to hold onto their prey, though he thought some of the people were crazy to attack the wolves with spoons and little sticks! Twice the wolves drove the people back and twice the people came again, and, then, suddenly, as in a dream, the wolf who carried him was thrust aside and his father, roaring and laughing, seized him, the fierce dark face suddenly tender and smiling. Confused but happy, the child felt himself carried back triumphantly to the village in those powerful arms, and into the great house of the winter ceremonial. Here the dancers, leaping and swaying, pretended to be wolves calling the other wolves outside. Here at last he found the comforting arms of his mother.

A few days later, he learned from his older brother, First Boy, about the trick that had been played upon him. Still he sensed that behind the trickery, the laughter and yelling and the tug-of-war between the people and the "wolves," the dancing and the solemn chanting of the spirit songs, there was some deeper meaning that he did not yet grasp. As he grew older, he learned that though there was trickery and some foolishness, the wolf spirits must come to the Wolf Dance so that they could be asked to help meet the difficulties and dangers of the year ahead. When the ice and cold of winter gripped the land, he heard the real wolves howling in the dark forest behind the village. He shivered then and knew, as his people did, too, that they were more than just animals, that they reflected ancestral spirits and that they had great powers.

Second Boy's life as a chief's son was far more rigorous than that of a son of the common people. In early dawn he was driven forth by a special slave servant to wash himself in the icy cold water of the nearest stream, then have his body switched with stinging nettles to bring the blood to the surface. He asked his older brother why they had to do these things. First Boy replied:

"To lead the people we must be stronger than they are, quicker both with our bodies and with our minds, able to withstand discomfort for hours without complaining. We must

sacrifice comforts and always be ready to do the most dangerous things. Then they will be willing to follow us and help us
as we help them in times of trouble or need. We also set the
example of how to live, by being clean in mind and body,
kind, strong, and firm when firmness is needed. We must
always hold our temper, not getting angry without good reason.
These are the teachings of the grandfathers of long ago and
of the Sacred Being who taught us how to live. This is why the
Nootka are a great people, why we live on the coast of the
great storms where other peoples fear to go, why we almost
alone are the hunters of the kings of the sea, the whales, why
we are the fearless ones who ride the wild waves."

So were both First Boy and Second Boy trained through
the years. They were taught to hunt, to fish, to paddle canoes
in the wind-whipped seas, to swim and dive without fear in
dark waters. Their bodies became strong and supple as the
otter's, and they grew as brave as the killer whales, whom
they called the "wolves of the sea." In the winter now they
danced in the winter ceremonial and were initiated into secret
societies like the seals and the wolves until they knew the
sacred ways. And then, finally, when they stood strong and tall
and straight after their spirit-seeking alone in the woods, each
in his turn was given the name he needed in manhood. First
Boy was called Splitter of Waves because of his skill with
paddle and canoe, and Second Boy was named Peacemaker
because of his love for the common people and the way he
stopped fights. One day, the fathers of two quarreling families
started cutting each other with knives. Many were amazed
when Second Boy threw himself between them like a whirl-
wind, singing the sacred song he had learned in the woods:

"I walk in a sacred manner between you. The Spirits have
told me to tell you 'Peace! Peace!' Do you want to die and be
forgotten? We will be a great people only if we are one! This
is the law of the wolves, and it must be our law!"

The combatants threw down their knives and listened in
awe to his words. He talked to them until they made peace
as friends. Later he was called to see his father, Chief Sea
Wolf Lord, who said:

"I have heard of your courage and your peacemaking; it is good! You know that your brother is taking his final training as a whale hunter, which also prepares him for the chieftainship. You will need some of that training, in case anything happens to him; but you will need some special training, too. What is your wish?"

"I would sit at the feet of the masters who use their knives to make wood take the appearance of life; I would learn from them. But my father's wish is my wish. I will always remember that Splitter of Waves is a chief over me, and has first choice in all things. I shall always be his servant!"

"I am glad," said Sea Wolf Lord, "that I have two such fine sons, true brothers, each wise and strong and capable. We have long known that the worst enemy among our people is not from outside, but from within, called jealousy. As long as you two brothers support each other, and you humbly give your older brother his right, we will be strong. In time I see you as a famous carver of wood. But first you must learn to lead in case the need arises. Your brother has already completed the first training, the learning of the sacred dentalium beds and how to find and harvest them. Now he is to follow me on the sea and learn to catch the noble ladies and kings (the whales). You will take his place in the dentalium beds."

Soon it was summer and the people had moved to the beach near the sea for the dentalium gathering, the fishing, seal hunting, clamming, and whaling. Here was the constant sound of the waves booming on the rocks and the wail of the sea wind, maker of storms. The rugged coast faced westward. Each day at sunset the people sang the sacred song as the sun plunged downward, a ball of red fire sinking off the edge of

MODERN NOOTKA MAN MAKING A CANOE IN OLD WAY. Notice adze marks on inner side of canoe; these are later sandpapered down smooth. (*American Museum of Natural History, New York*)

the world. At dawn the fog came in wet and dripping over the beaches, and the mysterious call of the sea was a chuckling murmur mixed with the screams of seabirds and the resonant booms of the waves. Boards had been brought down from the permanent winter villages, and the people made rough but adequate summer houses for the short season of good weather.

Peacemaker, who was now almost eighteen, questioned the man of late middle age, Sea Wolf Singer, who was to teach and train him in the ways of dentalium-shell harvesting.

"How do we find the secret dentalium beds?" he asked.

The older man's weather-worn brown face crinkled in a shrewd smile.

"We test the wind and the sea. When they give us the right signs, we go out to the beds and use the sacred cross sticks in the ways I will show you. But first you must learn how to make the dentalium traps we spear with and how to use them. The mystery of finding the beds is passed to us by our ancestors. Your grandfather's grandfather discovered the secret of the beds we are going to, and only by talking to his spirit on the night wind will he make it right for us to have a good harvest. We learn also the secrets of the sea and the mountains, for they point out the beds to those who follow the sacred way and to no others."

Peacemaker listened intently and was quiet as he followed the old man to the dentalium spear traps lying on the beach beside the great seagoing canoes. Sea Wolf Singer had him examine one of the spear traps carefully. It was made of several long, slim hardwood poles, each about fifteen feet long. To the end of one of these was lashed a circular series of sharp hardwood splints, cleverly arranged with underlashings so that all the points flared out from the central pole in a bristling circle. Placed over the pole was a wide square board with a hole in the center wide enough to slip down over part of the cone-shaped cluster of spears, but not wide enough to slip completely over it. To this were attached stone weights. Sea Wolf Singer explained that as the whole contraption was lowered down into the sea over the dentalium beds, this weighted board helped drive the pointed barbs firmly down into the beds. Then the dentalia could be broken off the rocks, a few of them caught between the barbs, and dragged up to the surface of the sea.

"But how do we keep these beds secret from others?" asked Peacemaker.

"There are several steps we take, each a secret to your family and mine. First we sing a song to our ancestors, the sea wolves, that they may help us each time we need to find and guard the beds from others. They tell us when is the right time to go, when no enemies are watching. Since the beds are found out in the open sea and no one except us knows how deep they are, we alone know how many poles to bind together to push our spear trap down to reach the beds. And we alone know the greatest secret of all, which mountaintops and hilltops on the shore and rocks in the sea to line up at certain angles with our sacred sticks to find the right beds."

One day Sea Wolf Singer touched the sea, felt the wind, studied the sky, and touched the earth. "It is time to go to the dentalium beds," he said, and called his two sons and another man to come with him and Peacemaker out on the sea. Sunlight glinted on the waters and the sky was blue when they pushed the twenty-foot canoe, deep-carved from a six-foot-thick cedar log, down over the sand and into the waves. Four men paddled while Sea Wolf Singer steered the boat over the sea. Above them the seagulls screamed, and ashore men and women lifted their hands to wish them luck. In the canoe's bottom ropes lay coiled, and the long poles and the dentalium traps were ready to be used. There was food and water and warm blankets in boxes in case of need, for the Nootka knew the vagaries and dangers of the sea. The canoe was small compared to the great whaling and war canoes, but it moved gracefully through the water as the paddlers dipped their paddles in rhythm, the high prow curling aside the waves. The body shape had been so well worked, first with adzes and next with sandstone and shark's skin acting as sandpaper, that its sides were smooth as glass, slipped through the water without friction. The blue water was so clear that they could see nearly a hundred feet down and watch fish swimming lazily far below, though not deep enough to see any dentalium ledges. They had to watch and wait until Sea Wolf Singer used the sacred way, the sacred songs, and the secret signals from land and sea that would guide them to the hidden treasure.

The long, spire-shaped shells of the dentalia, delicately fluted as if made by some master craftsman, were an ideal form of money in those ancient days. They were hard to get, as gold is hard to get, wrested only with great care from the depths of the sea, and their beauty of design was so great that none could doubt their high value. In the islands to the north a string of thirty of the longer shells, peerless in their perfection, was enough to buy a well-built canoe that might have taken three solid months or more to build.

When Sea Wolf Singer felt they were getting near the beds of shells, he stopped the canoe and asked them to close their eyes. Then he sang a sacred song, a song of the shells, asking them to grow well and quickly for the family and people of the Sea Wolf Clan, asking them to be easy to be caught, since their glory would be passed out to the world of men and be used for the good of the people.

After a final prayer to the spirits of the sea for calm weather while they fished, he opened his skin pouch and took out a strange collection of sticks tied together tightly at angles. This he began to handle as a navigator on a ship handles a sextant, pointing the different sticks to two different peaks on the land, and to a great rock that stood out to sea, and another to the distant summer village of the people just visible on the far-off shore. Now he told Peacemaker to steer while the others paddled, and gradually he worked the canoe over the sea in easy stages, giving directions until all his sticks pointed to the spots on land and sea they were supposed to point to. Smiling, he indicated the dentalium beds below, and a stone weight tied to a rope was tossed over the side as an anchor.

Soon they were tying the different sections of the spear trap together, sending down into the rippling waters first the head of the trap with its cone of sharp hardwood sticks, then another section and another section, until he held up his hand.

"At this point," he said, "the spear and the weighted box are hanging right over the dentalium beds. If Peacemaker and I together shove it down, it will hit one of the beds and perhaps capture some of the shells. Press down steadily and when I say so, strike hard!"

They pressed downward wth the long jointed poles into the calm blue-green sea, until the signal was given to strike, and then they suddenly pressed hard. Peacemaker visualized the heavy rocks dragging the square board with its hole down over the cone-shaped group of spines far below and forcing them into the bed. He prayed silently that some of the spines were grabbing shells and breaking them loose from the rock bed below. The only way to tell was to drag the several sections up out of the sea, and laboriously untie each as it was brought up. When the trap itself reached the surface, Peacemaker exclaimed in disappointment, "Only one!"

"Don't worry," answered Sea Wolf Singer, laughing. "Sometimes you will feel fortunate to bring up even one. If we did not fast long enough before doing this, if we forgot a word in the song, if the current is wrong in the sea, these and many other things can give us bad luck. There is one virtue above all that you learn from dentalium fishing. That is patience!"

All the rest of the day they fished from the slightly rocking canoe in a glassy sea, sometimes watched by a sea eagle soaring high in the sky, once observing the heads of curious sea lions all in a row watching from the direction of shore, and always the terns, gulls, and shearwaters flashing their snow-white wings as they circled and dove above and about them. Several times their down-driven trap of spines brought up a disappointing nothing at all, sometimes one only, less frequently two or three, and once, with a shout from all aboard the canoe like the whoop of cranes, the spear came up with a magic five! All were stored nestled in small baskets for taking ashore, while every hour or so Sea Wolf Singer brought out his strange sextant of bound and pointed sticks, lining up the mountain peaks and the great rock on the shore to make sure that even with their anchor they were still over the treasure-shell beds.

Several days of good weather allowed them to bring up more than two hundred shells from the beds. However, late in the last day they felt a change in the weather as dark clouds came up fast out of the northern seas and they bent their paddles into the water to head for home. They had covered little more than a third of the distance home when Peacemaker glanced back and saw to the northwest, in the gathering darkness, the high prows and sterns of some distant northern war canoes, heading at full speed for the shore to escape the storm. One prow, lit weirdly by the parting rays of red-gold light from the setting sun, had a great bird carved on it, a raven, which he knew was of the warlike Haida. A Haida war expedition to catch slaves, mainly women and children, and kill the men, could be a catastrophe to a tribe, as the Haida usually struck in the dawn with the greatest possible surprise and savagery. As Peacemaker passed the word, the small, swift canoe of Sea Wolf Singer pulsed with concentrated energy as the four paddlers drove it through the growing waves of the sea in a mad dash for home. All sight of the Haida had long faded behind them. They only hoped they had not been seen.

The first person they saw an hour later when they neared the village was Peacemaker's brother, Splitter of Waves, standing before a fire lit on the beach to guide them to safety.

"Haida!" they shouted, above the howl of the increasing wind, "coming out of the north!"

The word was enough. Within minutes, the village erupted into activity. The deep-shouted commands of Sea Wolf Lord could be heard above all the rest, and Peacemaker felt proud of his father and the way he took quick command. All knew that their village alone could not withstand the powerful attack of a full-size Haida war party of perhaps 200 to 300 fierce fighting men, so men rushed to the tops of nearby hills along the Kyuquot Sound to set fires of brush and drift logs already piled high for just such an emergency. Men also rushed away up the trails to be sure the word got through to their allies in the Kyuquot Confederacy, and a canoe raced across the sound to bring help from that quarter if possible. Meanwhile the villagers began to gather sea-drift logs from the beach to pile into barricades in front of the houses, and the women and older men sharpened spears and knives and gathered all available arrows into quivers for quick use when battle came.

The chief and his council soon decided the Haida would not attack until the fierceness of the storm had subsided, so they ordered all except the lookouts to get some sleep, and the village settled down for the night. In the new day the sun broke through racing clouds to pour light on the sand, but the seas were huge and rough. It was too dangerous for most canoes, even those of the Haida, greatest canoe-makers of all the coast tribes, and near to the Nootka in seamanship. During the blustery day, while the sea wind screamed, warriors came down the lee side of the sound in canoes from the upper villages.

At the dawn of the second day, just as the Haida attack came silently out of the sea through the fog to land, hidden war canoes of the Nootka came hissing out of the dark waters and fell with their armed men on the Haida rear. It was a complete surprise. Instead of a sleeping village ripe for slaughter, the enemy found another war fleet equal to their own, as well as the aroused villagers who came pouring down over the sand. As a flight of arrows struck among them, they tried to rush their canoes back into the sea. Although their elk-hide armor and wooden helmets deflected most of the arrows, they were disorganized and began running into one another as they tried to get the canoes into the water.

Peacemaker, a warrior now, and his brother, Splitter of Waves, rushed forward with their father and other warriors upon the sagging Haida. In the confusion of the dark fog-shrouded beginning of day the great roaring war shouts of the Nootka shook the air. The Haida gathered courage and roared back, as they desperately tried to get away by sea. In the confusion eight great canoes made it through the waves and turned seaward, fighting off the pursuing Nootka in a running battle northward. Four canoeloads of Haida were trapped on land, and these the Nootka fell on ferociously, eager to teach the Haida to leave their villages alone. But the Haida stood courageously to the attack, fighting like heroes, their tough armor giving them better protection than the lighter jackets of woven cedar bark worn by the Nootka.

Peacemaker saw about him the rising and falling war clubs and the jabbing spears. He drove his spear with all his might into the breastplate of a dark-crested warrior who rose in front of him. The spear point penetrated the tough skin enough to raise a howl of rage and pain. But in the next instant the spear was torn from his hands with giant strength, and a raised war club would have crushed his skull had not the equally giant Sea Wolf Lord, seeing his son in danger, come down from the rear. The chief crashed his own club into the other's, and the two clubs shattered in midair. The storm of battle raged down to the edge of the sea, where the waves, dark with blood, washed over the bodies of the last of the outnumbered Haida, fighting courageously to the end.

The following summer Sea Wolf Lord called his second son to come with him on a whale-hunting expedition. Days of purification, fasting, and strict continence preceded the expedition for all who were going on it. By dawn they washed themselves in ice-cold water and beat their bodies almost raw with switches of nettle to toughen the skin. By night they sought the power of the spirits, sometimes in the caves where the bones of their ancestors lay, sometimes calling on the great whale, the lordly spirit of all the whales, to give them aid, and remembering the heroic whale-hunting chiefs of the past, some who had given their lives that their people might live. When his father asked him to go whale hunting, Peacemaker had a

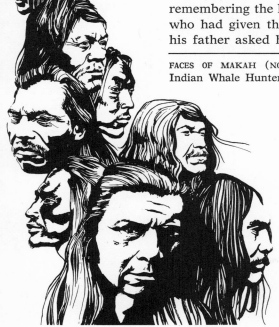

FACES OF MAKAH (NOOTKA TRIBE) WHALE BOAT CREW. (*McReavy*, Makah Indian Whale Hunters, *drawing by Robin Holmes*)

moment of fear. He remembered a childhood dream, a dream of terror when he had seen a huge whale smash a man to death with his tail. He fought daily against this fear with prayers and strove to drive away all thoughts of death in the sea.

On this expedition Peacemaker would be in charge of one of the two sealing canoes, thirty feet long and slim-carved to cut the waters swift as arrows. The two great whale-hunting canoes, captained by his father and brother, were over fifty feet long and broad of beam to give maximum control in a rough sea. He was glad that the wise hunter, Sea Wolf Singer, would be the steersman of his canoe, ready to give advice and explain the tricks of whale hunting to a rank amateur. The canoes were marvels of compactness, seaworthiness, and skill in building. Every square inch of space was either occupied by something useful or free for the moving of feet where such moving would count. There were coils of cedar-bark rope, spliced at intervals to tightly sewn sealskin floats, ready to be drawn into the water and form friction when the whale was harpooned. An extra shaft and extra harpoon heads were in each of the big canoes in case of lost shafts or heads when the whale was struck. They also carried spare food, blankets, warm clothing, extra cutting blades, and other items that might be needed.

Proudly the four canoes moved out into the blue-green waters of the sea in the dawn. Each canoe had been sanded to a silken smoothness so as not to create any friction in the water. The prows of the whalers carried carved wolf heads with fierce faces and teeth. The four great harpoons, each nearly twenty feet long and three to four inches in diameter, were made in three parts, joined with such careful binding that the divisions were barely visible. They were far too heavy to be thrown; only the most powerful man could lift one and plunge it into the side of a whale.

MODEL OF SECRET MAGIC SHRINE OF NOOTKA WHALERS: on Vancouver Island. (*American Museum of Natural History, New York*)

Two pieces of elk horn, expertly sharpened and with hollows inside through which passed the stout cedar-withe lines, were bound together with a sharp piece of giant clam shell, lashed with twine, and glued with dried spruce gum to form the blade and two prongs of the head of the harpoon. This combination was lashed tightly to the great shaft of hard and limber yew wood and covered with spruce gum. Once the whale broke it loose with his thrashings, the harpoon shaft floated free to be seized and used again. Usually the clam-shell point was broken by the power of the blow when the whale was harpooned, but the elk-horn prongs, firmly attached to the lines, stayed imbedded crosswise in the flesh and could be retrieved later when the whale was grounded.

In their songs and dreams the two harpooners had called on the spirit of the whale to swim out of the depths of the sea. They asked either the Noble Lady or the Noble King (they never called them by their true names), to rise to the surface and be still so the canoe could snake up quietly to the back side to deliver the first blow. Far back on the shore, as the canoes moved steadily seaward, the wives of the harpooners lay still in beds covered with red cedar-bark blankets, thinking of themselves as whales, moving only slightly and quietly, so that the whale to be harpooned might lie still and unsuspecting on the surface of the sea.

It was the time of the great migration of the gray whales from Alaska south to Baja California, and the hunters should have seen one or more of them moving slowly southward through the sea or basking in the sunlight for a short rest. But they criused for hours, always a little farther from land, searching and peering over the light waves of early summer. The two harpooners, Sea Wolf Lord and Splitter of Waves, father and son, grew more and more impatient. This explains why they were so recklessly eager to kill when they saw their first whales, not the dark-bodied splotched gray whales, but a

---

NOOTKA DRUM: painted to represent the Thunderbird carrying off a whale. (*American Museum of Natural History, New York*)

pair of the larger humpback whales, around forty-five feet long, a male and a female, swimming lazily through the clear waters. As they swam they touched each other lovingly with their extraordinarily long and white pectoral fins, their blow holes occasionally throwing up gushes of vapor. Their bodies were black above, with white undersides, especially the throats, which gleamed in the sunlight.

Peacemaker, in his slim, smaller, sealer's canoe, was actually closer to the whales when they were sighted. As his canoe came closer, his sensitive artist's nature understood the love between these two great beings, and he recognized them from his dream and sensed the danger. Rarely did the Nootka whalers attack humpback whales, generally choosing the more numerous and smaller gray whales, whose mates did not seem to be so closely attached to each other as with the humpback.

He signaled Sea Wolf Singer to steer their canoe closer to the great whaling canoe of Sea Wolf Lord, his father, moving it as quietly as possible so that the whales would not be disturbed. His father watched them approach and waved them away, eyes sparking dangerously. But Peacemaker insisted on coming closer and spoke softly.

"Father," he said, "I had a dream about these two whales and could see that you would be in great danger from them. Do not strike the bull. It could mean death!"

"Be still, my son, and drop your fear. You know nothing yet of whaling. This bull has been sent to us as a gift from our ancestors, the sea wolves. I also dreamed of two whales; we shall take one of them! Stay clear now, but be ready to help us when we need it."

Silently and carefully the whaler canoe maneuvered from the rear up to the left side of the huge bull humpback. It was necessary to come close enough to the body so the whale's eye would not see the approach, but not so close as to touch the whale. Inch by inch they moved forward. Sea Wolf Lord stood poised in the prow, his toes clinging to the gunwales of the two front sides of the canoe as he lifted the eighty-pound harpoon and directed it at the point just behind the left front flipper of the bull humpback. Then, as the canoe almost touched the whale, he drove the harpoon down and in with all his might. As he felt the strike go home, he dropped like a lead weight to the floor of the canoe.

Instantly the bull exploded, his whole massive body riding up out of the waves and twisting. The harpoon shaft whistled viciously through the air where the man had been a second before. Then the bull dove straight down and as he did so, his flukes rose out of the sea and struck at the water with a blow meant to demolish whatever had attacked him. But the paddlers and the steersman were prepared. At the strike of the harpoon, the steersman had twisted his large steering paddle, while the paddlers, as one man, dug into the waves as hard as they could to fling the body of the canoe out and away from those deadly flukes. The blow missed them by a hair. In the next instant they were trying desperately to keep the harpoon line from fouling their paddles or their own bodies, for it was hissing over the side as the whale dove with unbelievable speed. One paddler turned his paddle to ward off the line just in time to prevent it from whipping around his body and dragging him to death in the sea. The paddler behind him got the second coil ready to go over the side after the first part of the line. The power of the dive was so great that it ran out the whole length of the line without stopping, including the four sealskin floats, three of which were taken under the sea; but the fourth bobbed on the surface, telling them where the whale had gone. They had no more than noticed this when the female humpback charged.

Among all the whales of the sea the humpback couples seem to have the greatest love for each other. Among other whales, although the bull will go often to the aid of a female when she is injured or attacked, rarely will the female come to help the male. Usually she is too frightened and swims away. But the humpback is an exception. And this female was charging with all the fury of a bull.

Peacemaker saw the attack coming, but his first shouts were lost in all the yells of the other men and the loud hissing of the harpoon line. He signaled for his canoe to rush forward to help. Out of the corner of his eye he saw that his brother, Splitter of Waves, was commanding the other big whaling canoe off on a wild chase to catch the line that led to the bull and to try to get close enough to put another harpoon into him.

Suddenly Sea Wolf Lord and his men became aware of Peacemaker's shouts of warning, and turned to look to their rear. It was too late. Even as they turned, a great head loomed up beside them, butted forward with a powerful blow that sent the whole canoe rolling over and over in the waves. At the same time, the whale whipped her body around, waving her immense white forward fins, and brought her black tail flukes down in a blow aimed at smashing the canoe. The blow missed the canoe because by that time it had rolled out of her reach, but one central part of the flukes smashed down on a paddler struggling in the water and killed him instantly, while one corner of a fluke caught Sea Wolf Lord across head and upper body and knocked him senseless in the water.

Peacemaker signaled the other sealer canoe to decoy the angry female humpback away from the floating bodies and the overturned canoe, while he rushed to rescue his father and the others who had been thrown into the water. The sleek, fast, second sealer made itself obvious to the humpback now and she furiously charged it, led on a merry chase away from the others. Peacemaker asked two of his own crewmen to help, and they gently lifted the heavy body of his father out of the water and into their canoe, nearly overturning it in the process.

The chief was choked with water but still breathing. Peacemaker turned him face down in the canoe so the water could drain from him, and applied a little pressure on his back, gently, since he feared some ribs were broken. Meanwhile, Sea Wolf Singer directed his attention to the whaler canoe and its former occupants. Fortunately the blow of the charging humpback cow had caused the canoe to roll one complete turn and then come upright again. Cracks had opened in the side from the blow and the water was flowing in, but once they got the remaining five paddlers and the steersman back into the whaler, they were able to quickly use some pine pitch from a storage box to seal up the holes and then get busy bailing. The main harpoon shaft and the spare harpoon with its point intact were floating on the water and could soon be gathered in. Food and spare clothes and blankets in their boxes were still inside the whaler canoe, lashed under the paddlers' seats and hardly hurt by the water.

As Peacemaker began to get air moving into his father's lungs, the chief moaned in pain and opened his eyes. Feeling his ribs, Peacemaker realized that at least two were broken; his father would not be able to help any more with the whaling.

"What happened?" muttered the chief. "Where is First Boy?" The old name came out naturally at a time of danger. Peacemaker looked out across the waves for the first time and saw, in the distance, the second whaling canoe being pulled rapidly by the bull.

"Brother has put a second harpoon into the bull, and he is being pulled toward us. The bull is still strong, because they are coming fast!"

"You've got to get a third harpoon into him!" urged the chief. "Hurry and get into my whaler and get it ready!"

"Me?" Peacemaker was shocked and frightened. "I—I have never thrust a harpoon into a whale in my life!"

"You have harpooned seal lions and you have watched me. You are strong and you can do it. You were brave in battle; be brave now! It is the only way we can be sure to capture the bull, which I believe is the biggest our people have ever caught. I can do nothing. My chest feels like it is crushed!"

Peacemaker's head swam. He took a deep breath. The fierce look in his father's eyes told him he had to use the harpoon. Slowly he signaled to Sea Wolf Singer to bring their canoe closer to the whaling canoe, and when it came close, he leaped over and into it.

One of the sealer's oarsmen followed him into the whaler, and he explained heavily to the six paddlers and the steersman what they had to help him do. As in a dream, he saw them nod their heads, and he reached out to take the harpoon the steersman passed to him. The weight of the immense spear almost threw him off balance, and he wondered how he could ever get it aloft. Weakly he signaled them to take off after the whale, knowing his father's eyes were on him.

The great bull, visibly tiring, passed them on their port (left) bow about two hundred yards away. Far away to starboard (right) the humpback cow was still following the teasing second sealing canoe. Peacemaker saw his brother's startled face as the second whaling canoe came by, pulled by the bull. He almost laughed, suddenly feeling a surge of courage.

He signaled his steersman to head the big canoe for the bull and began steeling himself, hands still trembling, for the ordeal. He saw the bull sound again, tipping up his flukes to try to escape again into the depths, trying to get away from the pain that clung to him so tightly. Peacemaker felt pity for it and for the cow, but realized he must put all such thoughts from his mind if he was to serve his father and his people. He lifted his head toward the sinking sun, and softly sang his sacred song, calling in his heart for help from the spirits.

Swiftly and expertly the great canoe glided toward where the bull had sunk from sight. Soon Peacemaker saw the immense dark shape rising up through the waters until the heavy body broke the surface and the steaming moisture exploded in a long gasp from the blow hole to form a cloudlike pear shape against the sunset. Now the canoe moved more slowly, quietly, sneaking up on the left side of the great bull. They hovered silently just behind the huge left fin, fully fifteen feet in length, which lay flaccid on the water. The bull breathed heavily, tiring in the fight to live.

Straddling the prow of the canoe, Peacemaker lifted the huge harpoon, but his strength failed him and he could not lift it all the way. He stood there struggling to bring it up, feeling his failure like a dark cloud, when a strangled cry came from the sealer. It was his father's voice, twisted by pain, but the command was clear: "Kill!"

With a gasp of sucked-in air, Peacemaker suddenly lifted the harpoon, aimed it as he had seen his father do, and drove it with all his might into the side of the bull behind the left forward fin. He staggered under the impact and almost fell overboard as he sought to duck down into the canoe. A strong arm came out and slammed him to the bottom as, in the same instant, the harpoon shaft whirred by. There was a strangled bellow from the bull, for his immense eye had seen the shape of his enemy beside him. He turned his body, preparing to bring the great hind flukes down on this source of pain and terror and destroy it once and for all! The paddlers were digging their paddles into the sea with a superhuman effort to get the canoe free. But they were not fast enough. The blow caught the steersman square across the upper half of his body, tearing him out of the canoe into the sea. Then the whale sounded, but he had his revenge, a limp and lifeless body drifting in the waves. Sadly Peacemaker moved to the back of the canoe and reached out to seize the steering oar that floated in the water, as the other men gathered in the dead steersman. It was now up to the older brother and his men to finish the job. Peacemaker was shaking now, feeling like Second Boy again, but glad the ordeal was over.

The bull was failing, his strength visibly ebbing under the impact of three harpoon points driven into vitals. Prodding him with the extra harpoon shaft in his canoe, older brother forced the bull to swim toward the distant shore. His tribesmen sang "Going Home," the great song to tell the bull how the people would welcome him when he came, how they would thank him for giving his life for them, and how they would give his bones back to the sea so he might live again.

When the bull could swim no longer and lay still in the water, while his mate far off was hopelessly searching for him, the men of the second whaler got busy to end his suffering. First Paddler moved to chop off the flukes so the bull would be completely helpless. He swung a sharp stone blade attached to a four-foot shaft. When the flukes floated free in a skim of blood, older brother took the special heart lance, kept in the chief's canoe. This he drove repeatedly into the side of the helpless bull until it pierced the heart and, with a final groan, the huge beast spouted blood from his blow hole and mouth and died, his long day of suffering mercifully ended.

One man from the chief's canoe dove into the water, carrying a large bone needle and heavy twine to sew up the mouth of the whale; this was believed to keep it from sinking. Then all available floats were arranged around the body to make sure it would not sink on the way home. Dark night was all about them, and the wind whispered on the waves, as they started the long tow for home, the two whaler canoes pulling at the tow. A sealer canoe had gone earlier, bearing the wounded chief, to seek help from the mainland. They sang the song of the tow:

Home we go with the Sea King; noble was he and strong;
Fought he with us bravely, and the Noble Lady helped him;
Two of us they killed; one injured and living;
High we paid for the kill, but a prize we bring for the Nootka;
The greatest bull in our history, a Lord of the sea;
Meat for ten villages we bring, meat for the old and weak;
Meat for the dogs to fill them; tallow and oil for the lights of winter;
Strength for the winter ceremonial and the Wolf Dances;
Food for a year for our people, to be dried and smoked on the racks;
Kept in the storage boxes, hung from the rafters, making our people strong;
Thanks to the Sea Wolves, our ancestors, for the kill;
Thanks to the spirit of the sea that the weather was calm.

So they made up the new words to the song as they paddled for home.

In the early morning they shouted for joy when they saw four great canoes coming from the mainland to help with the towing, for their muscles were tired and they longed for home. By mid-morning the whale neared the beach, which was lined with happy people, shouting and dancing and laughing, except for the two families who had learned their sons were dead. These were at their homes in mourning, wailing the songs of death, waiting for the bodies.

When the whale came close enough, the people rushed into

the sea to drag the canoes ashore, help carry the exhausted men up onto the beach, and bring the dead ashore in honor. Then many men began to help get ropes around the whale so the whole tribe could help pull him as high as possible onto the beach. The chief, Sea Wolf Lord, had already been carried up to his apartment in the biggest house on the beach, and a medicine man, wrinkled and old, but knowing of touch, had worked to bind the broken ribs in place so they would heal properly. The chief would be all right, but would have to lie still for many days to mend his bones.

Splitter of Waves, as the oldest son, was given the chief's usual job of ordering how the cuts of meat would be made and distributed from the whale, while his mother proudly came down to see the whale, signifying the end of her own vigil that had helped bring the whale safely home. She watched as her older son, holding a patch of shredded cedar bark over his mouth to guard himself from the spirit breath of the whale, ordered the first great saddles of whale meat and blubber to be cut.

Already invitations had been sent on swift canoes to other villages, bidding them to come share in the meat. By afternoon visitors were arriving to watch the whale cutting. Each share was given by rank, first to the chief and his wife, then to each of the chief's sons, then to honored guests, then to the villagers—plenty and more for all who came. Meanwhile Splitter of Waves, half shouting, half talking, in the Nootka way, told of how his ancestors had first learned to hunt whales and told the great adventure of the past day, how two had given their lives to the taking of the Sea King, and even the chief lay wounded in his house from the great encounter with the largest whale ever known to be caught on this coast! When night fell and the happy people lay sleeping off the feast, the dogs and coyotes, raccoons and mice, scurried and fought for the last scraps of meat and intestines down at the beach, and stripped and gnawed the huge bones clean.

In the days and nights that followed, much blubber was rendered into oil and stored in large tight boxes for use in the lamps, for cooking, or for dipping food in, while meat was smoked and dried to be saved for harder times. Dances were given in honor of the Sea King and finally, the huge bones were taken far out to sea to be given back to the waves to create, the people believed, another monster of the deep.

When the chief was well enough, he called his sons and said:

"My sons, you saved my life when I was near to death, and you saved the whale for our people. You are worthy descendants of a great family. Splitter of Waves shall be known hereafter as Chief Harpooner, and he shall follow the lordly Noble Ones of the sea when our people need their flesh, and shall be the chief when I die. But you, Peacemaker, did a great thing when we saw you overcome your fear and strike the Sea King as hard a blow as mine. You can choose not to hunt whales, if you wish, and be, as I am sure you will be, a famous carver of wood, a maker of noble crests and designs."

6. The Coast Salish and Chinook

Evidently in some prehistoric time the Chinook descended the Columbia River and settled along its lower stretches, separating the Coast Salish into two divisions. The larger division was to the north in what is now Washington and southern British Columbia, and the smaller division consisted of the Tillamook of the northwest Oregon coast. These tribes, combined with a few small tribes of probably Algonquin and Penutian affinity, constitute what is called the Coast Salish and Chinook Province of the Northwest Coast Culture Area. See Appendixes B and C for the culture elements that help distinguish this province and its various divisions.

This whole province is distinctly subservient to the main Northwest Culture Center to the north, which includes the Kwakiutl, Haida, Tsimshian, and Tlingit. Culture elements from this more active and complex center diffused southward, becoming weaker as they got farther from the main area. Thus the potlatch, or giving-away-of-goods ceremony, was a major and frequent event among the Kwakiutl, somewhat weaker among the Nootka and the Coast Salish of southwestern British Columbia and the Puget Sound region, and began to fade out among the Chinook along the lower Columbia River. The art of painting and carving wood also became less complicated and expert to the south, while the capture and use of slaves was considered quite a bit more important in the north than in the south, fading to mere debt slavery in southwestern Oregon and northwestern California.

Most of the Coast Salish and the Chinook had flat heads, distinguishing them from both the people they enslaved, who were brought in from the south and west, and from the Kwakiutl to the north, whose heads were shaped and pointed upward in the middle of the back of the head. This shaping was done by tying boards onto the heads of babies while their skulls were

117

still soft and malleable; it was painless and evidently had no harmful effects on intelligence.

The Upper Skagit

The Upper Skagit are a Coast Salish people of northwestern Washington, inland from the present city of Bellingham, and some still dwell along the banks of the beautiful Skagit River, whose headwaters are in the high, snow-covered mountains of what now is the North Cascades National Park. In the old days this river, its nearby sea area, and the hunting lands of the interior furnished them with rich and diversified food and excellent wood in the form of red cedar trees for making dwellings and canoes. Unlike the interior Salish-speaking tribes behind the mountains, the Skagit had little danger from times of famine. Their yearly fish supply alone, particularly salmon, was sufficient to keep them alive and well even if most other food sources failed.

But they also joined with their cousins, the Lower Skagit, to hunt such sea mammals as the harbor seal, the sea lion, the sea otter, and the porpoise, and welcomed the occasional stranding on the beach of a whale. Inland they hunted mule deer, elk, mountain goat, grizzly bear, black bear, snowshoe rabbit, fisher, mink, raccoon, beaver, and river otter. Hunters, by fasting in the wilderness and praying, sought special powers from the spirits of the different animals (or guardian spirits as they were called) to aid them in their hunting. Some could even run down a deer or elk and kill it with a knife. Arrows and bows,

COAST SALISH DOG-HAIR BLANKET: from the British Columbia coast. (*American Museum of Natural History, New York*)

generally sinew-backed bows, were used in hunting, while noose traps, deadfalls, deep pits covered with branches and dirt, and nets were also used (see chapter 2).

The nature of the different food-gathering methods created a flow of trade along the river. People living downstream near the heaviest movement of river fish traded fish and fish oil for skins and meat from the people higher in the mountains, while both groups traded with the seacoast people for sea-mammal skins (particularly those of the sea otter), meat, seaweed, salt, and clams. People in the lower elevations, particularly the men, wore little or nothing during the warm months, and only robes or blankets of skin or woven dog hair for extra protection during the cold periods. The people higher in the mountains wove beautiful, warm blankets out of goat wool, and also sewed together tailored skin clothing of deer and elk hides; this they had learned from the Interior Salish. Down lower on islands in the river some of the Skagit raised a special kind of dog whose woolly hair was also used to weave blankets and robes. These blankets were similar to the famous Chilkat blankets of the Tsimshian and Tlingit (see chapter 3), but not so well decorated (see illustration). Weaving of dog-hair and goat-wool blankets was done on what is called a Salish Roller Loom, fashioned with two bars and two uprights made of hard wood. The wool was carded with a comb of wood, then spun with a spindle or flat circular piece of cedar. The weaver twisted the wool on her thigh and wound it into a ball, sometimes first mixing it with goose down. Raincoats of cattail matting were also woven, as were many forms of fine twined basketry.

The women wore skirts made of cedar-bark strips, sometimes reaching to the ankle, which were hung from a woven cedar-bark girdle. The skirts had to be thick, as it was considered immodest to show the legs. Women wore skin dresses, especially higher up the river where it was colder, buckskin in

COAST SALISH BASKETS WITH DESIGNS. Like most northwest coast tribes, these baskets are all done by the twining method. (*American Museum of Natural History, New York*)

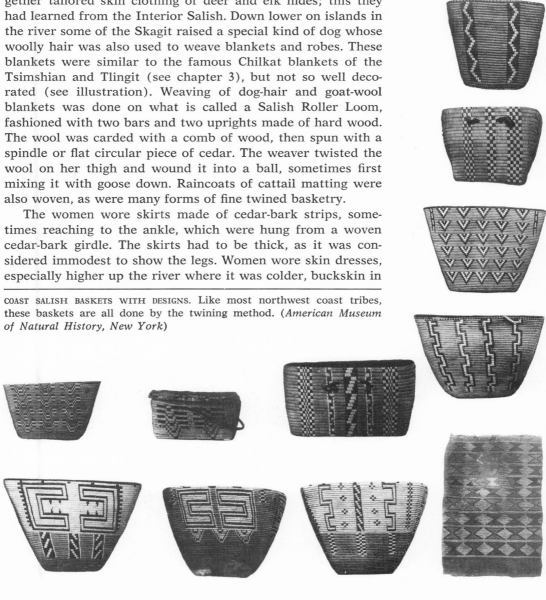

winter and doeskin in summer. Peaked basketry hats, mittens, and moccasins were also worn in cold weather. Well-woven mats were made from cattails, which were dried for several months to make the fibers ready for weaving. These mats would be used for many things, including beds, partitions in the large communal houses, and shelters on camping or gathering trips away from the main villages.

The rectangular wooden houses in the permanent villages had horizontal side planks and a shallowly pitched roof; a moveable board on top let out smoke. For better protection against rain, roofs usually had overlapping boards, held down by large rocks. The roofs were held up by six or more very large house posts. A large communal house could be as much as 120 feet long, made of three 40-foot sections, about 18 feet wide. Boards were split from large cedar trees with wedges of wood or horn and stone hammers; they were tied together with cedar-bark withes. Cracks were stuffed with moss. The door was a hole cut in a large plank; sometimes it was covered with a plank door.

Each of several families in the house had a large hearth where they could cook, and a continuous sleeping platform ran along most of the walls. Mats, dog-hair or mountain-goat wool blankets, and animal skins formed the beds. A higher platform or shelf held many things for storage in boxes made of steamed, creased, and folded cedar planks (see illustration), while above these, from large, heavy beams, hung dried meat, fish, and other foods and articles. House posts were carved and painted with designs of religious significance, usually guardian spirits or the stories of ancestors. The erection of the house posts was usually preceded by a special ceremonial potlatch, a time to feast and give away gifts.

Smaller wooden houses were sometimes built at good fishing sites away from the main village. At other times, simpler shelters were made of mats hung from or over a square framework

COAST SALISH BASKETRY CRADLE: with banded sides and slatted bottom. (*National Museums of Canada, Ottawa*)

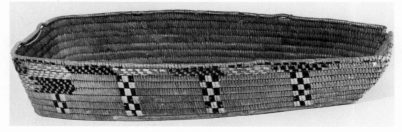

of posts and beams, or arranged in the form of a lean-to. Some sweathouses were built, too, although less frequently among the Coast Salish than among the inland people. The houses were usually circular in structure with a single center pole to which other poles were attached, then covered with brush. Hot rocks were placed inside and water poured on them to make a steam. A more frequent bath was taken by men and boys at dawn in the river.

Canoes were of several kinds: a small canoe for hunting ducks; a larger, shovel-nosed canoe for paddling or poling up and down the river; and a still larger canoe with sharp bow and stern for traveling on the sea. Each was dug out of a single cedar tree trunk, using fire, steaming, and adzes. Some canoes could hold as many as ten people. A ceremony that included prayers and fasting often prepared the way for canoe-making, which was usually done by one expert. Paddles were made usually of vine maple and ended with a T shape.

The Salish made buckets out of hollowed pieces of cedar trunks, and they carved wooden dishes. Spoons of horn and wood were also carved with animal and human figures, sometimes quite artistically.

Most of the Salish people were noted for their addiction to hard work and doing a good job, and this was particularly true of the Skagit. Those who did not work hard generally landed in the poor class and were looked down upon. Boys had a

COAST SALISH BOX AND LID: carved and painted. (*National Museums of Canada, Ottawa*)

Spartan rearing. Frequently they were driven by an uncle with whips to take early morning baths in the river, even in winter. Fasting to gain religious purification and power from the spirits, so as to gain wealth, was common.

Few men or women were specialists, although some men became mainly fishers or hunters. The hunting of mountain goats called for special expertise. Some women specialized in weaving blankets. If these people became very good at what they did, they were relieved of most other work. Although men were usually the shamans, women could learn to cure by supernatural means and even help return lost souls. As there was far more sharing of jobs between men and women among the Skagit and other Salish than among the great northern tribes, we might reason that the women had more freedom and greater equality.

Fishing was of prime importance in Skagit life. A weir was used, a sort of lattice-work dam of vertical poles and cross-pieces of branches, the poles often arranged in the form of tripods for greater strength, then interlaced with small branches to keep the fish from getting through except at the openings where the Skagit determined it was best for them to be caught. Most Skagit villages were on the main river or one of its tributaries where salmon, steelhead, and other fish could be caught with dip nets. A few villages were located near famous camass-bulb prairies where this delicious food could be gathered in quantities and traded for fish.

Sometimes fish were caught with large gill nets, stretched across streams. These caught the fish by their gills as they tried to swim through the holes in the nets. A set net was often put in the shallows and left there to catch fish in its closed end as they swam downstream. Some fish were caught with dip nets as they swam upstream; this was often done at night, with torches. A dip net was also used from a platform of logs built out over the river, from a canoe, or from a large rock near the bank. Many fish were dried and smoked for a winter food supply.

Property was continually circulating through gifts, sales,

and the potlatch. Ordinary gifts, as at a death or a marriage, did not have to be returned. Gifts given at a potlatch, however, were supposed to be returned in the form of other gifts at a later potlatch. All of this was to promote the prestige of the potlatch giver. Slaves were bought and sold and captured in war, but were comparatively few in number. Generally they were treated quite well, as part of a family; rarely did violent killing of slaves occur at the time of a chief's death as among the more northern tribes. A rich man usually had more than one wife. With the additional work of slaves, he could produce more goods for a potlatch, and gain more prestige. Exchange of property was mostly by trade, as the Upper Skagit did not use much of the dentalium money prevalent elsewhere. Houses and land were not sold, but were passed on only by inheritance. Land was usually owned by a village; trespassing by other tribes or villages could set off a war.

Skagit life centered on the extended family and the village. The head of each family had prestige based on his wealth and the numbers in his family. Skagit chiefs had much less power than those of the northern tribes. Family feeling was strong and the father and oldest brother occupied the pivotal positions.

The Skagit were strict with their children, constantly admonishing them to be good and have a high moral standard and

PADDLES, CANOES, AND VARIOUS IMPLEMENTS OF THE COAST SALISH AND CHINOOK: **A** paddles used mainly by Salish (1 and 2 odd-shaped paddles, probably with mystical or magical connotations): 1 sometimes called a sealer's paddle, 3 a woman's paddle (women's paddles are generally colored red, men's black), 4 a common woman's paddle, 5 commonest man's paddle, 6 steersman's paddle, 7 northern type paddle (probably borrowed from Haida); **B** canoes of various shapes: 1 Nootka canoe, 2 and 6 common Salish canoes, 3 Haida canoe, 4 Pelalt or "wide throat" canoe, 5 a vaguely Nootka-type canoe; **C** stone adze blade hafted in wood; **D** double-edged whale-bone knife; **E** Tillamook digging-stick handle with holes for shaft; **F** arrow with two-piece shaft; **G** one type of Salish snowshoe. (*Drawings A, B, and G from Barnett,* Culture Elements Distributions IX Gulf of Georgia Salish; *C from Collins,* The Upper Skagit Indians of Western Washington; *D, E, and F from Sauter and Johnson,* Tillamook Indians of the Oregon Coast)

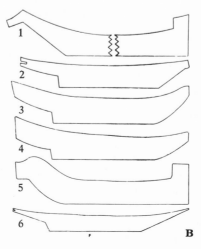

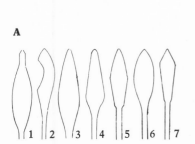

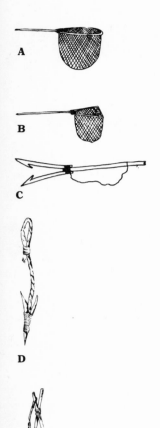

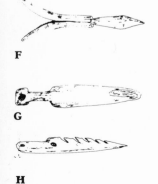

work ethic. A child was urged to uphold the honor of his family; children with bad manners or actions were considered to come from very poor families. There was little crime. An offender was either killed or banished from the territory. Marriages were usually made with people of nearby villages, so parents could keep a close check on their children. The married couple usually lived with the family of one or the other. Divorces were rare.

The Upper Skagit, like most of the Salish, were comparatively peaceful; in fact, peace and cooperation were constantly emphasized over war. They were far enough from the great warlike nations, such as the Haida and the Kwakiutl, to miss most of their raids, and their neighbors over the mountain passes seldom crossed the snowy heights to attack, although the Thompson Indians from British Columbia sometimes did. When Skagit war bands traveled to get slaves, which they did rarely, they killed the men and brought back women and children. There were roughly three classes among the Skagit: the ruling class, which actually included most of the people; a much smaller class of the very poor (by bad luck or inclination); and the slaves. The mountain Skagit probably had no slaves and looked down on the practice.

The Skagit, like most native Americans, were quite religious. Each boy and girl was to search for a guardian spirit, the most powerful of which could only be won by purity of heart and long fasts and searches. This was a very strong force for goodness of conduct. You could have more than one guardian spirit

FISHING AND CANOE EQUIPMENT OF THE COAST SALISH AND CHINOOK: **A** typical dip net; **B** triangular dip net (most dip nets have a bone or wood loop that can be used to close the upper part of the net); **C** upward impaling harpoon (slid down over back of fish then jerked upward to impale it); **D** harpoon head showing how cord is attached; **E** cross-handled dip net; **F** three-piece bone harpoon head; **G** salmon club of wood; **H** single-piece bone harpoon head; **I** Tillamook fish trap; **J** canoe paddle; **K** canoe bailer. (*A to C after Barnett,* Culture Elements Distributions IX Gulf of Georgia Salish; *D and E after Collins,* The Upper Skagit Indians of Western Washington; *F to K after Sauter and Johnson,* Tillamook Indians of the Oregon Coast)

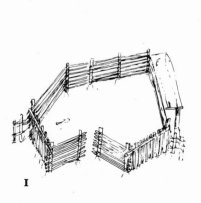

if you were lucky or tried hard enough. There were some spirits who helped with hunting, others who helped with fishing, wood carving, gambling, war, and so on. As most spirits came to visit the people in winter, the year was essentially divided into a more material time and a more spiritual time. In the winter the great winter festivals were held (see chapters 4 and 5). Then the spirits were called out of the darkness, and each person usually sang his special guardian spirit song to call his guardian spirit and to impress his listeners with his power.

The spirits used by shamans were supposed to be especially powerful. They were usually first met in dreams. Shamanistic spirits, unlike the ordinary kinds, were usually found all the time with their owners, helping them with curing, magic, and far-seeing. As a result, many people feared the shamans. Spirits were associated with certain animals; the bear spirit was supposed to be especially powerful. Wealth spirits were highly sought after. The Chinook had a culture similar to that of the Salish, but were most well known as traders and had developed a trading language, the Chinook jargon.

The Tamahnous Man (Chinook)

HYAK CHAK CHAK (SWIFT EAGLE) found his son, Kale Eena (Black Beaver), netting salmon with a dip net from a rock alongside the lower Columbia River. He admired the young man's technique, his slow sweep and quick dip, and his upward swing that flung the salmon unerringly in a long arc to the feet of his sister, Tokatie Tupso (Pretty Leaf), on the bank. His muscular brown body was a model of graceful action. The girl also was quick and deft with the wooden club with which she struck the head of each fish as she seized it by the tail and threw it lifeless but still wiggling into a large burden basket. Soon, when the basket was full, another sister would take her place. Then Pretty Leaf would put the tump line over her forehead, the great basket on her back, and carry the eighty or so pounds of fish to her mother higher up the slope near their tule-mat summer hut. Here the mother would cut the fish with an obsidian knife, clean them, and lay the fillets on an open-work platform through which the smoke was rising from a fire, curing them for winter storage.

Swift Eagle watched until the basket was almost full, then called out:

"Black Beaver, Pretty Leaf, you can stop your work now. I am taking Black Beaver on a deer hunt. I have found some good tracks."

With a yell, the young man leaped down from the rock and bounded toward his father, while the girl looked on enviously. She knew her mother would have plenty for her to do back at the camp.

The two men found sinew-backed bows and arrows at the camp and headed up into the hills. An hour later, when they found the deer tracks on a trail going through trees and brush, the father spoke seriously to the son:

"You have fasted and sought in the silence of the forest for your first dream. Now you have found it and your spirit helper. You are beginning to be a Tamahnous Man (one who has found spirit power), but it is a beginning, and you must watch and listen more closely than ever before to fulfill your spirit helper's guidance. On this hunt I want you to learn from me, not only for hunting, but how to handle men when we go on trading expeditions, for men can often be handled as we handle the wild animals."

As they followed the tracks, Swift Eagle showed his son how to find the signs. Even on rocky outcroppings they could see where a bit of grass had been recently bent by a hoof and was now slowly rising, the only evidence of a deer passing. The deer were heading into a large wooded amphitheater in the hills, and minutes later they sighted them below.

"Now we swing to the right," whispered Swift Eagle, "to get downwind from them so they cannot smell us."

They stopped when they had reached a good spot behind a large rock, about two hundred meters from the small herd of six buck deer. Swift Eagle reached into his pack and took out a deerskin attached to a cleaned and stuffed buck deer head with antlers.

"Now watch," he said. "I will pretend I am a deer to get near them. When near enough I will shoot. Meanwhile, you snake down as close as you can by staying out of sight, but off there to the left where the canyon begins and the deer may run. When I have hit one, spring up and run to get closer and try to get in a shot yourself."

With the deer head lashed on top of his own head and the skin flowing over his back, Swift Eagle moved cautiously toward the deer, sometimes crouching, sometimes on hands and knees. When they noticed him, he moved his deer head down as if he were feeding, but every few moments he would swing his head up in the typical motion of a deer watching and sniffing for enemies. The deer thought him another deer and continued to feed, as he came closer and closer.

Suddenly there was a pounding sound from the right, and both men saw a tawny figure leaping forward in great bounds. The mountain lion screamed viciously, striking terror in the deer, which had begun to run. Their stiff-legged pounding leaps carried them up and over the brush like bouncing balls. But a young buck was a little late in getting under way. He gave a strange moaning roar as he was struck on the haunches by two hundred pounds of driving fury. He tried to strike with his antlers, but the great cat clung to his back, inched forward, and, reaching out with one paw, dug its claws into his nose, and gave a powerful jerk with its forearm. The deer dropped as if struck by an avalanche, his neck broken.

When Black Beaver reached his father, the older man was calmly taking off the fake deer head. The son whispered angrily:

"He stole our deer; we should kill him!"

The older man replied: "The lion never saw us. He killed fairly, but we will take the deer away from him without any need to kill him. I want to show you the power of a Tamahnous Man."

Deaf to his son's objections, Swift Eagle took his obsidian knife and quickly cut two medium-thick, arm-length pieces from the branch of an elderberry tree, split each three quarters of the way down the middle, put a small stick at the bottom of each crotch, and bound it there with rawhide. Taking one clapper stick and giving the other to Black Beaver, while leaving both bows behind, he said:

"Do exactly as I do and show no fear. We will show him we have greater spirit power."

The two advanced on the mountain lion, who was snarling as he tore at the bleeding throat of the deer. Black Beaver trembled, but watched his father closely, doing as he did.

When they got close, the huge lion gave a deep coughing growl, his black-tipped tail lashing fiercely.

Swift Eagle did not look the lion in the eye. Instead, he looked at the ground and began a crouching, forward-weaving motion, much unlike a man, striking his elderberry clapper stick on the ground to make a loud clacking noise, and singing in a high voice:

"We admire you. You are very brave. We drink from your bravery. We honor you by coming to take your food, which is also our food. But we have a greater power. Listen to our power; it is in these sticks! Hear them beating our power. We will not kill you because you helped us. But you must go away; our power is greater than yours."

Black Beaver came close beside his father, doing exactly the same thing, trusting the older man. It was lucky he was looking at the ground, for the lion's tail was lashing so fast the eye could scarcely follow it and the ears were laid back flat on the head as the snarls rose in crescendo. But Swift Eagle was watching the beast out of the corner of his eye, and knew what to do. Suddenly he stood up tall, shaking the clapper stick as loud as possible and giving a penetrating scream. Black Beaver quickly did the same.

The overwhelming noise was too much for the great cat. With a frustrated scream of rage, he turned and ran, leaving the two men alone with the deer.

"Remember this lesson," said Swift Eagle. "Being without fear and doing the unexpected stops a fierce animal. It can also stop a fierce man."

Two weeks later, father and son and some kinsmen of their tribe, the Lower Chinook, were shepherding a line of about fifteen slaves they had bought, recently captured from California Indian tribes by the warlike Klamath of Klamath Lake, Oregon. All were on their way downriver to a trading center on the Lower Columbia River. The adult and teen-age slaves carried back packs loaded with finely tanned elk hides, beaver pelts, obsidian knives and arrow points, and dried bark of interior bushes used in medicine, plus food for the whole party. For the slaves and the other items, the Chinook had traded salt from the sea, dried salmon from the river, clam shells from the Oregon coast, and long, white, toothlike dentalium shells they had obtained from the Nootka of Vancouver Island. They had brought the slaves and their luggage around a series of rapids on the river and had come near smooth water at the end of portage where earlier they had pulled their canoes onto the beach.

The slaves were mainly Achomawi and Shasta peoples from northern California, mostly women, but also some ten- to twelve-year-olds, and three younger teen-age boys, sullenly bearing their burdens, their eyes sad with despair.

"I hate this slave trade business," said Black Beaver to his father. "Look at that girl, graceful as a fawn, and beautiful as the mountain lily. Some Haida or Tlingit chief, meeting us at the trading grounds, will want her for a concubine, since they never marry a slave as we sometimes do, or he may order her killed at a big potlatch to show how rich he is."

The father looked wisely at his son.

"Our people have been buying slaves from the Klamath, the Modoc, and the Yakima as far back as the generations remember and selling them at a profit to the northern tribes, and this will not change for a while yet. Frankly, I buy slaves so I can treat them well and win their respect, and my new policy in the last year is to sell them only to new owners whom I feel will treat them kindly also and may in time even free them, as the Salish often do. I know men and I know how they will act!"

"But what if some powerful northern chief wants some slaves and you deny them to him. You know they consider themselves the greatest warriors in the world, and he might just take them from you!"

"There may be something like that this trip. But wait and see what happens."

That evening they camped early, for the slaves were tired. Swift Eagle told them to bathe their feet in the river. Then he examined their feet and put healing ointments made from native herbs on those who had cuts or bruises, watching with amusement when Black Beaver rushed to salve and bandage one foot of the Shasta girl, Kawnie, who had caught his eye.

The slaves expressed amazement at this treatment and were astonished also when Swift Eagle had his wife and daughters, who had come up the river to meet the party in some canoes with some of their men kin, cook a delicious meal of fresh grilled salmon steaks, plus greens and roasted tubers, dug with digging sticks from the nearby meadows, and gave it to the poor tired slaves without asking them to move.

"Hwah wa!" exclaimed one slave woman in the Chinook jargon, the international language known up and down the coast among many tribes, and which a few of the slaves knew. "Kah-ta me-si-ka klose ne-si-ka?" ("Why are you so good to us?")

"Ne-si-ka til-i-kum kah-kwa ne-si-ka; tik-egh mamook me-si-ka hy-as kloshe!" ("You are people like us; we wish to make you very happy!")

"But you are going to sell us as slaves!"

"That is the way here and there is no turning back, but we will try to sell you to people who will be kind to you, and who will give you freedom when you can earn it. Be thankful. Many other slaves are sold to cruel masters, some who kill them."

Later, when Swift Eagle's party arrived by canoe at the trading center on the Lower Columbia River, the slaves were startled to see the great high-prowed canoes of the Tlingit,

Haida, Tsimshian, Kwakiutl, and Nootka come riding in fast and proud from the sea, filled with articles to trade, but also with the fierce-looking men of the north who could be warriors very quickly if needed. There were also some smaller canoes of such Washington and Oregon coastal tribes as the Tillamook, the Quinalt, and the Coast Salish from the Puget Sound region; it was a great gathering for trade, one of the greatest of the west.

Soon all about, up and down the beaches, furious bargaining was going on among all hues of copper-skinned men. They sat on their haunches, some with feathered capes on their shoulders, others with the beautiful sheen of sea-otter and fur-seal furs, keeping off the cold of the fog and the wind. The Chinook were the hosts, as this was their land, and they were the premier traders, their warriors ready in case any trouble began.

The Haida had brought the beautifully polished steatite stone bowls and cooking pots from their foggy islands. The Tlingit and Tsimshian showed their gleaming copper shields from the far north, worth fortunes, their Chilkat mountain goat's wool blankets, plus caribou skins and carved horn spoons and dishes. The Nootka brought abalone shells, iridescent as pearls, and the valuable white dentalium shell money, good as gold up and down the coast. The Coast Salish brought beaver teeth, fine for drills and chisels, and beautiful skins of mountain foxes and martens. The Tillamook had plenty of salt from their marshes, dried seaweed, and slaves from southern Oregon. Of course the Chinook were the middlemen, buying and selling all over the beaches. They were shrewd bargainers with their numerous slaves from the Dalles on the Columbia, plenty of finely tanned elk skin, and obsidian from the volcano country.

Swift Eagle and his friends tried to guide their slaves, loaded with trade goods, inland a ways to where the shyer Coast Salish were gathering, for they were likely to be much kinder to the slaves than the northern tribes. But before he could reach them, a huge eighty-foot-long Tlingit war canoe, its high, curved prow decorated with a carved grizzly bear's head, came hissing onto the beach, driven by the brawny arms of forty warriors. Leaping to the sand was a tall and haughty chief, his high basket hat topped with sea eagle feathers, an otter-skin robe glistening on his shoulders.

"Ni-ka chah-ko mah-kook mist-shi-mus!" he called in the Chinook jargon. ("I come to buy slaves!")

"Ah tyee," answered Swift Eagle boldly, "ne-si-ka mah-kook klas-ka ko-pa til-i-kum klak-sta klose nan-itsh kloshe!" ("Chief, we sell them only to people who take good care of them.")

Black Beaver gripped his bow tightly when he heard the Tlingit chief burst into a torrent of words in Tlingit, while the warriors behind him, armed with spears and clubs and fierce of face, grunted menacingly. An older Tlingit translated for the chief.

"He says, what is this foolish talk about treating slaves kindly. Slaves are to be bought and used as we please. If you will not sell them to us, we will take them without pay!"

Black Beaver knew the Chinook at this place on the beach were outnumbered four to one, for a new Tlingit canoe of thirty more warriors had just landed, and hearing the loud talk, shook their spears, while the chief stood confident and menacing. Black Beaver was astonished and proud to see his father draw himself up very straight and speak calmly and yet with force:

"Listen, oh chief, we are not children. We have a right to do as we please with our slaves just as you do. Look to the sun. Before it goes down tomorrow, if you attack and kill us, my spirit messengers will carry word to your enemies, the Makah, the Nootka, and the Bella Coola, just when and where you will be coming on your way home with your slaves. They will come in their hundreds against you, remembering their earlier fights with you, lusting for your blood in revenge for warriors and others killed in your night attacks, for I see they have already wounded you! Listen to my spirit voices telling me what they will do for me!"

The growl of a bear seemed to come up from under the sand

at the feet of the chief, and then the scream of an eagle from the sky where no eagle could be seen, and from up the beach the mournful howl of an invisible wolf. Stricken by superstition, the Tlingit warriors clapped their hands to their mouths in amazement.

The Tlingit chief hesitated for a moment. Then, realizing his men had lost all desire for an attack, he turned on his heel, humiliated but still proud, and told them, "We will find a better bargain elsewhere."

Black Beaver asked his father: "How in the world did you make those voices come from a distance, and where did you learn about the Tlingit's fights with the Bella Coola, the Nootka, and the Makah?"

"I am a Tamahnous Man!" laughed Swift Eagle. "I know all; I see all!" But later he drew his son aside and whispered to him:

"You too can be a Tamahnous Man, but you have to watch very closely. The Tlingit warriors were wearing ornaments taken from those three tribes, and I could see some Tlingit had been wounded lately. Also you did not watch my throat when the voices came from the beach, the sand, and the sky. My throat was moving, for I have a way to throw my voice when I need to and make it sound from another place. Someday I will show you how."

"Well," replied his son. "You are certainly a very strong spirit man. But there is one thing I know you don't know!"

"What is that?"

"I am going to buy and marry that Shasta slave girl you saved for me from the Tlingit chief!"

Swift Eagle knew this too, but he was a wise enough father not to say so!

7. The Yurok, Hupa, and Karok

The Yurok lived in the lower Klamath River Valley and its neighboring coastlands from Trinidad Head almost to what is now Crescent City in northern California. They were the center of a unique culture grouping in northwest California (see appendixes), although they had elements of the greater and more complex culture of the far northwest in British Columbia and Alaska. Yet there is something about the Yurok, Hupa, and Karok tribes—who still exist in northwestern California—that speaks to the best in all of us if we study them deeply. Without government as we know it, without chiefs who could be called chiefs, with no laws but word-of-mouth laws about the payments to be made for injury done, with nearly unlimited freedom to talk and go one's own way, these people produced men and women who by their character and their high standards of honor shamed and stirred others into following and obeying them. There was very little crime and almost no war. Perhaps this was because they were, in this beautiful country of rivers and vast redwoods, true masters of life.

The Yurok, Hupa, and Karok had widely different languages (see Appendix D). However, so close were they in the old days in culture, religion, and general outlook on life that we can easily discuss them together. The nearby Tolowa, Wiyot, Chilula, and Whilkut were very close too, in both social and religious culture, although their religious ceremonials were less complex. Farther north the southwestern Oregon tribes (see map) lost still more of the Yurok-based culture, though beginning to pick up some elements of Lower Columbia River culture from the Tillamook to their north. (See Appendix B and C for brief comparisons of the culture differences of all these areas.)

It was a land of heavy rainfall and heavy forest growth, with areas of sand dunes, marshes, and brushlands along the coast, and inland occasional areas of oak woods and chaparral in the driest hills and mountains. Where fog drifted in from the sea and blanketed the coast in summer, the redwood was and is the great and dominant tree, its majestic heights and trunks and deep dark quiet woods creating a special solemnity and mystery that must have influenced Indian character.

The great Klamath River and its branches, such as the Trinity and the Salmon, dominated the lives of these people in a unique way. Their world was made of the upriver and downriver (Karok means "upriver people," and Yurok, "downriver people"). Their directions were the directions of the river, not the east, west, north, and south of other tribes. They fished the river with ardor for salmon and other fish, and traveled it up and down by canoe, knowing the rapids with their dangers and their beauty as they knew their own blood and bones.

The Outcast—A Life Story

"M OTHER," Lost Star asked, "why do you always look so sad?" His mother's face was kind and beautiful, and as long as he could remember, he had always loved to lie on his mat bed in the evening when he was supposed to go to sleep and peek at her face from around the edges of his deerskin blanket. The light of the flames flickering across her well-turned nose and her high cheekbones emphasized the deep quiet of her eyes and the sensitive lips. Their poor little house with its one-pitched leaky roof was low down by the Klamath, and through the still of the evening before his mother answered he could hear the murmur and talking of the waters. At this time of year, in the late springtime, it was like her gentle voice, a song and a sound he loved.

"My son," she replied, "if I were to try to tell you why I am so sad I could never stop weeping, but I must stop thinking of myself and think of you and your future. You are asking many questions now. It is time you should know the truth and what you can and cannot do. I must take you to your grandfather,

for he alone of all our people still thinks kindly of me and of you, and he alone can talk to you as a father should to a son, for your true father is long passed away to the land beyond the sea. In three days I will take you to see him, but in the meantime I want you to prepare a present to take him, something you can make yourself, something that is from your own heart."

"Yes, mother," he answered and looked at her with love, while a smile spread over his finely featured face as his eyes closed toward sleep. Even in the half-dream state he was thinking of what he would carve for his grandfather.

Ah, clever mother, she knew well her son and his strange ability with his hands and also her father and his love for beautiful things. It was the two of them, her father and her son, who kept her spirits up through these dark days. Like her own son, she had become an outcast to whom other women hardly spoke and whom most men avoided, though a few sought to visit her secretly for reasons she despised and rejected.

The boy was happily busy during the daylight hours carving on a piece of soft redwood with his clamshell knives and using a piece of sharp elk horn and a beaver's tooth as chisels. He worked in his secret place on the edge of the woods, a place where the thimbleberry and hazelnut bushes and the glorious pink-cream azaleas hid him from the sight of man, and from which he could see the waters of the river sparkling and creaming in white caps on their way to Mother Sea. It was about the sea and its life that he thought and dreamed as he carved, for the greatest memory of his early years was a trip to the sea by foot at the age of eight. He had seen the sea lions sunning themselves on a huge rock on the Pacific shores. So the sea and

MODELS OF HUPA MAN AND WOMAN: showing typical costumes, including basket cap for woman and two-piece skirt. Notice large carrying basket. Man has beautifully decorated sinew-backed bow, typical of the fine sense of artistry known among these northwest tribes, particularly the Hupa, Karok, and Yurok. (*American Museum of Natural History, New York*) its life sang themselves into the work of his hands and the little flying chips of reddish wood.

On the third day he finished his work, but hid it even from his mother in a bag made of wildcat skin, his eyes sparkling with anticipation. After a brief meal of acorn mush, eaten with the carved wooden spoon of the poor, his mother led him through the village to see his grandfather. Lost Star was so eager that he passed by other boys without hearing the names they spat at him under their breaths, and his mother was glad that for a while he seemed to forget that he was an outcast.

The grandfather sat on a beautiful carved wooden stool, sanded until it glowed red-brown and rustic in the afternoon light. He was alone, for the other men of the big house, with its three-sloped roof of the rich and well born, had gone hunting, while the women were picking berries and finding other things to eat on the edges of the woods. He was a big man with finely muscled shoulders and arms, a well-shaped mustache, and a thatch of black hair beginning to gray. It was his face that drew the glance of the boy, a face carved in granite yet glowing with an inner compassion and humor that sparkled also in the dark eyes.

"I have a present for you, grandfather!" exclaimed the boy. "I made it with my own hands and my own tools." He carefully opened the wildcat skin bag and drew from it an object that caused both adults to gasp with surprise. Lost Star's face broke into a dazzling smile that turned to laughter.

"See, grandfather, I made what I saw when I was down at the ocean."

The grandfather held the carving gently and reverently in his hands. The boy had carved a canoe with two men in it, riding the waves, and one was about to throw a harpoon into a sea lion whose head stuck out of the water. It was roughly done, for after all he was only a nine-year-old, but he had caught the spirit of motion of what he had seen. The figures almost seemed to live!

The old man passed the carving to his daughter and looked at her gravely. "It is time indeed I talk to my grandson! You did well to bring him, and you have a right to be proud of him."

The mother cast down her eyes and moved her hands nervously.

"He is all I have to live for," she said simply.

"No, you are still young and beautiful, and the boy will be a passage for you back to a new life, for he has great possibilities. You must help him become strong and brave, and it will not be easy, for you must not touch him too much in love, but let him harden himself and become a man. Now listen, my grandson, and listen carefully so you will understand."

"My ears listen as the fawn listens for the doe in the forest."

"It is well, for all your future depends on following what I tell you to do. But what I tell you now is only a beginning. As you grow older and understand better, I will tell you deeper things.

"You know well what the boys call you because your mother never married and yet she bore you. But the boys and others forget the rest. Your father honorably sent the marriage money to pay for your mother to be his wife, and I refused it at first, demanding more because I valued your mother, my daughter, so highly. Your father found a relative who promised he would put up the extra payment to complete the marriage, but your father became so impatient waiting, he poled his canoe across the river one night to see your mother secretly. Going back to the other side that stormy night, his canoe was overturned in the rapids and he was killed. Thus the marriage was never quite completed, and you were born without a proper father. I have forgiven your mother and father for what happened, for they were very much in love and this made them foolish, but it is our unwritten law that children like you become outcasts."

"What does that mean, grandfather?"

"It means there are several things you cannot do until you prove yourself worthy. You cannot travel by canoe on the river and you will not be allowed in a sweathouse with the other men. If a man killed you, the price he would have to pay for it would be so small that most men would not worry about it. It will indeed be almost impossible for you to become a man, as we call a man a man, nor will any girl except one like yourself, an outcast, be able to marry you."

"Must this always be so, grandfather?" asked the boy. "And does my mother also always have to suffer for what happened?"

"For a while you both will have many severe trials, but there is a way to overcome this if you will listen very carefully, though it will be very hard."

"I am ready, grandfather!" Lost Star stood very straight and looked the old man squarely in the eyes. His mother looked at him surprised but proud.

"You must train your body, mind, and spirit. Every dawn you must sing a prayer to the sunrise, then run as far as you can until you sweat. Then down to the river to take a swim, no matter how cold the water is. And after you swim sing a prayer to the Woges, the little people whom most of us never see, the sacred owners of power that they give only to people who are good. And pray also to Pulekukwerek, the man from the north edge of the world, for he it is who taught us to be truthful, brave, and good. Say such prayers also at midday and at nighttime before you go to bed. Train your body every day to grow strong by doing hard work like cutting wood, by running, by lifting stones, and other exercises, and learn to shoot the bow and arrow or throw a rock with a sling until you can hit every mark.

"You must train your mind to be strong too. Don't reply and don't be angry if boys call you names. Pay no attention to them or to others who are unkind to you, but do good things for other people, even those who injure you. Help the old woman, the widow, the orphan, and anybody else who truly needs help, for the true man among us, no matter how rich he may become, puts the needs of the people before his own.

"If a boy attacks you, I will show you how to hold him so he feels pain but is not injured. When he feels your strength, he will not bother you again. Always speak well to people, be polite, saying only good things. When you eat, eat slowly and never in a hurry, for by eating fast you show you have no self-control, and it is not polite. And always think only good thoughts, for this will bring you the help of the Woges. A bad thought will drive them away.

"When you are older and ready I will tell you of other things to draw the spirit to you, to be strong and brave, so that people will finally recognize you as a true man, and your birth will be forgotten. Then your mother also will be recognized as a good woman and will be accepted. It is a long hard journey. Are you ready to make it?"

Lost Star put his hand over his heart.

"As long as my heart beats and my blood flows, I will do what you tell me to do, grandfather! But it is mostly for my mother. I want her to be happy again as she used to be."

The grandfather looked proudly at the boy, but the mother hid her face and wept. Then she wiped away the tears and seemed to gather new strength from her son. They left, walking together as one being.

Now Lost Star became like a ghost in the forest. No man would teach him the ways of Yurok men in hunting and fishing, and his grandfather could not because of an unwritten law. But the boy could watch the men from the edge of the woods or by secretly peering from behind trees in the forest when they went hunting, his steps softer than the whisper of the wind. Occasionally a man would glimpse a face looking at him from under a bush, but it would disappear so quickly and so quietly that he could not be sure what it was. Some said it was a Woge, one of the first people, the little people, and seeing such a face would bring good luck. But the boy watched and learned, for his eyes were sharp and far-seeing, his mind was quick and his fingers were clever.

He saw how a man made a bow. A straight branch of a yew tree was cut off and left to dry and season for a year or two in a dry cave in the hills. Then it was cut to the right length and chiseled and whittled gradually down to the right shape, thin and wide in the middle in the aristocratic way of Yurok bows. Finally it was sandpapered with equisetum or scouring rush stems until it was smooth and shining. He saw how they used a glue taken from the skin of the river sturgeon to fasten on strips of sinew to the back side. The bow was wrapped with sinew, especially at the grip in the middle, until it was strong and supple and capable of sending a hunting or war arrow two hundred yards or more.

The boy watched them making nets and harpoons for catching fish. The harpoon was made out of willow wood for the main part, with two hardwood foreshafts, one slightly longer than the other, that had sharp barbs of bone or horn glued to them with pine pitch and wrapped tight with sinew. The foreshafts were tied to the main shaft with short lengths of cord. When the large salmon were struck the foreshaft or shafts would come loose, but the man could fight the salmon with the cord if the prongs had caught in the flesh and bring it fighting back to the land to be hit by a salmon club of stone or whalebone. The boy also saw them making their twenty-foot poles and wide-angled dip or lifting nets, which were lowered into the water in an eddy where the current temporarily went upstream from a scaffold built out over the water. The fisherman sat on a stool on the platform, holding a bone button attached to the string that closed the opening to the net on its frame. A pull on the cord told him when a salmon had entered the net. Then the whole net was pulled up, the salmon clubbed and thrown into a basket, and the net lowered again. The boy watched all this carefully. They made the nets out of strong cord from the fibers of the wild iris leaf, something his mother could show him, as the women were the ones who usually stripped the two beautiful silky fibers from the leaf, then made them into strings that could be twisted and knotted by the men to make the net.

So in time the boy made his own bow and arrows. He made the arrows out of straight branches of a syringa bush, the foreshaft of hard wood, tipped with sharp flint or obsidian arrowheads he had to learn by long practice how to chip for himself. He made his own net and harpoon, but he had to be careful where he hunted and fished, for all the good hunting grounds along the river and for a mile inland were owned by various prominent men and could not be hunted without permission, and most of the good fishing places were also owned and jealously guarded.

So the boy had to hunt mainly far away from home, killing small game at first, wood rats and squirrels. Then one day, when he was eleven, he came close enough by silent stalking to wing an arrow into the side of a deer. The deer fled and he followed it hour after hour, by the footmarks, the broken twigs and bent grasses, and the drops of blood. At last it grew tired. He came close enough to draw the arrow far back in the bow, holding the bow crosswise to his body in the Yurok way, and then watched it hiss into the side behind the left front leg, hitting the heart and ending the hunt. As was the custom, he said a prayer that the deer might be born again. He cut the throat with his obsidian knife to bleed the carcass, then cut it up into parts as he had seen the men do. All he could carry back to his mother's house was the skin, one haunch, and the tongue, a big load for a boy. Later he brought back the head, which he had hidden up a tree, as this was important to clean and stuff to use as part of a camouflaging hunting outfit; thus he could look and act like a deer when stalking them. His mother scraped the flesh and fat off the skin and soaked it to get rid of the hair. She tanned it with the deer brains and a lot of chewing in the mouth and rubbing with the hands until it could be made into a warm, winter jacket for her son.

The boy became filled with a secret desire to kill a pure white deer, for a skin and head of one of these deer was, to the Yurok, the greatest treasure, worth many strings of the finest dentalium money. But his grandfather warned him that such a deer was found only by the pure in heart and only by those who were constantly doing good for other people.

Since Lost Star, now a youth in his teens, liked to make people happy, he was soon using his new-found skill as a hunter and fisherman to bring fish and meat to the poor and needy, to the widow and the orphan, the sick and injured. Many people had begun to look at him differently, with wonder in their eyes.

And all the time he was increasing his strength, by wrestling with trees and boulders, throwing heavy rocks, practicing with bow and spear and harpoon until his arms were steel hard and as supple as those of the wildcat. He learned to make special deadfall traps out of logs to trap raccoons, martens, foxes, wolves, and even bears, rubbing the traps with strong-scented roots and leaves to take away the man-smell. And he learned when hunting and trapping to sing the little hunting songs that the great hunters use, the songs that send out their breath along the hidden trails of the woods, luring the wild things in range of the bow and praying that their spirits may live again.

When he was seventeen he planned to build his first canoe. He found a recently fallen redwood tree about three-and-a-half feet thick, and prepared to work on it first by several days of fasting and praying, as he knew the old ones did, for a tree not treated with respect might split when turned into a boat. His mother taught him certain songs to sing as he worked on the boat. He cut and hacked at the log with stone knives, clam-shell adzes, and beaver-tooth chisels, using elk-horn wedges to split off the top part of the log. Finally he had a twelve-foot length that, laboriously, over many months of using fire to burn out the middle, and adzes, chisels, and mauls to hack away the burned wood, he had gradually hollowed. To make sure he would not come too close to the surface, he drilled small holes about an inch deep at intervals, making the holes the depth he wanted the canoe walls to be so he could stop cutting out the middle when he reached them. Each of these later was sealed shut with hot pine pitch that solidified when cooled. At the stern end he left a seat for the steersman and some little knobs on the bottom to give purchase for his feet, and another knob up near the prow for a foothold when poling the canoe up the river. Two long paddles he made out of yew wood, strong enough for swift currents and long enough to be used as poles for pushing when needed.

Finally the canoe was finished. He led his mother to see it in its secret place in the woods. She laughed with delight and touched it with admiration, acting for the first time like the happy girl she once had been.

"When do we go canoeing?" she asked. And then a sad look came to her face, and she said wistfully: "But maybe they will not allow us a canoe ride because we are outcasts."

When they asked the grandfather about riding in the canoe, he was silent for a while, thinking. Finally he said:

"Ride in the canoe. If they throw rocks at you, it is because you are not yet accepted. Then wait a while longer until the time is ripe. But if they do not throw rocks, you have won the hearts of too many to be stopped."

The two of them worked hard, using small logs as rollers, to move the canoe down a trail they had cut through the forest, until finally it splashed into the Klamath River. The next day, with trepidation, they pushed the new canoe into the river and paddled across to the other side and back again. Many people watched them from either bank, and many smiled and waved, so they knew they had many friends.

It was not far to the sea from the village of Turip where they lived. So a few days later they paddled downstream, some of the way through rapids where they had to use their paddles dexterously, and finally to the Pacific Ocean at Rekwoi, the big Yurok village on the coast. Here they used their canoe to ferry a family across the river. When the man asked the youth to go on a sea-lion hunt, he gladly accepted. Lost Star's mother was to stay with some relatives who would be glad to see her.

There were nine men getting three canoes ready to take to the sea after the sea lions. Just as the canoe with the youth was being shoved off to start through the breaker, a large man came running up and seized it angrily, shouting:

"You can't let this boy go with you! He is a bastard, and none of his name should be allowed to go on sea-lion hunts."

But the three men in the canoe turned on him, one saying:

"He helped my family across the river when we were in a hurry! He is our friend."

"I know him at Turip," cried another. "He has helped all

the poor families there with food when they were in need, and gathered wood for the orphans and widows and the sick. It makes no difference what you say!"

But the man who held the boat was very large and strong, and his eyes turned fierce.

"I won't let you go!" he yelled.

Suddenly Lost Star jumped out of the boat. Without a word he pulled it quickly out of the hands of the big man, shoved it through a wave and jumped into ride it out through the breakers. The men in the canoe watched open-mouthed, for he had shown himself more powerful than the bigger man.

"Look out for that one!" the man whose family he had helped yelled to him above the roar of the breakers. "He and his two brothers think they own the river. Because you are what you are, they may try to kill you, feeling no one can demand much money for your death."

"I won't make it easy for them," said Lost Star grimly.

Soon he was watching every move of the men in the canoe, for this was his first experience in the sea. Out beyond the breakers it was comparatively smooth, with only the long, even swells of a warm summer day. The Yurok canoe, with its small size and incurved thwarts, was not really meant for ocean work, though it was handy enough as long as the sea was fairly calm. But the youth gloried in the sharp smell of the salt air, the glistening of blue waters, the great brown jungles of kelp covering many meters of ocean space, and the shrill calls of the gulls and terns, shearwaters and other seabirds, as they wheeled and dove. He examined the sea-lion harpoon very closely, so he could later make one of his own. The head was detachable and attached to a long line that was wrapped tightly around the hardwood foreshaft. The point would break free from this shaft after it was struck into a sea lion and the cord would unravel while the harpoon shaft floated on the surface of the sea. The hunters would use this to hold their canoe in tow to the swimming but speared sea lion.

After several miles of paddling they came to a big rock whose brown sides glistened from the ocean spray. The three canoes moved shoreward on the lee side of the rock where the waves were lowest. A man dressed in sea-lion skin to look like the animal leaped onto a rock at the proper moment with a rope in his hand. He anchored the canoe to the rock so the steersman could play out against the rope and hold the canoe on the heaving sea. From the two other canoes a man from each leaped also onto the rocks with ropes and the three, all dressed in the sea-lion skins, were thrown clubs.

The men moved cautiously over the rocks toward where some sea lions were basking, some sleeping in the warm sunlight. Then the men began to act like sea lions, crawling on their bellies and throwing up their heads once in a while to look around as the watchful animals did. At first the sea lions payed no attention to them beyond a cursory stare. The instant the animals began to act uneasy, the three men suddenly jumped up and ran at them with the clubs. Three were clubbed to death before they could more than wake up, but one giant male sea lion rose up on a high rock, gave a roar of alarm, and sprang down to courageously attack one of the men, his ton or more of weight coming like a battering ram. The man leaped aside, although he was struck a glancing blow that sent him spinning. The great bull drove right on down to the sea, and the rest of the sea lions fled with him, their sleek brown bodies soon cleaving through the waves like living submarines, the spume from their leaps into the sea high in the air. There were three dead sea lions lying on the rocks, waiting to be skinned and bled and butchered for taking in the canoes. The three canoes were already chasing after the fleeing sea lions, the paddles churning water as the sleek boats dashed over the swells. Lost Star had been tossed a paddle and was working it madly in rhythm. His canoe closed in on the great bull that had knocked down the man; it evidently had been injured in the encounter.

Suddenly the man in the forepart of the canoe dropped his paddle to the floor, seized the harpoon, and rose in one fluid motion to stand poised on the prow, one foot on the starboard gunwale, the other braced against the wooden knob that rose slightly from the canoe's forward bottom. Lost Star and the other paddler redoubled their efforts to get the canoe alongside or near the swiftly swimming but wounded bull. The harpooner's shoulder muscles tensed. He drove the powerful weapon forward with his whole strength, sinking the elk-horn, reverse-barbed point into the animal's heaving shoulder.

As the bull roared and whipped about in the waves, the twenty-foot shaft of the harpoon was shaken loose, though still tied to the head or point, so that when the giant bull dove he took all with him below. As the cord unwound from the shaft of the harpoon, the harpoon bobbed to the surface. The paddlers raced the canoe up so the harpooner could seize the floating shaft. Once the harpooner got hold of the line he wrapped it around a knob on the prow of the canoe, and instantly, as the sea lion surfaced again, they were being pulled through the water at high speed, for the harpoon's head with its sharp back prongs was firmly lodged in the bull's shoulder.

The youth had never felt so exhilarated in his life. He could hear the shouts of encouragement from the men in the other canoes whose luck had not been so good at harpooning, but soon they were left behind. Toward noon the bull was visibly tiring and paused for a moment's rest. But as the canoe crept toward him with the harpooner readying another strike, the bull suddenly roared fiercely and charged! Coolly the man in the prow shouted commands. Lost Star and the other paddler dug their paddles into the port side's waters, swinging the canoe in an arc to port. Nimbly the harpooner worked his way rapidly back to the stern and arrived there just as the bull drove forward to attack, swiftly overtaking the canoe, his eyes glaring balefully. There was only one vulnerable place to counterattack. The harpooner balanced, poised himself, and drove the great harpoon down with its sharp point into one of those angry eyes. The shock of the blow nearly threw the man bodily from the stern, but his bare feet clung like a monkey's as he dropped to the floor and seized the gunwales with his hands.

Blood gushed from the bull's wounded eye and the dazed animal turned floundering in the water, bellowing with pain.

Lost Star felt a sudden strong sympathy for the gallant beast who was so badly hurt, and asked if he might kill it to put it out of its pain. The harpooner nodded and the young man dove into the water, elk-horn knife in his hand, its point honed to needlelike sharpness. Again he dove and came up beside the animal's left flipper, driving the point deep into the left side where he knew the heart lay. As he did so he swerved his body away with a powerful kick and arm stroke that took him out of range of the thrashing body. When he rose to the surface again he saw blood gushing from the bull's mouth and the good eye glazed in death.

So huge was the animal that they had no way to carry him inside the canoe, but had to tow him the long miles back to the land. The paddling was drudgery for the last mile, but was suddenly relieved by the two other canoes who appeared out of the waves to lend a hand. However, the crowd that gathered on the beach as they neared the shore and the shouts of welcome and joy were the best revivers of all. The two other canoes had brought back with them the carved carcasses of the three smaller sea lions that had been killed on the rocks, and the three men who had done the killing. There was enough meat for a great feast on the beach that night for all the villagers of Rekwoi and their guests, and plenty of meat also to be hung and smoked and dried over the fires and in the sun. The sea-lion skins would be prepared for cloaks and blankets, while the teeth of the great bull were given to Lost Star for that last blow of the knife that had killed it. Such teeth were valuable, especially as they were used by the flint and obsidian dancers at the Sacred White Deerskin Dance to make part of their spectacular headdresses.

Lost Star was told that the man who had tried to stop him from going on the sea-lion hunt had left the village to go up-river, but had sworn he would get revenge. "Beware!" the people told him. "It is not he alone you need to fear, but his two brothers also, famous warriors, who may try to waylay you. They are jealous of your grandfather and his influence and wealth, and may strike at him through you!"

All this, as well as the story of the hunt, the youth told his grandfather when he came upriver to his home at Turip with his mother. Both the grandfather and the mother looked worried.

"They are evil men," said the grandfather. "They have received fighting ability from the lake devils by diving into the waters. They have killed men and been wealthy enough to pay for the deaths. Now they live off the fear that others have for them. Even when they harm people, such persons are afraid to ask now for much of a payment, knowing they are so mean."

"Then if I stopped their power, many people would be glad?" asked Lost Star.

His mother gasped and paled.

"Leave them alone, son!" she pleaded with him. "They are three strong men who are experienced at dealing death, while you are only a seventeen-summers-old boy."

The youth did not answer his mother, but looked courageously at his grandfather. His eyes asked what he should do.

"It is time for you to go into the mountain to the sacred place of our fathers to fast and pray," said the grandfather gravely. "When you have found your help from the Woges, the little people, then you will be able to face anything that comes to meet you. You must train yourself by running up the hills, first in daylight and then in darkness, always praying for help, until you can run through the brush and your feet will have eyes. After that you will spend four days and nights on the sacred mountaintop without food, praying and fasting. It is the place where the great rocks were put by the ancient ones to give power to the true men. After you have found your power, you must dive at night into a deep, dark pool I shall tell you about. When you meet and overcome the evil you will find there and carry a rock back to the surface that shall be there for you to bring, then you will have the courage and strength to face anyone."

First came the running up the hills and the praying by daylight. Finally there was the night when he tried to run up through the bushes, but they hit him in the darkness and dragged him back, and the rocks tripped him and cut him until he lay bleeding on the ground in despair. Then he made a desperate prayer, a long one from the depths of his heart, asking the help not for himself, but for his mother, his grandfather, and for all the people, that he might be an instrument to overcome evil. So he called on the Woges, the ancient little people, who reflected the wonderful and powerful Spirit of the Universe, something too great and shining for the Yurok to name or ever see or hear.

Suddenly he was running up through the brush in the darkness as if there were eyes on all parts of his skin, as if he knew every place to step so exactly that every bush and rock and tree was dodged as easily as a snake slips through the grass. So he ran until he came to the sacred place on the mountaintop where the ring of great rocks was, where the moonlight came with mysterious beauty into the stillness, where all the mountains and hills and valleys stretched below him in dim ghostly masses, silvered by the moonbeams. He felt as if he stood at the center of the world!

So Lost Star prayed on the mountaintop to the Upriver Sacred People, who are supposed to live by the other ocean, and the Downriver Sacred People, the Woges, who live somewhere in the Pacific Ocean, and to the other Sacred People of his own rocks and hills and the river, and his whole mind and body centered on these prayers, many said over and over during the four days of his fast.

He did think also of money, the dentalium shells that came so mysteriously by trade out of the north from some far distant people on the edge of the world. And he prayed that he might have more of this money, not for himself, but for the power that money gives to help the people. And the Great Dentalium itself was a Sacred Being that had come down out of the north long ago to help the people, especially those who sought and obtained self-control. Thus his thinking of money was not the same as the greedy seeking for gold of the strangers who were to come, but something that came from the spirit world and had spirit meaning. This is why the truly great Yurok and Karok and Hupa rich men of the past were noted, not so much for their wealth, but for their generosity in helping other worthy ones of their people. Their wealth was given to them to give and if they truly gave then more would come back to them.

At last on the fourth day and the fourth night, he felt the spirit was beginning to talk to him. He did not hear words, but without knowing what he was doing, he went to one of the great rocks that surrounded him in the sacred circle and reached out in the pitch blackness to feel along its side. Suddenly his hand felt a hole. Fearlessly he put his hand inside, feeling around until he found something hard that fitted into his hand. When he pulled it out and felt it carefully, he found that it was a smooth piece of rock, carved in the form of a bull sea lion, the great head poised proudly above the powerfully shaped, muscular body. And he knew this was a sign of help from the Ancient Ones of the sea.

He came down from the sacred mountain feeling both humbled and proud. He was filled with a flowing power in his veins and arteries and through every muscle and nerve. And he prayed his thanks to the bull sea lion who had courageously faced the armed men and charged them twice, and whom he had killed not in the lust of the hunt but with the sincere desire to end his suffering. At a vale on the side of the mountain he paused to eat some dried salmon meat and other food he had cached there, as he knew he needed strength for the next ordeal.

So he came after a time to the deep, dark pool his grandfather had told him about and directed him to find. This final ordeal was to be faced with the courage of a man. So he took several deep breaths and dove down into the icy waters, down and down into the cold and the darkness, his arms stretched out before him and his fingers searching to find the bottom and the big rock he was supposed to bring to the surface.

And then he touched something slimy and smooth and moving, and his whole body reacted with shock and fear, his arms flailing and his legs kicking to drive him quickly to the surface. Flinging himself on the mossy bank, he gasped for breath and shivered all over. Every nerve shouted to him to leave this evil place and the terror that lurked in the cold, the wet, and the dark. So he started to leave, but stopped and took several deep breaths. Was this the final test and was he failing? He breathed again deeply and gradually stopped shivering. Then he reached for his belt and took from it his elk-horn dagger, the one that had killed the sea-lion bull, grasped it in his teeth, and dove again into the cold darkness of the pool and down and down. Suddenly again he felt the slimy touch and the wriggling movement with his fingers. But this time he did not explode in fear, but reached for his knife. And then he would have laughed if he could possibly have laughed thirty feet down in cold darkness and wet, for he realized he had touched a lamprey eel, and not a huge snake as he had been thinking. So he dove deeper and finally touched the bottom, felt around and found a rock a little larger than his head. He seized the rock and carried it to the surface, tossing it out onto the mossy bank where it lay still and glistening in the moonlight.

When he took the rock to his grandfather the next day and told him also of the carved figure of the bull sea lion he had left in the little hole in the rock, the old man's eyes gleamed and his hand reverently touched a deeply scribed wandering mark on the side of the otherwise smooth rock.

"The sea lion is the sign of your power," he said, "but this rock has equal power, for it goes back to the first grandfather, the first true man. Because you thought of no woman, nor of anything selfish, because you overcame your fear of the dark and the cold and the thing that moved, because you found this rock on your second dive, and because you found the carved sea lion and knew its meaning, you have great spirit power now, and you are a true man. Wealth will come to you to help your people, courage will come to you to overcome evil."

Somehow the word had reached the village, not by a sound, but in the strange way news sometimes used to come to the native people of long ago, that the youth had received his power. Men came then to him and invited him to the sweat lodge and, for the first time in his life, he crawled through the sacred round door into that secret place reserved for the men. Here was where the men spent most of their winter days and nights, the man of the highest rank sitting and sleeping in the tepolatl, the place directly opposite the exit and in the middle of the right side from the separate entranceway. As a guest the youth took the place directly in front of the door, called the legai, and it was while seated here, with the other men watching gravely, that he was given his new name of manhood, a name that is not uttered or named except among the very close of kin, and also his new nickname by which he would be known to most people. And that nickname was "Helper of All."

So he prayed and smoked and talked with them in the sweathouse and was accepted so well that they asked him to help with gathering posts for the great Keppel Fish dam, whose building would come before the World Renewal Ceremony and the famous White Deerskin Dance. And to each man present, to honor them, he gave what he had been working on in secret for just such an occasion, a horn spoon carved in beautiful geometric designs, work of the finest art that was touched with reverence. This was the kind of spoon that would honor a man's home, an example of the appreciation for beauty that marked the Yurok, the Hupa, and the Karok peoples. But there was one thing yet in his heart; he must somehow bring honor to his mother and make her feel accepted by her people.

So he climbed with the other young men into the mountains during the next week and climbed the high fir trees to cut their tops for the big stakes needed to build the great fish dam, the greatest effort of man ever seen in those days in northwest California. There had been three days of special ceremonies before the first work could start on the dam. The fourth day had heard the simultaneous sound of stone mauls hitting the elk-horn wedges against the fir tops on the hills to bring the stakes for the dam. The priest who directed the ceremonies and the building was called Lo, and he made sure everyone understood it was a time of great sacredness and

solemnity. When Lo walked through the villages near where
the dam was to be, none could watch him. All had to hide in
their dwellings. He himself could not look at a woman, let
alone think about one. And yet it was also a time of frequent
frolic and laughter, of joy in the great united effort of the
people to gather the sacred salmon. So from Ayto near Blue
Creek and the Pacific Ocean, upriver to Wahsek near the joining with the Trinity, the people came. It was a time when young
people from different areas got to know each other; it was a
time when the honorable met the honorable and the foolish
met the foolish.

So when Helper of All had finished the work in the hills
of bringing the great stakes down to be used on the dam and
was asked by new-found friends to help pound the stakes into
the river on the eighth day of the dam building, there were
several girls watching him with interest. One was called She
Dances with Dentalia. She was a girl from a very rich family
who had already felt the pain within her that told her she was
marked to be a medicine woman, a shaman. She would soon
be danced by the Shaman's Dance into new and great power,
which would add even more to her wealth. She Dances with
Dentalia knew she should not even look at Helper of All, for
her bride price would be far beyond his reach. Her family
would still call him a bastard and frown on even the slightest
mention of such a man.

But she could not help herself for she saw that he was
good to look upon, muscled like a giant, and that he laughed
in a way of no other young man. She watched when he moved
lightly and expertly out on the rickety falsework of poles and
stakes that formed a platform for driving the ten-foot main
stakes into the river to make the dam. When he began to
strike at the head of a stake with a heavy stone maul, she
held her breath, for she did not see how he could prevent him-

YUROK CARVED ELKHORN SPOONS. The elaborate geometric carvings are
typical of the fine artistry of the Yurok and contrast with the animal
carvings put on spoons farther up the coast in northern Oregon and
Washington. (*American Museum of Natural History, New York*)

self from falling into the river. Other young men often did so when hammering. Her breath went out in a long sigh when she saw that his footwork was perfect, holding him safely above the water as he pounded stake after stake with the smoothness of a powerful machine, his muscles rippling in the sunlight.

So the dam was built in a great V, its point heading upriver. There it was anchored by a very sacred stake called Wetspegar ("the one who has ears"), for the priest had prayed over it that not only would it anchor the dam firmly in the middle but would bring good luck to all the people, good weather when needed, lots of fine acorns in the fall, and plenty of salmon to be captured in the river. When the two wings of the dam, each working out from the opposite banks, and driven stake by stake into the gravelly bed through two to four feet of rushing water by the strong young men, finally came together at the Wetspegar stake, the people let out a great shout, crying "We are so glad!" The main part of the dam was done and it held.

It was a dam not to hold back the water, but to prevent the fish from going up the river for ten days, the sacred ten days of the Yurok. Seventy men hurried to finish it on the tenth day of building, for they could work no longer than that day, and it was necessary that ten fish traps be made at ten openings through the dam into which the salmon would swim and be captured. Already below the dam the water was alive with salmon leaping and swimming, trying to find a way through the dam, and when each fish trap was finished, they seemed to leap even higher. Last of all, the soft, furry branches of the redwood trees were brought to the dam by eager gatherers. These were wedged in around the bottoms of the fish traps so that the water would not wash away the gravel and make openings, or the fish find ways to nudge through the interwoven branches.

Then the fishermen came with their nets to the fish traps. Salmon churned the water with silvery bellies and dark backs, so close and in such hundreds that some traps seemed filled solid with fish. Down into the traps the great nets dipped, taking up the squirming fish in silence but with many smiles. The salmon were killed with wooden clubs and thrown into baskets that were carried to the shore. There the people split them with flint knives into fillets, saving even the backbones and the heads, for these would in the end be thrown back into the river to make new fish for the new year. The fillets were pierced with sharp narrow stakes, driven into the sands of the river banks next to the fires, turned from side to side toward the flames until the juices ran and the aroma of salmon cooking filled the air. The people ate and ate until they could eat no more. The women took the rest of the salmon and smoked and dried it to save it in the great storage baskets that lined the insides of the houses with food for the dark days of winter.

She Dances with Dentalia was helping with the cooking. She looked up and saw Helper of All watching her, and she grew confused and bowed her head while her cheeks flamed with color. Suddenly she was more beautiful to him than any other woman in the world, and the feeling he had for her was a very great tenderness. As the days passed, some of them in fun and frolic, and the others with the sacred seriousness of the White Deerskin Dance, they had moments to talk to each other. Her father, who was a very important man and very rich, was a sponsor of one of the dance teams, and his wife was very busy helping, so they did not at first see where the eyes of their daughter were straying.

So Helper of All had time to find out that she shared his friendship for all people, that she too liked to watch the ripples in the water and the movements of life in the streams and pools, the trees and bushes and grasses, that she admired the beautiful elk-horn spoons he carved and the wood he fashioned into plates and bowls, and that most of all she loved him. And then she told him sadly that probably there never could be any marriage, for her father was asking an almost impossible bride price for her, two large red-and-black obsidians for the White Deerskin Dance, four headdresses ornamented by twelve each of the bright red giant wood-pecker scalps, and much more.

"If you will wait for me," he told her, "I will get it all my-self to pay for you in one to three years."

"I will wait and I will take no other man save you," she promised, But from others he learned they were planning to make her into a healing shaman, as it was women who mainly became shamans among the Yurok, and, if this happened, there would be still more to pay. However, he had seen the glowing look in her eyes, and it was enough for him!

But a friend, when he heard of this, warned:

"How do you expect to do this? You have nothing now, for you give away everything you get or make as gifts, especially to the poor. It will take many years, and meanwhile rich men will be wanting her, for she is indeed a great prize. They will offer far more than you can offer and there will be much pres-sure on the girl from her family."

"I will pray and I will work," said Helper of All very simply.

Places are all important to the Yurok. Certain localities in their land have great and sacred meanings that we find hard to understand. But the Woges, the ancient, wise, former people of the land, they say, used these places in the old days for their ceremonies and dances, giving the earth sacred mean-ing where their feet had walked, so that the same ceremonies were repeated as it was believed they had done in the morning of the world.

At the same time, though also sacred to the people, the White Deerskin Dance was a chance for the rich to display their wealth. Usually two competitive groups of dancers from separate villages moved about to the ancient sacred dance spots, showing not only their dancing abilities and their songs, but displaying the extremely valuable white, black, gray, and otherwise uniquely marked deerskins that were signs of prestige and wealth. In front of the line of deerskin holders in the dance there marched, back and forth in tune to the shrill sounds coming from whistles made of crane bone, the holders of large black-and-red obsidians, some over a foot long and beautifully chipped. These valuable obsidians had usually come in trade from far-off peoples to the south and east and were valuable in proportion to their size and the perfection of their craftsmanship, some of the best of them so valuable that no money could ever pay for them. The obsidian dancers wore striking headbands lined with sea-lion teeth. Back and forth they moved in front of the other dancers, holding up the great obsidians, proudly shaking their sea-lion-teeth headbands.

Helper of All remembered when he was young, watching the deerskin dancers at a distance, from his mother's side. The rhythmic nature of all the movements and sounds, the blowing of the crane whistles, the clacking of the wood clacking sticks, the stamping of the dancers, the concentration of the dark faces like people in a dream, the high, wild voices of the three central singers, rising in tremolos and accentuated by deep grunts from the side dancers, the bowing forward and backward of the beautiful and striking deerskins, had a never-to-be-forgotten effect on the child. It all gave him the feeling of

WHITE DEERSKIN DANCE ON THE HUPA RESERVATION: summer, 1937. The white deerskins and the large osidian blades used in this dance were symbolic of the wealth and prestige of certain leading men. The dance was part of a world renewal ceremony to keep the good things of life repeating for the people, particularly acorns and salmon. (*Photo by Vinson Brown*)

his people, their connection to the earth and its life, their deep concern that the good things, material and spiritual, the salmon and the acorns, the food of life, would continue to flow. There is something magical and deep that the Indian child feels on those days and nights of the great ceremonials that the white child lacks and may never understand. Indeed the earth is renewed and the people's spirit is renewed for another year, and it is sad these days that so much has been forgotten.

When the White Deerskin Dance and the Canoe Dance were over, Helper of All went down to get in his canoe and paddle his mother home to Turip. Suddenly the three mean brothers faced him on the trail, three big men with small gleaming eyes and heavy shoulders, and the largest and oldest said:

"I am paying the marriage payment asked by the father of She Dances with Dentalia, and she is soon to be mine. You are not to talk with her anymore."

Helper of All stood very still. The rage fought to rise within him, but he held it down and took a deep breath.

"She will marry whom she pleases," he said quietly. "If she wishes to marry you, it is all right with me. I will wish you well."

His calm, friendly manner and answer made them look at him in astonishment.

"And what if she does not?" asked the largest brother, glowering at him.

"Then I will bring the marriage price and see if she will have me," he replied calmly, looking at the ground, but his body relaxed and ready.

"You have no money and no family to help you. Besides we would never let you," said another brother.

He had been praying silently. The power came to him suddenly, the power given to him on the mountain and in the depths of the black icy pool. He stepped over to a large rock that may have weighed eighty pounds and lifted and threw it as if had been a bowling ball.

"Throw that back to me," he said, "and I may let you stop me."

The largest brother walked down to the rock and started to lift it. His muscles stood out like cords, but he could only lift it, not throw it.

The three brothers were seething inside. They came together, shoulder to shoulder, like one man, and the older one spoke again:

"You can never pay the marriage price, and we will kill you before you can. Our arrows can come from anywhere and nobody will know!"

Suddenly there was a whispering all through the woods, and out from behind the trees came the people, many dozens of them.

"We have heard your words to Helper of All!" said an old man to the brothers. "We have been listening, for we came when we heard the great rock thrown, and some of us saw it thrown. If you kill Helper of All, we will kill you, for he is a friend of everybody but you. He has helped so many of us. He has given everything he has!"

"And I," said a man whom all knew was rich, "will help him pay the marriage price."

"And I also!" announced another rich man, "for there is more wealth for all of us in this young man than we can ever repay him!"

The three brothers walked away without a word, but their shoulders were bent. And they did not dare again to do evil on the river.

Helper of All was indeed an outcast no longer, and his mother was accepted by the people, too.

8. The Pomo and Other Natives of Central California

It is hard to draw the line around the Central Californian Culture Area, as there is considerable overlap along its borders. The southern tribes, such as the Yokut and the Salinan, picked up many traits of culture from southern California, with its missionarylike Tóloache or Chingichnish religion, while the northern tribes, such as the Shasta, northern Maidu, and Wintu drew many of their culture elements from both the Central California Culture Area and the Northwest Coast Culture Area. For some of the basic elements of these cultures, see the appendix.

Before the white man came, central California was one of the most peaceful places on earth. War was not glorified and peace was promoted. People lived with very little crime or violence, with neither policemen nor armies, for many thousands of years. It is a triumph of human existence we would do well to learn from.

The natives of central California were noted for craftsmanship in only three arts: basketry, fishing, and dance regalia, but it is the fine basketry that is the gleaming light of their culture. Their bows and arrows, their tools and other utensils were well done and very usable, but they rarely showed the intense creativeness found to the northwest and the south, and in their home building, for the most part, they were only modest creators, building what was adequate only and with the least work possible. An exception was in their meeting or dance houses, which the whole community usually united into making firm and substantial buildings, far above the norm in quality of work.

The women, though, took hold of basketry and made of it

an act of true creation. Even the poorest basket makers in this region could make baskets so tightly woven that they could hold water. The women were also clever at working designs into the weave, often striking and beautiful ones that used different materials for different colors and effects.

Two main basketry techniques were used, twining and coiling, both clearly shown in the illustrations. In a number of these tribes, one technique in basket-making was used almost to the exclusion of any others. Thus, all the tribes of northernmost California down to the Wailaki on the coast, the northern Wintun in the upper Sacramento River drainage, and the northwestern Maidu in the northernmost Sierras, used the twining technique (see illustations) in their basketry. And most of the tribes to the south of this used mainly the coiled basketry technique, though they were forced by necessity to make their large more open-work baskets, such as large carrying baskets, baby-carrying baskets, and fish traps, with twined basketry because the tightly coiled baskets did not allow the use of open spaces. (See illustrations.) The Yana, who lived on the border of the two great basketry areas, used both twining and coiling about equally, but the work of these isolated mountain people was coarser and poorer. Most of the rest of the coiled-basket-making people to the south used a base for coiling of three willow rods in the warp, though the Yuki used one rod and a welt or welts (usually strips of grass), and some tribes to the south, such as the Yokut, used a multiple foundation of several different plant withes or roots.

The Pomo, on the other hand, were outstanding in the

NORTHWEST COAST VILLAGE. Because of woman doing twining basketry and woman carrying typical Pomo baby basket, this is probably a central California village of long ago. (*Painting by Arthur A. Jansson, American Museum of Natural History, New York*)

use of many basketry techniques and seem not to have allowed themselves to become limited in their creativity. They also developed clever methods of fishing in Clear Lake, and were noted for their beautiful ceremonies of the Kuksu religion, the strongest spiritual force in the old days in central California.

She Came from Komli

IT WAS a lovely spring day, flashing with the colors of new flowers, earth smells coming up with the breeze from the river, the sky so blue it filled the eyes with glory, and the thrilling "kee-dee-dee" cry of the killdeer mother sounding

Opposite, top COSTANOAN OR OHLONE SHELL MOUND GROUP ON SAN FRANCISCO BAY SHORE. Shown are the usual round grass huts, one in the process of construction; shells thrown out, after being eaten, which increased size of shell mound each year; two balsa or tule canoes pulled up onto beach and another out in the bay. (*American Museum of Natural History, New York*)

Opposite, bottom MIWOK MEN SUCCESSFULLY RETURNING FROM DEER HUNT IN THE YOSEMITE VALLEY. Notice the bark tipis common to California mountain peoples and the many baskets for storing or cooking. (*Diorama by Elizabeth Mason, Southwest Museum, Los Angeles*)

Below CLEAR LAKE POMO, "MOCK BEAR ATTACK." A man, dressed in a bear skin, is pretending to attack the village and is frightening the women and children. Some Pomo "bear doctors" did sometimes attack and wound or kill people. Typical grass and brush-covered hut is shown. (*Diorama by Elizabeth Mason, Southwest Museum, Los Angeles*)

from a sandbar. Eyes Awake and her younger sister, Little Bit, were happily helping their mother dig for sedge roots in the sandy damp soil near the river. Opening up the soil first with their digging sticks made of hard wood from the mountain mahogany bush, they used their small, tough fingers to feel out the roots, then pull out one as long as possible from the ground. Each such root, split in half and shaved laboriously to an even thickness, would make two long cords in the woof of a Pomo basket.

"Mama!" cried Little Bit. "Look at this one! It is six widths of my hand, the longest yet."

"Wonderful!" warmly answered her mother, Far Seeing Woman, as she herself carefully pulled another long piece of root from the resisting soil. "You are going to be a great basket maker woman, someday, Little Bit!"

"Really?" asked the nine-year-old girl, tossing her long black hair and laughing joyously. "Is that one of your visions, Mama?"

"Not really, Little Bit, but it is one of my good guesses."

"And will I be a better basket maker than Eyes Awake?"

The large, well-formed woman chuckled fondly at her daughter's words.

"No, Little Bit," she answered with a slight sigh. "No one will ever be a better basket maker than Eyes Awake when she grows up, but she will have a lot more trouble than you about getting married until she learns to be humble. That *is* one of my visions!"

Little Bit's fairylike face puckered in a frown for a moment, but then she laughed again.

"I'm glad I am going to have a happy marriage."

"Yes, you will be a very beautiful woman and you will make some fine man dance right around your little finger!"

"Mama! Stop telling her such things!" exclaimed Eyes Awake. "It is she you are making have the big head! Besides, I don't believe you. It is I who am going to have the happy marriage, and she who will be the great basket maker woman. So there!"

Far Seeing Woman laughed and laughed. "Always my strong-minded one!" she cried. "But you have both helped me enough for a while. Be off, both of you, to play down in that meadow. I will call you when it is time to go home."

So the children played happily and without fear under the watchful eyes of their mother and another woman of the village of Komli, Cascade Woman, whose two boys were playing on the edge of the woods. Eyes Awake, as usual, led the direction of the play. They started building a miniature village, looking like Komli, on a sandy area in the beautiful meadow. With rocks and twigs and leaves they wove and constructed their dream village, the twelve rectangular shaped, willow-framed brush huts, in each of which several families supposedly lived. They made an especially big one for the chief and his relatives, the sweathouse almost all under ground except for its stick and bark roof, and covered with dirt except for a hole in the center of its roof to let out the smoke of the fire, and the great round dance and ceremonial building, as usual built with far greater care than any of the lesser structures. It too was partly below ground, with a ramplike passageway leading through an outer hall down to the big room, supported in the middle by a thick pole, and with seven radiating rafters going out to the lesser poles on the sides.

"Down this passageway," said Eyes Awake gravely, "the Kuksu dancers go backward into the dance hall."

"Why do they go backward?" asked Little Bit.

"They say it is the sacred way so as not to see where they are going, but I say it is because those big long branches with feathers on them that stick out from their head nets might get caught in the passageway if they went frontways!"

"Oh, Eyes Awake!" exclaimed Little Bit in fright. "Don't say such things about spirit people. They may hear you even here!"

Eyes Awake looked frightened herself at her own temerity and was quiet for a few minutes. Then suddenly, with a whoop and a holler, two red-earth- and mud-painted small warriors dashed down from behind them and through the tiny village, kicking houses and even the great dance house, so laboriously built, right and left. "War! War!" they shouted.

Little Bit burst into a flood of tears, but Eyes Awake, in outraged eleven-year-old dignity, jumped up and chased after them. "I'll get you for this, Coyote Boy!" she almost roared, her strong long legs flashing beneath her. "And you too, Duck Under!" Being boys, they would have got away, however, if Coyote Boy, the larger of the two, had not stumbled badly on a root. In a second, Eyes Awake was upon him! She knew better than to come face to face with him, as he was bigger and stronger, so instead she grabbed him by his long black hair, whipped him around and down on his back, then dragged him over the ground so fast he had no chance to get away. Bump, bump, bump went his body over the uneven ground and grasses.

"Take that and that," shrieked Eyes Awake, "for breaking our village!"

Bump, bump, bump he went over some rocks, yelling himself.

"And that for making my little sister cry, you bad boy!"

Suddenly Cascade Woman, the mother of the two boys, was there, shaking Eyes Awake free from her son. Far Seeing Woman appeared the next instant and the two women glared at each other. There might have been a grown-up war except that both at the same instant saw the woebegone faces of their two children and both burst forth into laughter.

"Let's end the war!" they said almost together.

"She nearly tore my hair off!" wailed Coyote Boy, "and my back is bleeding!"

"They wrecked our nice village that took so long to make!" screamed Eyes Awake.

Far Seeing Woman, as the older mother, spoke calmly, but with a glint of amusement in her eyes:

"Let's do this just as if there had been a real war. You know in a real war payment has to be made to both sides for any damages, wounds, or deaths. Let's go to our chief. He hasn't ever had a war to make peace about or exchange payments for damages, so it's about time he had some practice.

"We'll see what he says."

Suddenly the children had forgotten their quarrel and were all excited about making peace. They could hardly wait to tell the other children.

When the two families reached the village of Komli, they notified the chief, whose name was Wind Caller, about the war, and, with great dignity, he agreed to meditate between the two sides the next morning. Within an hour the whole village was bubbling with laughter and talk about the battle and the peace efforts. There was much surprise that Eyes Awake had been so brave and so fast. As for Coyote Boy, many felt from previous experience with him that he had received exactly what he needed!

In the morning the chief started the peacemaking:

"We are aware that the village of Little Komli, built and owned by Eyes Awake and her sister Little Bit, was destroyed by the two warriors, Coyote Boy and Duck Under, but that in the battle Coyote Boy was severely hurt by Eyes Awake."

"He wasn't badly hurt!" objected Eyes Awake. "Just his head and body bumped a little on the ground."

"My hair was nearly torn out of my head!" insisted Coyote Boy.

The eyes of the chief twinkled as he investigated Coyote Boy carefully.

"He was hurt some," he intoned solemnly. "I see a couple of good-sized bumps and some scratches. So I now proclaim the following payment of indemnity for injuries done. The two warriors are to completely rebuild the village of Little Komli under the direction of the two owners as payment for the loss and to leave it alone thereafter. The two people of Little Komli are to repay the injury done to the warrior called Coyote Boy by cooking him a loaf of acorn bread, flavored by manzanita berry sauce."

When all payments had been made as ordered, by law of the tribelet at Komli, all grievances were to be forgotten and peace and good will were to prevail. Since the prestige of the chief was at stake, he did a little private persuading of both parties with some sugar pine syrup from the mountains to get the two parties to the "war" to keep the peace thereafter, though Coyote Boy was heard to mutter darkly once that if he ever married Eyes Awake he would make sure she obeyed him and not the other way around! While Eyes Awake was heard to sniff once that she "didn't see how he figured she would marry him anyway!"

At the Kuksu Dance that summer, following a wait of about four years, all the children between eight and twelve were to be initiated into the tribelet, and the older youth had their fun scaring the little ones about all the terrible things that were going to happen to them. In fear, Little Bit asked her mother: "What really is going to happen and what really is the Kuksu Ceremony all about?"

"It is the yearly renewal of the spirit ceremony. Kuksu and Shalnis come to us as spirits to help us keep well and be good. Long ago they were great heroes who came, one from the south and the other from the east, to destroy bad people and creatures and help our people. They come to dance for us and to sing us songs. Sometimes we cannot understand the songs because they are sacred spirit songs, so the chief or his assistant tell us how we are to live, and what the songs mean, so we can help each other instead of harm each other. Behind all this is Great Spirit, He who lives in the sky. We never see Him or hear Him, but He speaks to us through these messengers."

"But what of the children being initiated? What happens to them?"

"They are initiated to help them become good members of the tribe, to have long life, to help us all get food, to build our homes and be happy. They have to suffer a little pain to teach them to be brave. You are a girl, so you can cry out if you have pain at the initiation, but boys are supposed to be braver."

The ceremonies and dances lasted for four days. On the first day the children were initiated. They were driven into the large dance house with its long, tunnellike entranceway, its great solid roof of pine slabs, thick brush, and dirt piled on top, and its large posts holding it all up. They had to lie down on the cleanly swept dirt floor in the semidarkness. There they were covered with fragrant branches and the older people filed in to make a circle around them. Then an old man came with a sharp knife made out of a clam shell.

"Don't look up!" he warned them. "You will lose your sight if you do!"

Eyes Awake and Little Bit lay perfectly still under the leaves. Suddenly a girl let out a yelp, and Eyes Awake felt all her muscles and nerves tighten as the footsteps of the old man sounded nearer. Then, deliberately she made herself relax, as her mother had told her to do, and her nerves did not jump even when she heard the scream of Little Bit next to her. The smaller girl lay still, weeping softly, but Eyes Awake did not cry out when a sharp pain suddenly creased down her own back.

When the old man had finished cutting the children, he said:

"This cut you have each had is not to harm you, but to help you. I have used a sacred knife to make the cut. It is blessed by the spirit, and if you have been brave and not looked up it will give you health and long life. But it is a warning also from Kuksu that you will have much worse pain than this if you do bad things in your life. So be good. Do not tell lies; be kind and helpful to your mother and father and relatives and all in the village. Be brave and help the weak and helpless. If you learn to obey those who are older than you, when you grow up you will be worthy to have others obey you. You will be worthy to have a family. If you do not, you will cause harm to other people and nobody will like you. You may even be driven away as we sometimes drive away those who are very bad, and then the hand of every man will be against you! Watch now the Kuksu dances; they are spirit dances. They come from the greatest spirit of all, and if you listen to the songs, they will tell you how to live."

In the next three days the Kuksu spirit dancers came out of the woods, called by men who shouted for them from the top of the dance house. Eyes Awake and Little Bit and the other children did not know they were men disguised with paint, feathers, and leaves as spirit impersonators. They thought they were real spirits and they were frightened at first to see these strange-looking beings, with their brilliant feather headdresses of bright orange-red flicker feathers, their dark-painted faces and bodies, their deerskin aprons, their circles of leaves and girdles of wooden sticks, as they rushed down out of the oak woods and entered the great dance building backward with their long feathers sticking out in front of them.

As they came in, a strong man began to beat with a heavy stick up and down on the great hollow log drum at one end of the dance room inside the sacred round house. The deep beat of the drum, the songs of the dancers, and the beat of their feet, their strange bowing and swaying motions, the clacking of the clapper sticks in the hands of two old men, the whistling of the bone whistles, all these made the children aware that something wonderful and powerful and magical was happening. Deep into their hearts the strange sounds and songs went, deep into their consciousness went the feeling of oneness with all their people. It was a sacred ceremony that came from the sky spirits and the earth spirits, from the four winds, and from the Greatest Spirit of All. The effect of these dances would be with them all their lives, and most of the effect was good.

On the third day was the throwing of the older boys and youth by the Ash Devils. This was a kind of second initiation for the older ones, but also a powerful warning. The chief and the elders had talked about the youth, and said to each other: "This one is telling lies!" or "This one is mean to the small children," or "This one thinks he is too smart for us to catch him at what he is doing behind our backs." "Let the Ash Devils warn them and give the warning strongest to the worst of them, telling them we know all about them, and they will have something much more dangerous happen to them if they keep on!"

The Ash Devils, with stripes painted all over them with ashes, came running into the room shouting and grimacing at the audience, playing tricks on people by throwing bits of fire at them or teasing them with long branches. Then suddenly they shouted and began to seize the older boys and youth one by one, whispering to them warnings of what they knew about them and that they were going to burn them in the fire, but it would be lots worse for them if they did not heed the warnings. Then they would throw a big boy right through the middle of the flames, after wood had been thrown on the fire to heat it up, and catch him on the other side. They did this several times, throwing one of the worse offenders quite low, so even his hair began to singe. Coyote Boy was so thrown, but even Eyes Awake hoped he would not be hurt too much! It was a great lesson, however, and there was many a chastened young man after the Ash Devils got through with him!

On the fourth day, when the feeling of the spirits in the air of the round house was very strong, there came the healing ceremony of Kuksu. A little girl who was sick was brought forward and placed where the light fell upon her, and all watched in hushed silence as the dancer who represented Kuksu, the hero god from the south, danced down to her and around her. He had a pole with the bright red feathers of a pileated woodpecker attached near its tip, and with these sacred feathers he touched her here and there on her body, singing at the same time. Then he touched her on the head

THREE EXAMPLES OF CENTRAL CALIFORNIA DANCE HEADDRESSES. (*American Museum of Natural History, New York*)

with his hand, and Far Seeing Woman whispered in the ear of Eyes Awake, saying:

"If her heart is right, the spirit will touch her and she will be cured!"

As our modern doctors are learning, such psychosomatic healing often works as well as do medicines if the patient truly believes!

As Eyes Awake grew older she needed a healing of something inside of her that even her wise mother despaired of finding for her. Far Seeing Woman explained the trouble one day to her neighbor, Cascade Woman.

"She is such a good girl in every way except one thing. She learns nearly everything so quickly and well I can hardly believe it."

"Then what is the matter?" asked Cascade Woman.

"She can't seem to make a good basket, and worst of all she is not really interested! She just goes through the motions."

"She is eighteen and looking for a man to marry," suggested Cascade Woman. "Maybe that is her trouble."

"Maybe," said Far Seeing Woman, "but I really think she has heard so much about my vision of her becoming a great basket maker, that she is stubbornly determined to prove me wrong! But meanwhile no young man from a good family is going to want her for a wife, and certainly not his mother!"

"Look!" cried Cascade Woman suddenly, pointing down toward the river. "Strangers are coming. We must let the chief know right away!"

The two ran toward the chief's house and shouted. Soon the dignified old man appeared and snapped:

"What's all the noise about!"

"Strangers from the east; looks like both men and women, but you had better make sure they are not dangerous!"

The chief's stentorian voice was soon calling the men of the village, a dozen or more of whom came running, snatching up bows and arrows as they came. Weapons were lowered, however, when they saw the group approaching. It was small, only about ten, half men and half women, all carrying large basket packs on their backs with tumplines across their foreheads.

Now all the people of Komli were gathering to meet them, waving friendly greetings, the children peering from behind their mother's skirts, everybody curious. Eyes Awake ran to her mother.

"Who are they?" she asked.

"From the big lake!" some of the people of Komli cried.

"Yes, we are from Kashibadon near the lake," said a thick-set man, stepping forward from the group. "We bring dried fish and magnesite and obsidian," he said, naming some of the things he knew the Russian River Pomo most valued. The pinkish magnesite ore was drilled and ground into beautiful beads that were highly valued as money, while the obsidian was excellent for knives and arrow points. "But," he continued, "we have to save some of these things to trade down at the ocean at Kalaili." He spoke a dialect of the Eastern Pomo, different from that of the Northern Pomo, but still understandable, as the two Pomo divisions did much trading with one another.

As they opened their packs on the ground by the village and began to spread out the things they had brought, Eyes Awake and Little Bit ran to get something to trade. Little Bit brought a well-done, brightly decorated basket she had made, quite a prize from a sixteen-year-old, and Eyes Awake brought a beautiful brown-furred quiver made out of well-tanned mink skins. Both objects brought exclamations of surprise from the newcomers from Clear Lake, and two tall young men who looked like brothers reached at the same moment for the mink-skin quiver, while an older woman, apparently the wife of the leader of the expedition, reached for Little Bit's basket.

The two brothers laughed when they both held the quiver and the younger withdrew his hand politely, saying:

"You look at it first, older brother."

Eyes Awake looked at the two closely and felt strongly

attracted, especially to the younger brother. "He looks and acts so kind and polite," she thought. The older brother disturbed her by his calm assurance. "Maybe he is stuck up!" she thought.

But it was the older brother who said:

"I can see you really like that quiver, younger brother. You trade for it with the pretty girl, but I'll take this basket. Did you make this fine basket, young lady?" he asked, looking straight at Little Bit.

Little Bit blushed and was too shy to answer except by a nod of her head.

Younger brother was looking at Eyes Awake so sharply that she felt her heart flutter.

"I'll bet you can make a fine basket too!" he said.

She was too confused to answer even by shaking her head.

That night in the round house, by the light flickering on the walls from the flames of a big fire, the women danced the Lole and Eyes Awake was among them, wearing one of the usual thick forehead bands with little mats of orange feather quills that swayed with her body. Most of them were large, plump women, as befitted the Pomo idea of beauty, but standing in line and moving their feet rhythmically, they were very graceful, their hands waving feather fans in tune with the slow beat of the huge hollow log drum. Eyes Awake felt a stir of jealousy when she saw Younger Brother watching Little Bit among the spectators, but he suddenly turned and gave her a dazzling smile that melted her heart.

When the men danced with the women they were separate but equal, doing the Momimoni on one side of the room and the Yo, or southern dance, on the other. Strangely, the men had the long bustles of leafy branches on their rear ends, which they swayed violently in all directions. And stamping the ground with the greatest vigor of all were the two brothers from Kashibadon on Clear Lake.

"Ah, there is a man!" sighed Eyes Awake to herself, looking at Younger Brother, who was so quick and agile, he seemed like a bird.

In the morning, the expedition from Kashibadon prepared to get under way on its long trip to the distant ocean, and the old leader of the group asked if any volunteers from Komli would like to go along. To her great disappointment Little Bit was told she was too young. Altogther four from Komli came, Eyes Awake, Cascade Woman and her husband to act as chaperones, and their oldest son, Coyote Boy, who now had the man's name of Eagle Catcher.

"Be very careful not to be alone with any young man," Eyes Awake's mother warned her. "Stay close to Cascade Woman at all times. Remember your virtue is your greatest fame and will win you a good husband!"

"Oh, mother!" Eyes Awake stamped her foot. "You should know me by now!"

"Yes, but I saw how you looked at the young men from Kashibadon! I think they are honorable persons, but I want to be sure."

It was about forty-three miles by trail, a rough trail up the ridges to the top of the pass, with 60 to 180 pounds to carry in each load, but Eyes Awake fairly danced down the trail into what is now Dougherty Creek Canyon, so eager was she to see the ocean. At last, on the late afternoon of the second day, they could see the sparkling blue-green of the distant Pacific and the white line of breakers hitting the beaches. When they reached the coastal Pomo town of Kalaili in the valley of Little River and heard the roar of the sea, Eyes Awake could hardly bear to stay for a few minutes to talk to the people who came out from the village to welcome them. Soon she was dashing down through the coastal brush to the sands of the beach. There she stood, as though anchored, her face turned glowingly to the far blue waters, her long black hair streaming in the wind, her nostrils sniffing deeply the wonderful salt smell, and her eyes drinking in the long white lines of the combers with eyes that could never see enough!

Soon the two brothers, whose nicknames were Fish Chief and Wedge Maker, stood beside her, also gazing at the sea with wonder.

"It is so beautiful!" they breathed together, watching the waves breaking in white foam on the rocks and the white-winged seabirds wheeling and screaming. But soon Fish Chief was standing on a rock amid the breakers, immobile as a bronze statue, fish spear in one hand, waiting for the moment to drive the spear point deep into a pool and pull it out with a California bluefish wriggling on the sharp prongs.

During the days they spent at the beach the people of Kalaili joyfully taught the visitors how to gather clams by digging in the mud flats by the river's mouth, also mussels, limpets, and turban snails from the high- and middle-tide pools, and the highly delicious abalones and octopuses from the low-tide pools. The first time Eyes Awake saw an octopus being dragged out from its hole under a rock by Fish Chief, she let loose a scream that could be heard half a mile away, and had the children and youth of Kalaili rolling on the beach with glee!

That night the two brothers talked together in their beds of deerskin blankets that lay side by side in the sand.

"That girl, Eyes Awake, does something to me!" sighed Fish Chief, "but I'm afraid she has eyes only for you!"

"She's a wonderful girl all right. But haven't you heard, they say she is a terrible basket maker. Our mother would have fits if she heard either of us were interested in her!"

"You mean you are not interested in her?"

"Oh, I like her all right and I especially like to tease her. Did you see that look on her face when I told her she was chewing on a piece of octopus? She nearly spit it out, but then she decided she liked it after all. I nearly died laughing! But the one I am crazy about is that little sister of hers. She's the real basket maker and what a beauty!"

The older brother heaved a deep sigh. "Thank coyote" he exclaimed, "that she's off your list! I would not care if Eyes Awake couldn't even do a fish net. She's got a spirit that sings to me; her movements are like flowing water; and her voice like the thrush's song."

"Brother, you sure have it bad!" exclaimed Wedge Maker, "but watch out for our mother. She'll be rough on you if you try to marry Eyes Awake!"

"That's one of my lesser problems. I've got to convince Eyes Awake that I am the man for her!"

The next night they sang around the campfire the old, old songs of their people, and danced to the light of the flames, until the great constellations of glowing stars had wheeled a quarter of the way around the sky and it was time for sleep. The next day all in the expedition worked hard at collecting seaweed, then drying it on the rocks. They also cooked and dried other sea foods they could take back over the hills as a treat for the home folks. There was also salt to be gathered in the high pools where it had dried in crusts under the summer sun.

The next morning they had the last trading of things from the sea that the villagers had, principally clam-shell money that came up from Bodega Bay and some sea-otter pelts from the kelp beds out in the sea. In exchange they traded the fine bright saffron beads of magnesite money that were worth hundreds of clam shells. They also bargained for the iridescent shells of abalone with a few fine skins of mink, land otter, gray fox, and mountain lion from inland. At last, happy, but heavily loaded, the visitors started on their way back after a last exciting swim in the breakers that Eyes Awake would always remember, and how the two brothers held her high when the biggest waves came.

A weary, heavily loaded group came into Komli in the valley of the Russian River three days later, eager to put down their great packs and lie in the shade. But Eyes Awake, after she threw down her load, ran to her home, a brush-thatched house about forty feet long that sheltered four families, and, finding her mother alone there, threw herself into her arms, weeping.

"Oh, Mother!" she exclaimed. "It was all so wonderful and the ocean was the most exciting thing in the world, and everything was nice until Wedge Maker told me that he loves Little Bit and not me! And then it was terrible! Do you think it was because he learned I cannot do good baskets?"

The mother was wise and held her daughter tightly, saying softly:

"The love of a man should be deep enough not to depend

just on the making of baskets. What about Fish Chief? He seems like the best of the two to me. He is a strong quiet man, and such often make good husbands."

"Perhaps he smells too much like fish to me. I don't know, Mother. I just feel very lost right now. Leave me alone for a while!"

"Rest and time will heal many wounds."

For three weeks Eyes Awake listlessly moped about the house or out under the summer oak trees in the shade. The longer this lasted the more bored she got, so that suddenly one day she took up an unfinished basket she had barely started two years before and looked at it. It was the simplest kind of twined basket, of the sort, however, that can hold water if well done. To start it, three willow withes had been crossed over three other willows to form an X. Each piece of willow had been shaved carefully down with a knife so it was as exactly even from one end to the other as possible. Two pieces of sedge root, each a half a root with a flat side and a round side, and also shaved to evenness with a knife, had then been wound in and over the four sets of branching-out willow withes, keeping the flat edges of the sedge roots toward the willows until the willow withes were tightly bound together with four spokes of three willow withes, each emerging from a center. (See illustration.) From this point on, the two sedge-root halves were separated as one was wound under, the other over, a set of three willow withes, so continuing around and around, building up the basket.

Eyes Awake examined critically what she had done before, remembering what her mother had said about making every

INTERIOR VIEW OF MAIDU HOUSE: made of cut branches tied together and fastened to sapling posts, then covered with brush and often dirt. Inside are baskets for storage of acorns and pine nuts, also in the water-tight baskets for cooking with hot stones placed in water. (*American Museum of Natural History, New York*)

move with the sedge-root halves as tight as possible. She saw that she had not done a good job, and remembered that even while she had been doing the basket she had been daydreaming. Now she felt an overwhelming urge to make a good basket, so she took the beginning basket apart and started over, watching carefully every move she made and making the weaving as tight as possible.

Out of a desire also to be creative, she searched until she found a coil of some finely shaved, evenly shaped redbud withes, bright reddish-brown in color. As she worked away she began to weave these into the basket, working into the weave the forms of a pattern of diamond-shaped rattlesnake heads she had envisioned, the bright red heads standing out against the white of the sedge roots. When it grew late in the day, she hid the basket so she could take up the work on it the next morning. Day after day she worked, the feeling of making something beautiful and fine taking hold, her fingers literally coming alive and knowing in their delicate tips the act of a unique creation.

When the basket was finished and the last ends wound around tightly and shaved off closely to form the top, Eyes Awake gazed at it a long time. She knew she had done a good job, but how good she could not tell until she put water into it. It held the water tightly except at one point where it developed a small leak. She studied this place carefully to see how it had not been quite tight enough there when she was weaving. She knew what to do next time. Then she showed the basket to her mother, and felt a glow of conquest warm within her when she saw the look of pleased surprise on her mother's face.

"A great improvement!" exclaimed Far Seeing Woman. And then she showed the girl exactly what to do to make the basket still better.

The art of making coiled baskets, instead of twined, Eyes Awake had to learn next. She knew something about it, but had been so clumsy and uninterested before that her mother had given up. This time she watched closely and listened. To start, four sedge-root halves were tied together tightly into a knot to start the center of the basket. Then each two sedge-root halves were tied together into knots to make a thick hard center. Now a new root was added and tied around just one sedge root in the knot. This started a curving section of wrapped-around knots developing into a circular coil. To make a one-willow coiled basket, this circle was completed and then carried a bit beyond, whereupon a willow withe shaved to exactly even thickness and with a sharp point was inserted into the end of the coil and the two tips wrapped with the other half sedge root to hold them together tightly. The willow withe then was started in a coil as it was wrapped (see illustration) and the coil continued around and around with added willow withes at each ending of a withe until it was wide enough to form the bottom of the basket. Then it was tightened still more as it was wrapped to cause the basket to turn up on its sides in an even way. All this and more Eyes Awake learned from her mother until she finished her first fairly good coiled basket. The mother held the basket up, critically examining it.

"This is a good ordinary basket," she said, "but it has not the spirit in it yet. You must fast and pray for a few days before you start a really fine basket. Call on the Great Spirit and the lesser spirits to help you; call on the spirit of the sedge root, the spirit of the willow, the spirit of the redbud tree and the bulrush root, so you will be one with them when you weave and they will help you."

She showed the girl how to take the bulrush root and soak it for many days in water mixed with ground black walnuts. The walnut stain made the roots very black and then allowed them to be woven into black designs on the baskets, while the redbud was used for red designs. Ordinarily the two colors were not mixed on the same basket, but used separately.

It was the touch of the sky and the earth that the girl sought when she fasted and prayed for two days. Soon she forgot about

POMO MONEY. Mrs. Elsie Allen, a modern Pomo basketmaker, shows many strings of brilliant white Pomo clam-shell money, each bead bored out of the most solid part of the clam shell, cut and polished to perfect roundness. (*Photo courtesy of Mrs. Elsie Allen*)

everything else, about Wedge Maker and any other man. She thought only about the touch of her hands on roots when digging them, on willows and redbuds when cutting them from the trees, on bulrush roots in the moist ground, and on all four of these parts of the basket maker's art when she worked on a basket. She could feel their smoothness, their evenness, their roundness, and the flat sides of the sedge-root halves that had to be placed so tightly against the willow. She could see the beauty of black arrowhead designs made with the blackened bulrush roots, the red circles and dashes of rain clouds made with the redbud withes, the rhythmic turning and turning of the coils in the coiled baskets, the over-and-under rhythm of the plain twining technique. She learned about wickerwork, and the technique unique in California of lattice twining for carrying baskets. She learned diagonal twining and three-willow coiling. Then she turned to designs and experimented endlessly, using horizontal, banded, vertical, radiating, isolated, diagonal, and many designs crossing each other. It was wonderful to combine walking in the countryside on beautiful days, generally with her mother or other women, gathering materials, and the rest of the time by or in the house weaving baskets of all kinds, including canoe baskets, boiling mush baskets, catch-everything-in-them baskets, giant pest-proof storage baskets, tiny little doll baskets for the children, and many others.

But the greatest advance came when she started her first feather basket, the supreme creation of the Pomo woman basket-weaver. Her fingers had a delicate touch now, like the breath of a warm summer breeze. Her lovely tawny face puckered in concentration when she applied the tiny feathers between the weaves. Easy feathers she used at first like the bluebird's stiff quills, then harder ones like the feathery down-feathers of wild geese or of ducklings that made a basket look like a drifting cloud of sun-drenched rainbows. Soon she was using also the brilliant red feathers of the giant pileated woodpeckers, the orange feathers of the oriole, the golden-yellow feathers of the meadowlark, the emerald-green feathers of the mallard duck, and the glossy black feathers of the male blackbird. Most of these came from dead birds she found on her walks; others were brought in and traded for from hunters, who hid in trees and used the blunt-tipped bird arrows and much patience.

At last she showed her mother a basket that was drowned in a sea of feathers, the colors like running waves, the glow of them in firelight and sunlight like fire opals, a basket so lovely even her mother could only cry "Oh!"

She was so concentrating on her mother's face and the awe in it, that she neither heard nor saw anything else, until suddenly there was one standing beside her mother. She looked up into the strong and rugged face of Fish Chief. Beside him stood his younger brother, Wedge Maker.

"Oh!" she cried, almost in fright. "When did you two arrive?"

Fish Chief, looking at her imploringly, was speechless.

"Speak up, elder brother!" urged Wedge Maker. "Tell her we just arrived to see her and Little Bit and their father and mother."

"You tell her why we came, younger brother," whispered Fish Chief, his face very red and his eyes on the ground.

"See, a beautiful girl can make him shake like a leaf!" laughed Wedge Maker, "and just a day after he killed a grizzly bear with a single spear thrust!"

"Oh!" cried the two girls with one voice, for Little Bit had just come running up. "How could he?"

"Yes, I would like to know too," said a deep voice just behind them, and all turned to look in surprise at the girls' father, Hunter of the Bear, a man almost as big as Fish Chief.

"We were in the brush up toward the Mysterious Mountain, looking at traps we had set for deer, because we needed their skins for gifts to your father and mother, when we came around a corner of the trail and almost ran into a big grizzly. He reared up high, growling, and we should have run for our lives, because you know it takes at least five men to kill a grizzly. But Fish Chief called to me that he wanted the skin for a present for Hunter of the Bear. I yelled to him not to be foolish and to run, but he just stood there with his back to a big rock and his spear in his hand pointing at the bear as it charged. Before I could even get my own spear ready, the bear came roaring up to him and I thought he would, quick, be a dead brother! But he had the butt of the spear pressed against the rock to take the shock and when the bear rushed him he kept the spear steady, but ducked a blow from the huge paw, and the point went right into the bear's side and through his heart, killing him."

"Do you have the skin here?" asked the older man skeptically.

Fish Chief ran off without a word and returned in a few minutes with his enormous pack basket. Out of it, slowly and with some struggle, he drew a folded and finely tanned bear hide, enormous enough to cover a large bed, with the claws dangling from the skin of the feet. Then he drew out a buckskin bag and tumbled from it onto the ground a pile of large teeth, four of them almost the length of a man's hand and sharp.

"So you can hunt bears and deer as well as fish," said the old man with considerable respect. And then, pretending he did not know, he asked: "And why are you bringing my wife and me all these presents?" Fish Chief was still too tongue-tied to answer. So he drew forth two beautifully tanned deerskins, and a necklace of magnesite beads worth a small fortune.

"A girl has him by the tongue!" laughed Wedge Maker. "He wants to tell you these are gifts for your family, and at the same time he wants to marry one of your daughters." The Pomo are exquisitely courteous when a marriage is being arranged. There is no actual buying of the girl as in some tribes, but an exchange of gifts.

"Which daughter?" asked Hunter of the Bear, his eyes twinkling.

"He's got to say which. I'm not going to do it for him," replied Wedge Maker, "though he had better not say the one I have chosen!"

Fish Chief drew a deep breath. He was shaking so that the grizzly's skin fell from his hands to the floor, but at last he stuttered:

"It's—it's Little—I mean, it's Eyes Awake!"

"It better be that one!" growled Wedge Maker, but almost instantly everybody but the sheepish-looking Fish Chief were bent over with laughter, the girls so convulsed that tears poured from their eyes.

As Eyes Awake began to control herself, she felt a thrill of delight course through her generous body. This huge man, she thought, this brave killer of a grizzly, is actually afraid of me! With growing maturity, helped into being by her earlier sorrow over the loss of Wedge Maker, and helped also by her year of strict training and effort in basket-making, she sensed that Fish Chief's love for her was very deep indeed, far deeper than her girlish infatuation with Wedge Maker had been. With some humbleness she wondered if she could adequately return such a love. She looked then into the understanding eyes of her mother. My mother knows, she thought, and I know too!

Now Wedge Maker was bringing his gifts and it was Little Bit's turn to be blushing and confused by the rippling furs, fine rabbit-skin blankets, and the obsidian spear points and arrow points for Hunter of the Bear.

"We will think about this and let you know in two days!" said the father gravely. "Maybe my girls will not like these gifts." He hid his twinkling eyes.

"Oh, Father!" exclaimed the two.

With the agreement two days later of the father and mother and their promise to give gifts in return when the family visited the other family in Kashibadon, the marriages were consummated. Both bridegrooms came to stay first with the in-laws at Komli for about a month before the trip of new gifts was made.

A month later, at Kashibadon, the two young wives met for the first time their in-laws, Dawn Hunter, a big man like his biggest son, and Meadowlark Woman, quite small for a Pomo, but merry of face and quick in her movements. There was much laughter about how the little woman really ran the big man. The girls were delighted to find that the usual strict Pomo rule against talking to or even looking at your parent-in-law did not hold very strongly among the Eastern Pomo because they enjoyed talking to Meadowlark Woman, who was full of fun like Wedge Maker.

"Can you take me fishing with you on the lake?" asked Eyes Awake of Fish Chief one evening.

"Yes, if you can get up an hour before daylight and fish with me for a day and a night, and if you can remain absolutely still when I tell you to." He said this laughing and yet testing her, touching her long dark hair tenderly.

She gripped his arm hard, and said: "I will be as quiet as a bittern when the hunter comes near!"

So he took her down that evening to watch him prepare his boat made of bound bunches of tules and also all his fishing gear. The balsa canoe was made by tying together large bunches of tule reeds tightly at both ends with tough twine made from the vine called Virgin's bower. Then these groups of bound tules were again bound together in larger form to make the raft or boat. The Clear Lake Pomo also built and shaped the boats so they had prows, sterns, and seats.

When Eyes Awake stepped into the boat and sat down, she gasped, for the cool water of the lake came right up through the reed stems and touched her below. Fish Chief laughed.

"Don't worry, dear wife," he said. "The boat won't sink. The tules all filled with air and keep the craft buoyant even when you feel water creeping through them!"

He took the long-handled, thin-bladed paddle and began to move the boat across the lake. The first light of morning was just beginning to glisten on the water, while the bright morning star flickered its bright face in the dark waters. First he showed her how fast he could go, the paddle cleaving the water and driving them forward so rapidly that the frightened girl gripped the sides tightly.

Out a ways from the shore he let the boat drift and they began to fish with hooks and lines, the hooks made out of carved freshwater clam shells, the bait worms and insect grubs. As the eastern hills flamed with the sunrise, and the snow on the great peak to the north blazed with a thousand mirrors, they began to feel tugs on their lines. Soon Fish Chief pulled in a kom, the great yellow sucker with horns, while Eyes Awake lost her first fish when she tugged too quickly. The boat was drifting slowly shoreward, the water about them smooth as glass except for an occasional leaping fish, and one by one, almost machinelike, Fish Chief drew the wriggling splashing shaghal or blackfish, the behowuk or small blackfish, and the tsawal or goldenside, squirming in on his hooks, so they could be killed with a club and thrown into the big basket in the middle of the canoe. Soon he was catching otonodo, the long-nosed pike, but these larger fish fought him back and forth across the water, beating up tiny waves, splashing as they leaped, and his wife watched him with eyes aglow. Always he handled the fighting fish calmly, smoothly, giving just enough line to prevent them from losing the hook, or just the right pull to tire them. Eyes Awake tried to copy him, but it was like a beginning painter trying to copy a great master.

When the big basket was full, they brought the fish to the shore where the two families were camped, and soon excited voices were exclaiming over the catch. Little Bit was astonished at what her sister's husband could do.

"Wait till you see what Fish Chief can do tonight!" boasted Wedge Maker.

That evening the water of the lake was like a lovely limpid mirror, the thick clusters of tules and other water plants just off the shore nodding gently in the slight breeze. As the sun dipped below the hills to the west and a full moon began to rise from the east, a line of fishing boats formed about forty boat-lengths out in the water. Then slowly they moved toward the shore, one man paddling in the rear of each, while in the prow a second man knelt on the prow seat, extending forward as far as he could a deeply-built dip net. During the late after-noon Fish Chief had coached Eyes Awake at the paddling until he felt she could handle the canoe correctly. In the evening now she tensely watched the other paddlers, noting their slow careful dips of the paddles, making no dripping and no sound, and she copied them carefully. Every so often Fish Chief would dip the long sacklike net softly into the water and down, coming up with fish that he dumped expertly into the large holding basket behind him.

Later in the night, when slight movements in the water told the fisherman that the shaghal, the blackfish, were coming shoreward to spawn before the dawn, the line of men reversed itself and moved from the shore outward. There helpers had meanwhile set up a long row of gill nets, fastened to long stakes driven into the shallow water about fifteen to twenty canoe-lengths from the beach. These open mesh nets, woven out of iris stems and designed to catch the fish by the gills when they pushed their noses through the mesh, formed a trap into which the fishermen in their boats slowly began to drive the shaghal. Fish Chief held in his hand a queer double paddle shaped like a cross with which he beat the water to foam, driving the frightened fish before him. When the nets were reached, all was excitement as the fish leaped and struggled to escape, and the fishermen worked frantically to enclose the nets completely over them.

Suddenly the lunging body of Fish Chief jerked his boat so hard that it threw Eyes Awake out of the tule raft into the dark waters. She sank, choked on water, and came up again screaming. The piercing scream rang across the lake, and Fish Chief dove into the black water to rescue her, although she was perfectly capable of swimming and had been simply too frightened and startled to react properly.

But as Fish Chief started pulling her up on the balsa, someone else was choking and screaming near the shore. When they got near her a few moments later, she had disappeared beneath the surface. Fish Chief dove and dove until finally he found a body and dragged it up. They took her to the shore and when they turned her face up, Eyes Awake screamed, It was her mother, who had jumped into what she thought was shallow water to save her daughter; she could not swim because of a frightening experience in childhood which had prevented her from learning.

Eyes Awake fell over in a dead faint, and when she came out of it in the arms of her husband, she began to weep uncontrollably. Fish Chief could not seem to comfort her, for, like most Pomo, she took the death of a dear one very deeply. The next day she singed most of her hair off in mourning while the other women prepared her mother's body for cremation. When the men put her mother's body on the pile of wood and set fire to it, Fish Chief had to grab Eyes Awake in his strong arms to keep her from leaping into the flames. At last she calmed; as the embers descended to a soft glowing, and the body turned to ashes, she asked for the beautiful feather basket, glowing with purple, red, and yellow colors, she had recently made. Saying a prayer for her mother's spirit, she took the lovely creation of her hands to the dying fire and tossed it on the coals. It burst suddenly into a ball of flame. Thus do the Pomo often give honor to their dead, giving their best creation in loving memory to the departed to follow her on her journey to the other world where the Great Spirit waits for all his people.

9. The Chumash and the Tongva

To many native Americans, the eagle is a symbol of greatness of the spirit, of rising above earthly limitations on the wings of powerful thoughts and noble deeds worthy of our destiny. Among two former great peoples in southern California, the Chumash and the Tongva or Gabrieleno, there are hints that there were two such great heroes. My story here is about them as I imagine them and how they affected their peoples.

The two premier centers of culture in southern California, the Chumash of Santa Barbara and Ventura counties, and the Tongva or Gabrieleno of what is now Los Angeles County, faded and died very quickly under the impact of white conquest. Their sensitive natures were unable to withstand the callous indifference of people who were sure they were superior and destined to rule America. Some of the hardier mountain and desert tribes, in pockets in the wilderness and on reservations, have preserved some of their past. These people were influenced by the two great culture innovators, the Chumash and the Tongva. Only from them do we have glimpses of what used to be. The appendixes show some of the more distinctive culture elements of the different tribes of this area.

Some hundreds of years ago, nobody knows exactly how long ago, Shoshone-speaking tribes of the great Uto-Aztecan

Opposite, top CHUMASH INDIAN VILLAGE NEAR THE SEA. Notice the framework of partially-built, round, grass-covered hut; finished hut with skin door on right. Coiled basketry is used for carrying, storage, and cooking with heated water. Steatite (soapstone) bowls can be used for cooking directly over fire. (*Los Angeles County Museum of Natural History*)
Opposite, bottom ATAHUM (LUISEÑO) VILLAGE: showing earth-covered house (kicha), sweathouse, religious enclosure (wamkish), and villagers; sweathouse is partially underground. (*Diorama by Elizabeth Mason, Southwest Museum, Los Angeles*)

Language Family came streaming out of the deserts, through
the mountain passes, and into the fertile plains and valleys of
coastal southern California. By their movement they pushed
aside, to the north and south, peoples of the Hokan Language
Family who had occupied this land before them. We know this
because today we find Hokan-speaking tribes, the Chumash and
the Kamia, to the north and south of the Shoshone speakers.
At the forward point of this great wedge were the Tongva, a
people who grew in appreciation and wonder at the mysteries
of life and the foundation of the universe, and who sought
spiritual answers. Their search culminated in the appearance
of a hero, Chingichnish, on what is now Santa Catalina Island
and was at that time a seaborn colony of the Tongva. By the
time the whites came, this man was worshiped by the Tongva
and by neighboring peoples, who accepted their religion, as a
god, or at least as the direct representative of the Great Spirit,
Nocuma. A very brilliant and persuasive human being, he
deeply touched the hearts and minds of his people; of this we
can be certain. But who knows whether he was inspired by a
greater spirit or not?

The story of Father Geronimo Boscana, the Franciscan friar
of San Juan Capistrano gives us inkling of this. He wrote that
this man had reached the hearts of the native peoples so
deeply that the natives were more obedient to the teachings of
this religion than to Catholicism. Chingichnish warned that
avengers would destroy those who did evil. Why were the people so deeeply afraid of these avengers? In my story I try to
answer this question.

Another great mystery of southern California is the fantastic and colorful cave paintings of the Chumash. One of these
paintings is extremely beautiful and interesting, possibly the
most beautiful native American art in existence. One can
imagine the genius who did it also leading his people spiritually
and teaching them a way of life. Campbell Grant, who wrote a
beautiful book on these paintings, *The Rock Paintings of the
Chumash*, feels their beauty and design somehow expressed religious feelings and symbolism of rich significance. What this
is I have tried to answer.

Silent Falls the Eagle

HIGH SWALLOW, of the village of Takuyo, lived by a creek on the north side of the great mountains, the mountains that were all white in winter and kept their snow on some of the north slopes through half the summer. He was of the Tokya speakers of the Chumash, the far northeast people, farthest from the sea, guardians of the passes, guardians of the border with the Tulamni, the southernmost tribe of the San Joaquin Valley Yokut. The Tokya were rude compared to the Tsumwich and the Mishkonaka Chumash who lived on the slope by the great ocean, who had big houses ten times the length of a tall man, and whose towns sometimes stretched for three times an arrow's flight above the beaches. But among the Tokya were some famous painters in the secret caves of the hills, the Silent Ones who knew the spirits of the skies and the winds. Greatest of all was old Wise Otter, to whom many came seeking.

Wise Otter was an uncle of High Swallow and when High Swallow was ten summers in age, Wise Otter came to see his family. He took the boy into the woods and had him tell what he saw and heard. He left him alone for a while on a rock by a stream and watched him from a distance. When he brought him back, he said:

"The boy has promise. He really hears what is in the woods, what is under the leaf and the rock. He will learn to see the

CHUMASH PREPARING ACORNS: by pounding in natural hollows in the sandstone rock with stone pestels. Acorn meal is then leached in warm water poured over them in a hollow in the ground and later boiled for mush or baked for bread. (*Diorama by Elizabeth Mason, Santa Barbara Museum of Natural History, photo courtesy of Southwest Museum, Los Angeles*)

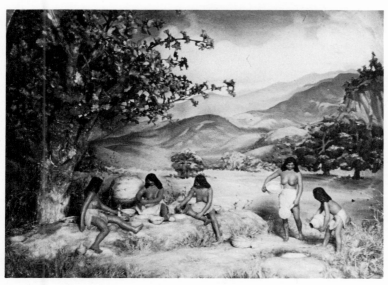

little people of the forest and learn their wisdom. He has fine long fingers and keen eyes; he listens and he learns. Someday also he will paint as the great ones paint. Someday he will be one among the Silent Ones, and I will train him."

The mother had tears in her eyes when she watched her youngest son leave her, but she could not help but be proud of the jaunty way he walked with his head held high and alert, his shoulders back, his feet silent on the leaves, as he had learned from the hunters. She knew his eager eyes were on the trail ahead, and that already he had forgotten her, for, unlike all the rest of her children, he had eyes that lifted beyond the hills and ears that listened to every tale about the great world beyond the mountains.

Miles to the west of the village in a land of high grassy hills and many oaks lived Wise Otter. He had a hut near the hilltop cave where he painted, but he came to the village of Takuyo and to other villages when he was needed for the healing. The people loved him. He knew every medicine of the woods and fields, and his touch was gentle but firm and quick when he set

CHUMASH PAINTED CAVE WITH ARTIST AT WORK. These caves, hidden in the hills and mountains back of Santa Barbara and Ventura, contain many beautiful paintings in abstract art for the most part, some in several brilliant polychrome colors, probably done for religious purposes. (*Diorama by Elizabeth Mason, Santa Barbara Museum of Natural History, photo courtesy of Southwest Museum, Los Angeles*)

bones and relieved sprains. He sang songs that brought back blood to the cheeks and light to the eyes, and his voice was kind and wise. The children sat around him fascinated when he spun his stories of the lands beyond the mountains, the great islands and the greater seas, and the ancient legends of the people.

So he trained the boy in the ways of the good shaman, the healer, the keeper of the way, the one who learns by prayer and fasting and purity of heart how to be a helper of the people, saying:

"We who paint the great pictures in the caves are called the Silent Ones, because we paint on the walls of rock the meanings of our dreams, but we do not tell that meaning to others, save for a special few. This is our power. The people look and wonder and are afraid. This fear is good when we do them good, for they respect us and listen to us. When they fear us then they do what we tell them to do to get well and to lead good lives. In most of our pictures we put the circle, often many circles. These are the circles of power, the circles of harmony, of being one with the spirit beings and especially the Greatest Spirit of all."

"But aren't there sometimes evil doctors, shamans who could use the powers in the pictures against others to make them ill or kill those whom they hate?"

The old man was silent for a while, too astonished at first to speak.

"Yes, there are such ones, and we who are of the Silent Ones must use our power to destroy them or they will destroy the people. In fact, one is doing much evil now, a boy I once trained to paint and who paints beautifully, but who turned against me

H

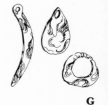

G

F

E

ART OBJECTS AND TOOLS USED IN SOUTHERN CALIFORNIA: **A** money beads made out of Pismo Beach clams, cut, drilled, ground, and polished; **B** bone whistle used in dances; **C** knives for carving wood and bone, each with sharp stone head, inserted in wood and glued to it with asphaltum; **D** stone mortar and metate for grinding paints or acorns; **E** ring made of the vertebra of a large fish; **F** turtle shell rattle; **G** abalone shell pendants; **H** men's hair ornaments. (*Drawings by Gladys Fox*)

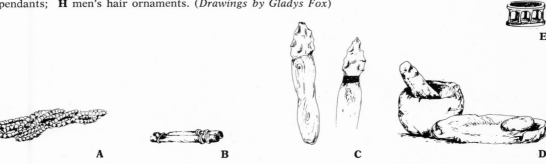

A   **B**   **C**   **D**

when I prevented him from having his way with a girl. That is why I am training you to be a good shaman, for I will not live much longer, and there must be one who will be strong enough to stop such an evil one. There is much that is bad in the world, but there will always be good men who will fight and overcome it."

High Swallow learned woodsmanship from Wise Otter, the following and unraveling and understanding of the maze of tracks on earth, in mud, and on snow, the language of the plants spoken in their healing and food-giving powers, the ways to build clever traps of snares or deadfalls when he needed food, but the ways also of being understanding and kind to all life when he did not need it for food.

He learned to be as soft-footed as the fox and as quick as the wildcat. He learned to build his muscles with hard work and exercise until he was almost as strong as the bear. He learned where to find paint for the sacred paintings in the caves, the black rocks that could be ground down to fine powder, or the charcoal from fires that would do if the rocks could not be found, and the very white soft stone (diatomaceous earth) that makes the very finest of white paints. He learned how to find and meet the Tulamni, the south valley Yokut, and get from them different shades of yellow and orange rocks they had at their hot springs, and how to use a binding to make a lasting paint with the white from bird's eggs or from the juices of two plants, the milkweed and the chillicothe. And he hunted until he found the fine red rock that makes dull red paint when you grind it, but makes a paint as brilliant as the brightest vermillion when you have it over the fire.

He learned to carve and grind steatite, the soft grayish soapstone that the Chumash and Tongva used to fashion into many things of beauty, including dishes. It was also very good for making small paint cups.

And one day when he had learned all these things and many

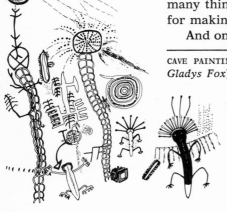

CAVE PAINTING SHOWING MEN WITH FEATHERED HEADDRESSES. (*Drawing by Gladys Fox*)

more, Wise Otter took him to the high cave in the top of a great rock where Wise Otter's great paintings stood in glowing colors on the walls and ceiling.

And here the old man spoke:

"I have had my last dream and made my last painting of that dream, and I am soon to die. Here on the ceiling I have drawn nine circles. On their right are two dark beings who have broken the circles, while in the middle of the circles is the sign of two storms. Standing on the eighth circle is a man with a face as pale as the moon. I do not understand fully my dream, but I do know this, there are two bad times coming, one lesser and one greater, and I think you will have to do with the lesser. The pale-faced man I think has to do with the greater darkness. When the ninth circle is completed, I am told a new light will come, and our people will be a sacrifice to help bring that light. The only other thing I know is that you are immediately to go on a long journey to the south; you will have a dream that will tell you what to do. Don't worry about me, but go, for somewhere south of here you are needed badly. You are of eighteen summers now and strong in body and spirit. I have taught you much of what I know and how to paint the sacred paintings. When you have dreams you will paint them and you will be one of the Silent Ones. I soon will be no longer on this earth, but my spirit will always be with you."

M

L

K

J

I

Overleaf SOUTHERN CALIFORNIA FEATHER BLANKET: made by very closely attaching duck feathers to a net made of native twine. (*American Museum of Natural History, New York*)

Below VARIOUS ARTIFACTS USED IN SOUTHERN CALIFORNIA: **A** wooden bailer for boat; **B** spear head of stone, probably flint; **C** self bow (without sinew backing) and hunting arrow; **D** two kinds of single tube smoking pipes; **E** arrow straightener; **F** sandstone pestle for grinding acorns; **G** basket mortar showing outline of basket as it is placed into stone, hole at bottom allowing grinding action with pestle; **H** fish hook, probably of bone lashed to wood; **I** medicine tube made of steatite; **J** special steatite toloache mortar for grinding jimsonweed in preparation for Toloache ceremony; **K** stone mortar and pestle; **L** carved steatite effigy of killer whale; **M** miniature steatite (soapstone) canoe. (*Drawings by Gladys Fox*)

H

E   F   G

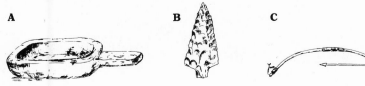

A   B   C   D

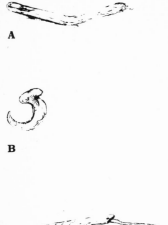

A

B

C

D

When High Swallow left the village of Takuyo two days later, his mother gave him a package of acorn bread to eat on his way south, and dried and smoked deer meat and chia seeds to chew on. It was the month of many flowers but the trail he followed southeast took him higher and higher into the cold of the great pass (Tejon Pass) that led to the southern valleys. But he sang the song of his adventure as his feet carried him quickly upward, and the pack on his broad shoulders never felt too heavy, for he was in the flower of his young strength. On the other side of the pass he went singing down into the green and misty valley of the Piru River, and the Alliklik, a branch of the Marangayam tribe, to whose villages at Kauvung and Hugang he came, heard the joy in his voice and gave him welcome as one who came in peace.

It was in Satikai on the big river (presently called the Santa Clara), in the land of his father's people, the Mishkonaka Chumash, that he found his first trouble. He expected to find a welcome from his father's brother, White Crane, but instead he found a great fear. The older man literally shook with this fear when High Swallow appeared at the large thatched communal house in the village where this uncle's family dwelt.

"Haven't you heard the word?" he whispered, looking around fearfully. "They are killing the Silent Ones among the Mishkonaka, and are saying this will spread to all the Chumash. They have heard of you, that you are a servant of Wise Otter."

"Wise Otter may already be dead, but who is it that is doing this killing and why?"

"It is a shaman called Walking Thunder, who proclaims himself a great chief sent by the spirit beings. He makes his thunder with a huge stick so that all are afraid of him. The young men are blinded by the tricks he does and follow him,

E

ODD ITEMS OF SOUTHERN CALIFORNIA CULTURE: **A** throwing stick, used like a boomerang to hit and kill rabbits; **B** abalone shell fish hook; **C** bull-roarer. The stick has holes in it that give off a roaring sound when the stick is swung round and round at the end of the cord; **D** Atahum (Luiseño) feather headdress; **E** bone awls with holes in their ends, used in sewing. (*Drawings by Gladys Fox*)

killing all who are against him. He is telling all the people that the Silent Ones have wrongly hidden the secrets of the paintings, that he knows these secrets and can make his followers powerful over all the rest."

"Does he do any painting himself?"

"Yes, he has a painting that everybody says is the most powerful one they have seen. It shows two beautiful comets in the sky and figures with giant feather headdresses like those he and his followers now wear. He says in his dream he was given the power to rule all the Chumash, and that these headdresses and the comets are symbols of the power to rule. Already he has taken several young women of the powerful families to be his wives, and these families are either very much afraid of him or have decided to join him."

"He is indeed the evil man Wise Otter warned me against," said High Swallow, "but I will not run away in fear!"

Suddenly there was a noise at the door and a slim girl dashed in, her eyes flashing fire.

"Walking Thunder has told my father he wants me!" She stamped her foot. "I will not go! He will ruin all of us if he can!"

"This is my best friend's daughter, Light Fawn," said White Crane, introducing her to the young man. She looked at him keenly.

"You are one of the Silent Ones!" she exclaimed. "I can tell. You must escape before they kill you!"

"I am not a Silent One yet," replied the youth, "as I have not had my great dream and the power. But you must escape too if you do not want to marry Walking Thunder."

The door burst open again and inside, ducking low, came a huge man with a dark fierce face, followed by several young men armed with spears. All wore tall feather headdresses.

Light Fawn quickly hid behind White Crane, and, using him and some other people as shields, she slipped away and out the back door. But the eyes of Walking Thunder were on High

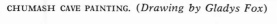

CHUMASH CAVE PAINTING. (*Drawing by Gladys Fox*)

Swallow. He struck together two quartz rocks, producing a great shower of sparks, and pointed commandingly at High Swallow.

"This is the disciple of my enemy, Wise Otter," he said angrily. "My spies told me he had come here. Seize him! It was Wise Otter who told me long ago that I could never join the Silent Ones and be a mystery painter. Now I am making all the Silent Ones truly silent!" He laughed grimly at his joke. "And now it is I who am doing the most powerful paintings."

The young men sprang forward and grabbed High Swallow. Realizing he would waste his strength by fighting so many, he submitted docilely to their hands, but his eyes were proud and wary.

"He shall die tomorrow at our big meeting," said Walking Thunder, "for all the Silent Ones must die and give their power back to the people!"

"Power to the people!" shouted all the young men. High Swallow was amazed at the way these people acted. He had always thought of his people, the Chumash, as friendly and kindhearted, but there was a strange cruelty and arrogance here that he would never have dreamed possible. He was very tired and hungry from his long walk, and felt helpless and lost as he was dragged away to the large dance and ceremonial building in the middle of the village. He was taken inside and tied securely to a post at one end. It was very uncomfortable for the first two hours, but later they untied him and retied him to the same post so he could lie down on a mat. Many of the headdressed warriors kept coming and going, but no one offered him any food or drink.

"It is exactly as if I were fasting for a dream," he thought, and began out of old habit to concentrate and discipline his mind to dwell on spiritual things. From his mouth came whispered prayers to the Great Ones in the sky, the ancestral spirits of the heroes of the past. In the night, as he prayed, and sang softly to himself and to the spirits, all fear left him. He felt his own spirit purifying and strengthening until at last he fell asleep. In his sleep a strange dream came to him. He saw a darkness like a cloud descending on his people. He knew it was made of the schemes of Walking Thunder, but to the south across the sea he saw a light hovering over a far-off island, and under the light was a man talking to an eagle that he held on his wrist. He knew without being told that this was the man he had to find.

Later in the night he felt something tugging at his ropes. He woke with a start and found himself staring into the anxious face of Light Fawn, just visible in the glow of a dying fire. She held her fingers to her lips, and whispered: "I have come to set you free. You must get away to bring help to stop this terrible man."

She cut his ropes and quickly led him out to the darkness. When safe, he told her about his dream of the man on the island.

"It is the island of Himinikots. I have heard of a man there who talks to eagles. It seems a long way to go, but I hope you will find help."

"What of you? How can you be saved from Walking Thunder?"

"My father is sending me away immediately to the far northwest edge of land where the water is cold, at a place called Lompoc."

"As yes, that is where I get my white paint from. Will you wait for me if I come to see you there?"

"Yes, I will wait!" There was no question in her eyes, only a soft glowing. "And now I will do something for you. You need strong and willing hands to help you. I am sending with you across the sea my brother who is a famous fisherman and boatman. He loves adventure, and I am sure he will take you. I wish I could go too!"

Later, down the river, they met her brother, White Wave, whose eyes flashed at the prospect of adventure over the great south sea.

First High Swallow needed food to give him strength, then the two men trotted away through the early dawn, down to the village of Ishwa by the blue sea. Here White Wave found his

Chumash board canoe, the whalebone wedge-split boards bound tightly and almost invisibly together by cords of milkweed fibers and Indian hemp, and well caulked with black asphaltum from seeps in rocks along the edge of the sea. But White Wave said they would need another paddler, as well as a boy along to act as bailer when the boat leaked.

White Wave found the man and boy, eager to go with them, and then threw four baskets of food, four skin blankets, plus two narrow-necked water baskets, caulked with asphaltum and full of clear spring water, into the boat. High Swallow was handed a double-bladed paddle, and soon all three men were paddling vigorously toward the southwest. Although High Swallow was laughed at for a while because of his clumsy paddling, he was amazed at the speed with which the light and well-shaped board boat sped over the waves. Like a giant dolphin, it bore them toward the first island they would land at, Michumash (today called Santa Cruz Island).

When they reached Michumash that evening, they pushed the boat up on the beach at the little village of Swahul. Greeting them as they pulled the canoe higher on the beach was one man whom High Swallow felt he recognized by his calm and wise face as one of the Silent Ones. Almost immediately the two fell into earnest conversation about Walking Thunder. "Tell all the people in the island about this evil shaman!" warned High Swallow. "I am sure he will come out here too with his warriors to kill our brothers if he gets a chance."

In the morning they headed southward for Himinikots (Santa Catalina), with a bright and sunny day to speed them on their way. High Swallow, greatly enjoying the journey in the fast canoe, kept calling to White Wave to identify the gulls, terns, frigate birds, cormorants, and other seabirds that often circled or dashed above them.

"Watch the terns!" shouted White Wave above the wind. "Those over there are diving into the water for fish. We'll catch some too!"

When they came paddling swiftly to the scene, the white-winged terns set up a great screaming.

"They are mad at us!" called White Wave, but quickly he drew a large dip net from one end of the boat, and, as they got nearer, High Swallow saw the water actually boiling with the leaping and writhing bodies of many small white fish. White Wave expertly dipped his net into the water and gracefully tossed numbers of the fish from the sea into a large basket in the canoe. "Those will make friends for us among the people of Himinikots when we land there!" he shouted gaily.

Late that summer evening they landed at Himinikots and almost immediately were surrounded by laughing, singing people, happy to see the fish they brought and suggesting that a big feast was in order. Fires were started on the beach and soon both the Chumash and the Tongva-speaking islanders were smiling and eating and joking together in the greatest friendship. Many knew White Wave, who had been often to the island on trading trips for the beautiful steatite bowls, pots, and dishes for which the islanders were famous, and who could speak their language. The deliciously fried fish disappeared very quickly into hungry mouths, and everybody soon rolled over on the sands to watch the sunset, the islanders asking White Wave why he had come. So he asked them about the man who talked to eagles, assuredly a powerful shaman.

"That is Chingichnish, but we believe him to be not a shaman, but a god, so powerful is he," one islander replied. "He taught us how to live in obedience to the Great One in the sky, and now he is gone to the mainland to teach them the same. There are many evil people there, but he will conquer them! He will send the avengers to punish them, the rattlesnake, the great bear, the mountain lion, the wolves, the eagle, and the fierce winds."

"We will go to the mainland in the morning to find him."

"Be careful that you treat him with respect!"

They nodded their heads; yes, they would be respectful to one so powerful.

In the morning they again launched the beautiful canoe upon the blue-green waters, and sped toward the mainland. The waves increased for a while under a brisk wind, but High

Swallow laughed at the lifting seas and paddled furiously till the boat fairly danced over the waters, so eager was he to meet this strange being, Chingichnish.

They landed near the village of Mayo (Newport Beach today), with dunes where waves of beach grass tossed in the wind. The village people were friendly, giving them acorn mush and seabirds' eggs for lunch. They told them that Chingichnish had gone into the mountains to seek power, but no man of course would dare follow him.

The two young Chumash smiled secretly at each other. But they left in such a way as to not disturb the villagers, going back to their boat and leaving word with the boy and the other paddler, West Wind Man, to await them at the village until they came back.

The way to the mountains was easy at first, up over the flood plain of the river we now call the Santa Ana, and then up a big creek (Santiago Creek) until they came at nightfall to the first of the deep canyons, Sierra Canyon, that leads up into the mountains. Here they decided to camp for the night, building a fire over which they roasted a young rabbit High Swallow had shot, eating with it some greens and bulbs gathered nearby.

The next day, as they climbed higher and higher up the canyon, they came to a place where it widened to make a beautiful dell, bright green with the new grass of late May. Here they paused, straining to listen, sensing a menace in the air.

"Be still!" whispered High Swallow. "Do you see that little black thing moving up behind that rock?"

"I see, but what is it?'

"It is the nervous jerking of the tip of a mountain lion's tail. He is watching us, maybe getting ready to charge."

The two men gripped their bows tightly and slowly drew arrows from their quivers, one each for the bow, three to hold in their mouths for quick use. Then they heard the sound of falling rock and, looking higher on the slope, saw an immense bear heave into sight, a grizzly whose heavy shoulders moved with the hint of immense power.

"Be absolutely still!" whispered High Swallow. "Let me handle this. I think Chingichnish controls these animals."

White Wave nodded his head slightly, and High Swallow began to sing a song in a high voice, the tone of the song saying more than the words:

"Peace, peace! We come in friendship. Our blood is the same; let us be friends!"

So he sang, relaxing his body, controlling his fear, so that White Wave also gathered strength from him. But still the mountain lion crept on toward them, sliding over the rocks almost on his belly, and the great bear rocked his way down the slope, rumbling inside like a hidden volcano.

Suddenly there was a large man standing on a rock high above the bear and the lion.

"Who are you?" he called, "and what do you want?"

"We have come to see Chingichnish to ask help for the Silent Ones among the Chumash," answered White Wave in Tongva. "This young man is preparing to be one of the Silent Ones. Have you heard of them?"

"Yes, I have heard and I understand. The Silent Ones know some of the mysteries of the spirit and try to do good. Stay there and I will come talk to you. My brothers will leave you alone now." He gave a high piercing whistle, and the two huge animals turned and went back to him, then, at a wave of his hand and a grunt, disappeared up the canyon behind the bushes.

When he came near they saw a face that at first was stern and forbidding, and yet when it broke into a smile was kind. The dark eyes seemed to pierce their hearts and brains, but the fingers were long and artistic, the mouth sensitive. He touched their hands and then their foreheads lightly as if seeking something, then spoke gently:

"I am Chingichnish, the servant of Nocuma, the supreme, invisible One, who dwells among the stars. Your faces are good, your hands are good, your minds are good. I am glad you have come; tell me your story."

White Wave explained carefully their mission and High Swallow's dream.

"Yes," said Chingichnish, "I was born on the island of Himinikots, and that is where I had my great dream. The people there now believe in me and have peace; they follow the sacred ways. But here on the mainland I have come to teach the Tongva and all others who will listen how to be in harmony with Nocuma. Many have forgotten; many seek selfish and evil desires; they become like mad animals who must be killed. Children are poisoned by them, so I bring the avengers, the rattlesnake, the grizzly bear, the mountain lion, the eagle, the wolves. But they do not kill until the people understand and make the judgment. When they understand that you cannot continue to let these people poison the land and the children, then they give them three warnings. If the last warning is disobeyed, then the elders say: "He is lost, he must be killed!" and I send the avengers. The children can see with their own eyes what happens when wrong is done. They fear the avengers, they fear the power of Chingichnish, the servant of Nocuma, and they obey!"

"May we see your animals and how you train them?" asked White Wave.

"Yes. Come with me and I will show you." He led them higher, to a beautiful dell below a waterfall. He whistled, and soon a pair of mountain lions, the great bear, two pairs of wolves, and an eagle and a raven came to him as if they were his children, the lions purring loudly under the soft touch of his hand.

"The rattlesnakes I handle differently," he said, "but these creatures I have raised from when they were very young and trained them very carefully to follow my whistle and word signals. Some are more intelligent and quick to learn. Hunar, here, the great bear, knows my mind almost before I speak to him, and does quickly what I wish. But Tukut, the lion, is very nervous, and unless I teach him over and over what to do he could make bad mistakes, like killing the wrong person. Panes, my eagle lady, is larger than her mate and more dangerous. But she has learned to love me and obey me." He held out his wrist and the great eagle flew from a nearby branch and lighted on the wrist with a squawk of pleasure.

"It is good what you are doing," said White Wave slowly,

"but already on the great island they are talking about you as if you are a god. Could this not lead to evil?"

"Not if I remain humble before the true Great One, Nocuma. He sees into my heart and knows that I wish only good for my people. It is true many of these simple people are begining to think of me as a god because of my powers. Maybe it is necessary for them to look at me like this so they may more strongly believe and obey. When the time comes I shall go away and none shall see me when I die, but I will promise to return when times are bad again. However, it will not be me who comes back, but another one like me."

All that was said between them, White Wave translated to High Swallow. At last High Swallow said:

"Ask him what can he do to help the Silent Ones against Walking Thunder, whose power for evil is so great that he can kill us with impunity and fool the people."

When this was translated, Chingichnish was silent for a few

SOUTHERN CALIFORNIA INDIAN WOMEN CARRYING GRASS SEEDS AND WATER IN SPECIAL CARRYING BASKETS. (*Peabody Museum, Harvard University*)

minutes, thinking. But they felt a warm friendliness flowing from him.

"Walking Thunder must be destroyed for he does great evil. I will go back with you to the land of the Chumash and help you against him. But first you must see how I am helping the people here, and watch the ceremonies that I teach them."

High Swallow watched the great man very carefully in the days that followed and learned to approach the wild creatures with the same courage and calmness as Chingichnish, so they became his friends. White Wave stayed away from them. "I do not trust them," he said, "and I guess they do not trust me."

When they went with Chingichnish out of the mountains, the animals were always perfectly controlled by whistles. They stayed in the distance and hid in the woods when the three men approached the village of Hutuh on the other side of the river. Hutuh-vik, the chief, came to greet them, and Chingichnish asked him what had happened in the village that was wrong.

"We have a young man here who was caught three times stealing and he has taught some of the boys to steal for him."

"Did you warn him?"

"Yes, each time. The Council of the Elders, the Puplum, warned him that the avengers would punish him if he kept on with his ways, but he laughed at us."

"Bring him here."

The young man was brought forward with two guards, hands tied behind his back, but his eyes were defiant, a sneer on his face.

"Have the Puplum weighed the evidence and found him three times guilty of stealing?"

"Yes we have."

"What do you say about this, young man?"

"I did it," said the young man indifferently.

"What is the Puplums verdict for such a guilt?"

"Death," said the Hutuh-vik.

A great raven came winging out of the sky and lit on the shoulder of Chingichnish, and all present looked startled.

"What does the raven say?"

The raven ruffled his feathers, then pointed his beak straight at the bound figure. "Krak!" he said loudly.

"Let the young man go free. If what the raven says is true, the Great Being will send the avengers."

A man untied the young man's hands and he started to walk away. When he had gone about a hundred lengths of a man's arm from the crowd, he turned and shouted. "I will steal again from you in the dark. Catch me if you can." And he began to run.

The raven leaped from the shoulder of Chingichnish and flew over the running figure, croaking loudly. But suddenly two great figures burst from the edge of the woods, Hunar, the grizzly, and Tukut, the mountain lion. Across the field they raced, as if seeing who would be first. The young man suddenly saw them and put on a burst of speed, letting out a scream of fear. He had no chance. The lion hit him first at the end of one gigantic leap and sent his body rolling. The bear caught him on the rebound and tore his chest open with one ripping blow.

"You can cremate him now," said Chingichnish, and he blew his whistle so the two great beasts slunk away into the forest. From the people came a sigh of wonder, and the children stared with mouths and eyes wide open, the sight of death to the evil one inscribed forever in their minds.

"So shall the Great One above deal justice to those who do evil, but if you do not see this happen right away, and the Puplum deems a man guilty who has been warned three times, then let the whole village rise against him and kill him, for poison must be destroyed or it will poison others."

On the following day the people fixed a Yabagnar, a large circular enclosure of brush, that would be the sacred place of the Toloache Ceremony, the beginning initiation of boys into manhood in which each was given a vision. Chingichnish had taught them the details of this sacred ceremony. The original youth ceremony at puberty had its beginnings thousands of years before. As Chingichnish explained to White Wave:

"We have to impress the boys deeply in this ceremony, just as we impress the girls in their ceremony, at puberty, when they are heated over warm sand. It is important for each boy to have a vision, to give him strength to be good and to work for the people, not against them. So we give each boy the Toloache (jimson weed root), ground up and mixed in a drink, which he takes from the sacred steatite bowl. Watch during the days to follow and you will understand."

They watched the boys as they went through their long ordeal, first without food or water, then a little meal, but dancing and dancing, men often holding them up to keep them going. Then on the third night they were given the Toloache drink that threw them very quickly into a stupor, followed by a deep sleep. In their sleep each would see an animal or bird or reptile, or perhaps a power like the lightning or the wave. Each boy would know this forever after as his personal spirit power to protect him from danger as long as he was good in heart and deed.

When they awoke they were fed again and then had to dance some more. Finally they must step from rock to rock through a sacred pit where, if they missed a rock, it would signify early death. After this all the boys gathered around the sacred sand painting where the Paha, the chief priest, second to the chief in rank, spoke to them and warned them:

"Here in this pit in the center is the sacred center of the world and all around it are the sacred circles of harmony and spirit. Here is the door that leads out of the circle into the world of evil. You make your own choice. You walk out to where you become a lost person and soon to die in a terrible way, or you stay in the circle and grow in goodness like a mighty tree. These circles surround each of you who becomes a good man. Some of you will become heroes who will rise up to

SOUTHERN CALIFORNIA INDIAN WOMEN IN ACTION: **A** carrying baby on back; **B** carrying pack sack with tumpline and using basket hat to protect forehead; **C** using triangular wooden tongs to lift red-hot stone from fire to drop it into water in basket for boiling food. (*Drawings by Gladys Fox*)

A

B   **C**

become stars in the sky. The star means purity, because it is pure with bright light. The outer circle is the Milky Way, the second circle is the night sky, and the third circle is the sign of your blood. If you keep your blood in tune with the two great circles, you will be safe, but if not, in time the avenging animals, such as the rattlesnake, the bear, the wolf, and the mountain lion will destroy you or a terrible sickness will come. Beware that you do not break the laws of life, given to us from above.

"Be kind to the old ones, the widows, all children and women; be polite and speak well to those older than you, meaning them well, and obeying those who are your superiors. At all times be careful not to enter a house or visit a person in anger, or eat secretly or speak a lie. Always Chingichnish will be watching you. You will know he sees what you do that is bad."

After the ceremony, the Paha took the sand painting up in his hands and threw it into a central pit, which was then covered over with sand, for the sacred ceremony was over. Every boy knew he would be watched closely to see if he took his guardian spirit faithfully and followed the Way of Honor and Goodness for the rest of his life.

The next day they had the whirling eagle dance or moharish. All the wild spirits of the young men were let loose as they whirled in circles, the long eagle feathers that hung about their

EAGLE OR WHIRL DANCE (MORAHASH) OF THE ATAHUM (LUISEÑO). The eagle feathers are whirled wildly when they dance. (*Diorama by Elizabeth Mason, Santa Barbara Museum of Natural History, photo courtesy of Southwest Museum, Los Angeles*)

middles whirling with them until they seemed the very incarnation of flight, while the girls and women clapped and sang in tune with the clapping sticks and the rattles.

Then that night they had a great central fire. All the men and youth of the tribelet danced the fire dance with bare feet, recklessly pushing dirt forward with their feet, then jumping back as the heat became unbearable, but dancing in again to shove some more dirt, until late in the night they could finally stamp out the whole fire down to the last glowing ember and only the light of the twinkling fires of the sky remained. High Swallow and White Wave both danced in this dance, the two young Chumash exulting like their fellow dancers in the steady pounding of feet, the singing, the beat of the stick clappers and rattles, until every heart seemed to be one, lifting up and up to the Great One in the sky.

The next day Chingichnish told the two Chumash that he would go with them now to the Chumash country, to Ishwa and Satikae, to meet with Walking Thunder and test his power.

"We will have to walk," he said, "so we can take with us the animals, Hunar, the great bear, Tukut, the mountain lion and his mate, Wishawa, three of the great gray wolves, and Tecar, the eagle."

So they left Hutuh in the morning, and White Wave sent a messenger to tell West Wind Man and the boy to take the canoe back to Ishwa and wait for them there. On the hot days of summer they traveled north and west, resting during the greatest heat under a group of shade trees by a spring, then traveling on in the cooler hours of the evening and during the early morning. So they came to different villages, Shua (near what is now Long Beach), Engva (just north of Redondo Beach), Saan (just below Santa Monica), then to Maliwu, the first Chumash village on Malibu Creek. So on and on, past Shulawahu and Muwu till finally they arrived at Ishaw from whence the two young Chumash had started their journey. Here they learned that Walking Thunder had traveled north and west in the last few months, spreading his evil to all the coast towns, and ordering his warriors to kill the Silent Ones wherever he found them, until he reached Mispu (near what is now Santa Barbara).

So westward they had to travel some more, like trackers following the huge footprints of a great and dangerous bear. By now the quick mind of High Swallow had learned many words in the language of the Tongva, and his ability to know and love and lead the animals and birds drew warm words of praise from Chingichnish. They had to be careful now with the animals and make sure they stayed in the surrounding woods, for the villages of the Chumash were so numerous along this fertile and lovely coast that they met one every quarter of the day.

When they reached Mishpu they found that Walking Thunder had gone up the mountainside to Ushtahash, near a famous painted cave, and there he was having a great ceremony to show his power. As the three friends strode higher into the hills, they came to a place where they could look downward in the late afternoon into a great natural amphitheater. Here they saw hundreds of people gathering.

"Now," said Chingichnish, "I have a plan. You two go ahead, first making your faces dirty so you are not too recognizable, and then mingling with the crowd to watch what is happening. I will circle around with the animals to a place above the meeting place and will watch for the best time to appear. But if you need help or see that the time is ripe for me to act, give the long whistle I have taught you and I will come."

So he left them and the two young men dirtied their faces and arms to make themselves look rather disreputable and then followed the trail to the vast assemblage. There they saw a huge flat rock that was a stage, for standing on it were many young men with tall feathered headdresses. As they got closer, High Swallow gasped and pointed, whispering:

"Do you see that? There are five men there bound with ropes, and all five of them, I am sure, are Silent Ones. See how they hold their heads up. They are too brave to show fear and I can tell some of them are praying."

"And here comes Walking Thunder!" exclaimed White Wave

as the huge man walked up onto the rock. He also wore a tall headdress of many feathers that made him look truly like a giant. He held up his hand for silence and his majestic appearance quickly quieted the crowd. He spoke:

"We are here to celebrate our growing freedom from the Silent Ones. For many years they have not told the people the secrets of their magic in the paintings of the sacred caves; they have hidden their witchcraft from the people. We will kill five of them today so that they will no longer do their dark magic!"

A great shout went up from the tall-feathered and well-armed young men who surrounded him, but many of the common people were silent. Perhaps they were remembering the kind things and the healings the Silent Ones had done.

"You see," whispered High Swallow angrily, "how he twists things, making good people seem evil and himself good, and darkness is light. He is far too clever! It is time for me to speak."

"Hold yourself in," whispered White Wave urgently. "It is not time yet. Wait until we see Chingichnish on the mountain behind this place. When he is ready, it will be time to act."

Walking Thunder began to harangue the people in his deep, magnetic voice, urging them to find out and kill the Silent Ones. He told them all about the wonderful things he would do for the people. Then he began to show his powers that fooled and frightened many people, his ability to walk through and over fire (using a secret coating of powdered rock and glue on his feet), pretending to stab himself to death, with blood (animal blood from a hidden bladder) gushing from his wounds, and then bringing himself back to life, and other wizardry. Then suddenly he commanded the five Silent Ones to be brought forward, and five young men raised sharp knives to plunge into their hearts. The men came bravely, but this was all that High Swallow could stand. He rose to his feet and shouted:

"Walking Thunder is telling you lies about the Silent Ones! Who has been harmed by them? Down through the years they have given their lives to helping and healing people. This is the secret of the beautiful paintings they make in the caves: simply, that in painting their dreams in beauty they are telling us that the Spirit of All That Is has given them the power of healing. They would lose this power if they foolishly told you their secrets. This alone is why they are silent. It is Walking Thunder who is trying to steal your freedom and make himself into a big chief who runs your lives!"

"Grab him!" roared Walking Thunder. "He is a spy of the Silent Ones. I know him. He is the one who escaped from me at Satikae!"

People rose around High Swallow, some to defend him, others to grab him. White Wave knocked down a man who was rushing at him. Then a new wave of shouting came from the people. They were pointing up the mountainside. Down came the strangest group the Chumash had ever seen: a man as huge as Walking Thunder and, by his side, a massive grizzly bear, three giant wolves, and two slinking, snarling mountain lions.

Though Walking Thunder seemed as astonished as the rest for a moment, he soon showed himself brave and resourceful. He seized a large stick filled with holes, to which a cord was attached, a giant form of what is called a bullroarer, far too big for the ordinary person to handle. Walking Thunder grabbed the end of the cord and swung the hollowed-out log around his head at high speed. Instantly a tremendous roaring noise filled the amphitheater, so loud that the ears of the mountain lions flattened in sudden fear and they turned and ran, followed by the three wolves. Only Hunar, the monster bear, remained with his master. Taking advantage of this change in the situation, Walking Thunder seized a large heavy spear and threw it like a javelin up the hill at Chingichnish. The other giant sidestepped like a cat and, catching it with a lightning move, whirled it around his head and hurled it back so quickly that Walking Thunder just barely had time to make the quick move he needed to save himself, seize the spear, and hurl it back once more. The rapid moves and countermoves of the seemingly equal contest so paralyzed the audience that everybody watched frozen in place, each holding his breath in amazement. Four times the great spear whizzed through the air. Then, Walking Thunder, sensing that he was weakening because of his uphill throwing, caught the final throw, held it, and shouted to his followers:

"I need twenty heroes with me, spears in hand, to charge up the hill and kill man and bear!"

His magnetism raised a shout around him and several tall-plumed young men grabbed their spears and rushed forward at this stirring command. From Chingichnish came a shrill whistle and the single word "Tecar!" shouted to the sky.

In the noise and confusion, everybody but White Wave and High Swallow were watching the rush up the hill. They, however, looked to the skies and saw a black dot growing larger and larger. It was an eagle coming from the blue with the tearing speed of a rocket. Walking Thunder was in the lead of the rush on Chingichnish and Hunar, standing out above all the others, and it was he who was the target. One moment there was a living giant man, furious with war rage, the next second Tecar had checked his plunge just enough to aim well, then six claws like raking razor-sharp knives tore across the face of the giant, two of them penetrating through the eyes into the brain. Walking Thunder fell as a great tree falls, dead on contact with the ground!

Completely awed, the rushing warriors stopped to gaze in horror at their fallen chief. Down went their weapons and they fell to their knees.

"Whew!" exclaimed High Swallow, with a great sigh. "That was close! But now I can go up to Lompoc!"

"What in the world for?" asked White Wave in amazement.

"To see your sister, of course," replied High Swallow calmly.

A hand tapped High Swallow on the shoulder, but the voice that spoke shook him loose from his calm.

"You don't have to go that far!" she said. "I'm right behind you!" And then with a big sigh in her turn: "I would not have missed this for anything!"

Appendix A. Tlingit Monthly Activities

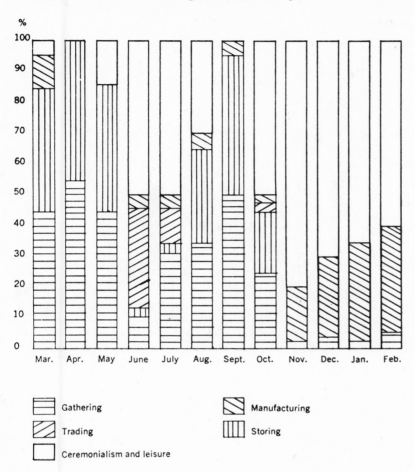

Gathering

Trading

Ceremonialism and leisure

Manufacturing

Storing

RELATIVE AMOUNTS OF TIME SPENT EACH MONTH ON IMPORTANT ACTIVITIES
(*Oberg*, The Social Economy of the Tlingit Indians)

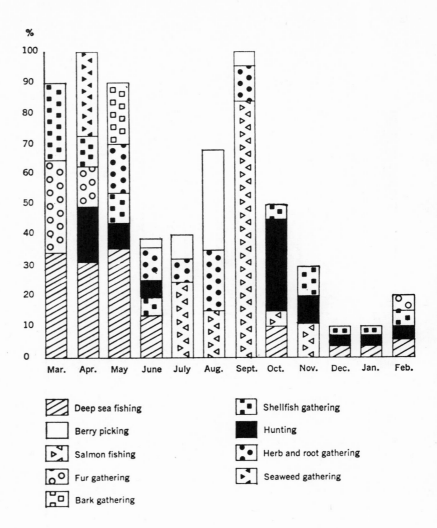

RELATIVE AMOUNTS OF TIME SPENT EACH MONTH ON GATHERING RESOURCES
(*Oberg*, The Social Economy of the Tlingit Indians)

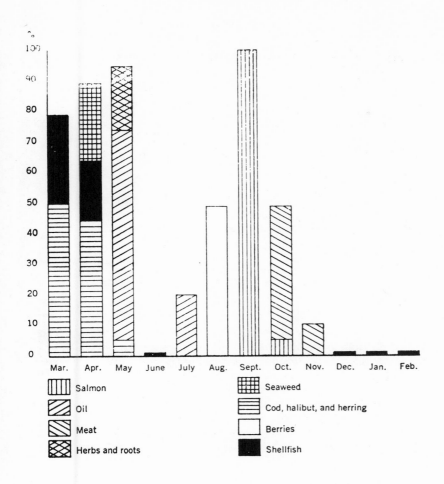

RELATIVE AMOUNTS OF TIME SPENT EACH MONTH ON STORAGE ACTIVITIES (*Oberg,* The Social Economy of the Tlingit Indians)

Appendix B. Definitive Material Culture Elements of the Pacific Coast

Elements Common to Whole Pacific Coast

WEAPONS AND TOOLS Bow and arrow, spear, harpoon, digging stick, wedges, stick tongs for lifting hot rocks, bone awls, stone hammer, twirling stick and base board for producing fire, stone scraper.

OTHER ITEMS Baskets, mammal-skin blankets, dip net, fish hook, root digging by women, food boiled with hot stones in water, whistle, tumpline to help carry loads, skin pouches or bags.

Elements Common to Southwest Alaska, part of Aleut-Eskimo Culture Area

WEAPONS AND TOOLS Throwing stick, 3-pronged bird arrows, bird net for catching auklets, murres, etc., slate-tipped lances which are poisoned for whale hunting; paddles point-tipped for use in combat; walrus ivory commonly used in tools.

OTHER ITEMS Skin kayaks with round body holes on top, larger skin boats (umiaks) for general transportation; ivory used for decorative items and toys; caribou- or seal-skin parkas with hoods, high quality closely fitted sewed clothing, clothes sometimes attached to rim of kayak hole to keep out water, carved wood hats for men, hats made from seal intestines for women, seal-skin boots, large seal-skin bags; pottery vessels; food dipped in seal oil for flavoring; cylindrical wooden quiver; whale bones used in construction of part of house (usually roof), partially hollowed stone lamps used for light and heat (oil burning); some rather elaborate and clever traps for trapping mammals; labrets of wood or bone worn in lips of some men; tobacco smoked in pipes, not chewed.

224

Northern Interior Forest Culture Area

Athapaskan Division (mainly Tanaina)

DISTINCTIVE CULTURE ELEMENTS Usually part bark, part board houses, partially underground and banked with dirt or snow, but sometimes all board and post houses with gabled roofs, copied from nearby Tlingit; sewed and tailored skin clothing, superior to that of northwest coast culture, but more loose-fitting than that of Eskimo; sweathouses usually made of skins covered with dirt or partially underground covered with slabs and dirt, hot stones sprinkled with water used to make steam, practice of steam bath more frequent than in neighboring cultures; birch-bark or other bark canoes used for major transporation; dogs carry loads in saddlebags and also pull sleds (as with Eskimos).

Elements Common to Northwest Coast Culture Area

WEAPONS AND TOOLS Salmon harpoon with single point, arrows made with two kinds of wood-joined foreshaft and main shaft; more artistic and finer work shown in weapons and tools than in surrounding cultures (except possibly the Eskimo).

SHELTER AND TRANSPORTATION Rectangular plank houses with log posts and beams; houses made of cedar or redwood; hollowing of log canoes by cutting with adzes or chisels, steaming or burning; canoes usually with cross-beams and thwarts.

OTHER ELEMENTS Twined basket hats; mats of shredded cedar or redwood bark; some clothes made of shredded bark; women usually wore 2-piece skin and/or cedar-bark skirt; elk- or caribou-hide armor or armor of wooden slats or rods (except in Puget Sound area) worn by men in war; tidewater fish traps catch fish when tide goes out; a wide variety of fishing nets and traps (common also with Eskimo); fish eggs stored in boxes (except in south-western part of area); food dipped in fish oil for flavoring; dentalium shells commonly used for money; wooden dishes common (also with Eskimo); no pottery.

NORTHERN PROVINCE

DISTINCTIVE CULTURE ELEMENTS Men wore belted robe of sewn skins, sometimes with undergarment, rarely went naked; sides of houses usually vertical boards, central smoke hole with adjustable shield, house framing and sheathing together, central fireplace for everyday use; sweathouse usually board hut over pit, often earth-covered, water poured on hot rocks to produce steam (similar to Athapaskan but not as frequently used); northern-type canoes with extreme upper parts of high curved and sharp-pointed prow and stern attached to rest of canoe so joints can hardly be seen, canoes spread first by steaming and then putting in crossbars; chopping adze used to cut down trees; hot-stone boiling of food in baskets; berries stored in eulachon fish grease; caribou hunted (also by Eskimo and Athapaskans, but not to the south); puffin-beak rattle used in dances; tobacco chewed, not smoked; labrets of wood or bone put into lips of nearly all women; head deformation rare or absent.

(In the following divisions, distinctiveness is shown by the combination of culture elements as well as by unique culture elements found in only one division.)

Tlingit Division (includes Eyak)

DISTINCTIVE CULTURE ELEMENTS Salmon split down belly before cooking or smoking, fish eggs stored in seal paunch, sea lion speared on rocks, mountain goat and grizzly bear hunted; some squared posts in houses, board floor in house; cedar- or spruce-bark canoe used in rivers; basketry quiver; copper anklets; wooden helmet; goat wool woven into blankets, woven wool belts and packstraps; fire drill with bow for ease in twirling, fire also by percussion or hard rocks struck together; tobacco grown.

Haida Division

DISTINCTIVE CULTURE ELEMENTS Fish eggs stored in seal paunch, clams eaten; zoomorphic (animal) decorations on house posts, bark sometimes used on roof, board floor in house; split-stick rattle used in dances and shaman ceremonies; copper display plaques named; boxes decorated with realistic carvings; basketry quiver; fire drill with bow for ease in twirling; both wooden and skin helmets; copper anklets; yellow cedar-bark blankets woven; tobacco grown.

Tsimshian-Haisla Division

DISTINCTIVE CULTURE ELEMENTS Salmon split down belly before cooking or smoking; porpoise harpooned, mountain goat and grizzly bear hunted, waterfowl hunted by torchlight; clams eaten; hot-stone boiling in waterproof bark vessels; bark dishes; zoomorphic (animal) decorations on house posts; round posts in house, bark on roof (sometimes), earth floor in house; cedar- or spruce-bark canoes; stone chisel; boxes decorated with realistic carvings; skin helmet; yellow cedar-bark blankets woven, also goat wool woven into blankets; woven wool belts and packstraps; split-stick rattle; tobacco imported.

WAKASHAN PROVINCE

DISTINCTIVE CULTURE ELEMENTS Men wore belted robe of sewn skins but often went naked in good weather, conical rain cape generally made of plant fibers; sides of house usually with longitudinal boards, earth floor in house (also with Tsimshian and Coast Salish), roof board movable to let out smoke, central fireplace for rituals only; elk hunted instead of caribou, deer caught in deadfalls, rectangular wicker-work fish traps, waterfowl hunted by torchlight (as with Tsimshian); raccoon eaten, clams eaten (also by Tsimshian); D-shaped adze, stone chisel (also used by Tsimshian); trees chiseled down instead of cut down by chopping adze; pear-shaped stone hand maul; baby's head often deformed with boards but not as flat as salish (coming more to a high point or knob in back); cylindrical wooden quiver; tobacco not used.

Kwakiutl Division (Southern Kwakiutl, Xaihais, Bella Coola, Comox, and Pentlatch)

DISTINCTIVE CULTURE ELEMENTS Eulachon fish grease stored in kelp bulbs; mountain goat hunted (also by Tsimshian and Coast Salish), grizzly bear hunted, eagle caught with noose on pole; seaweed eaten as medicine; zoomorphic (animal) decorations carved on wooden dishes, spoons carved from mountain goat's horns (also by Coast Salish); northern-type sea canoe, Kwakiutl war canoe, cedar-bark canoe bailer with cross handle, canoes spread by steaming (as in northern tribes); boxes decorated with realistic carvings (as with Tsimshian); yarn spun on spindle.

Nootka Division (Nootka, Makah, Quileute, Hoh, and Quinault)

DISTINCTIVE CULTURE ELEMENTS Dip net on double crossbar frame; fish eggs stored in seal paunch; sea lion hunted with harpoon, whale hunted with harpoon using seal-skin floats and long lines played out from canoe, dead whale carved up with mussel shell blubber knives; dentalium shells used for money (fished from private sea beds owned by important families); Nootka-type canoe with fine, fin-like stem and flat top in rear; wooden triangular bailer; house sometimes with suspended mat door, house often as large as those of Kwakiutl but cruder in design and structure; pear-shaped stone maul; men wear dentalium pins in nose; twined or sewn tule mats; yarn spun on thigh (no spindle).

(Some of the Coast Salish tribes, such as the Comox and the Quinault, have been placed with the more complex northern cultures of the Nootka and the Kwakiutl. Because of their close proximity to the Nootka and Kwakiutl, they picked up many of their culture elements.)

COAST SALISH-CHINOOK PROVINCE

DISTINCTIVE CULTURE ELEMENTS Robe of special dog hair (more rarely of mountain goat wool); hat with brim; fiber petticoat for women; round to oval entrance to house instead of rectangular entrance of more northern tribes, house roof usually shedlike or low fore-and-aft pitched, some gabled houses found in more northern parts of province; mat beds on platforms around central pit; mat-covered shelters in summer camps; canoes of several types including 2 borrowed (Nootka-type and northern-type) and several definitely Salish with very elongated prows, largest canoes 45–50 feet long (usually smaller than the largest canoes of the northern and Wakashan provinces); basketry traps for fish; spoons usually carved from goat's or mountain sheep's horns; wooden cradle; some coiled basketry, wrapped twined basket with false embroidery; tobacco little used; baby's head deformed by flattening with boards.

Puget Sound and Southern British Columbia Division

DISTINCTIVE CULTURE ELEMENTS Men's robes of woven cedar bark or dog's hair; planks usually placed horizontally on house but sometimes vertically, adjustable roof board to let out smoke, house larger (up to 60 feet wide and several hundred feet long) than houses in the south of province, house more crudely made than those in provinces to the north, plank partitions; spoons carved from mountain sheep's and goat's horns either plain or, more rarely, with animal carvings; trees for canoes felled mainly by burning; cedar-bark canoe bailer; double-pointed digging stick.

Columbia River and North Oregon Coast Division

DISTINCTIVE CULTURE ELEMENTS Men's robe of skins; some use of acorns as food, though not as common as to the south; planks placed vertically on house, house smaller than to north (up to 30–40 feet wide, up to 100 feet long), temporary summer house of rushes or bark; sweathouses partly underground, covered with boards, water poured on hot rocks for steam; spoons carved from mountain sheep's or goat's horns with geometric carvings; canoes often bought from northern tribes; tremendous quantities of salmon caught on Columbia River, dried and smoked for use in trade with interior tribes.

NORTHWEST CALIFORNIA AND SOUTHWEST OREGON PROVINCE

(The center of cultural diffusion for this province was the Yurok in northwest California. The farther tribes were from the center the less complex their culture.)

DISTINCTIVE CULTURE ELEMENTS No head deformation as in north; men have measuring stripes tattooed on arm to measure dentalium money strings, men wore deerskin robes, dentalium nose ornaments; women wore brimless basketry caps, wealthy women wore dentalium necklaces; planks placed vertically on sides of house, sliding door on most except those of poor people who used mats, houses mainly for single family, rarely as large as those farther north; sweathouse partly underground, board covered, no steam used; most beds on floor; dugout canoes generally of smaller size (less than 25 feet) than canoes to the north, with blunter prow and stern and without painting or carving; twined basketry with hazel or willow warp, weft of split roots, generally of conifers, white patterns of *Xerophyllum tenax* (bear grass), red patterns of dyed alder; basketry cradle; conical burden basket; mortar hopper used in grinding acorns; acorns much commoner food than with above tribes; 2-pronged harpoon; a long mush paddle; tobacco cultivated and smoked.

Southwest Oregon Division (Tututni, Takelma, Umpqua, Coos, and Siuslaw)

DISTINCTIVE CULTURE ELEMENTS Men wore fur caps, deerskin shirts; women wore petticoats of plant fiber and sometimes had deerskin gowns, women had 3 stripes tattooed on chin; planks of houses made of cedar (poor people used bark), house up to 12 feet wide and 15–20 feet long with one ridge (sometimes flat), excavation of the floor for the whole house; girls' beds on a platform above floor; brush hut used at summer camps; sweathouse rectangular with planks, earth-covered; armor of elk hide over wood rods; hide helmets; stick seed beater; spoons carved from elk antlers (no design).

Northwest California Division (Yurok, Karok, Hupa, Tolowa, and Wiyot)

DISTINCTIVE CULTURE ELEMENTS Men didn't wear hats or deerskin shirts; women wore petticoats of deerskin, women shaman's petticoat of plant fibers, women did not wear deerskin gowns, women had almost solid black tattoos on chin; planks of houses mainly of redwood, houses up to 20 feet wide and 23 feet long or almost square, excavation of house in center only; sweathouse heated by fire; armor of elk hide or wooden rods; no helmet; basketry seed beater; spoons carved from elk antlers with geometric designs; most tools, weapons, artifacts, and art finer and more perfect than among surrounding tribes.

Material Culture Elements Common in Both the Central California Culture Area and the Southern California Culture Area

TOOLS AND WEAPONS Wedge or chisel made from antlers used in working wood, mortar and pestle for acorns, arrowheads generally of chipped flint or obsidian; to the north, bone, horn, and ground stone arrowheads were more common.

SHELTER AND TRANSPORTATION A brush- and earth-covered semi-subterranean sweathouse used by most men for a clubhouse or for making sweat (from fire), sweat followed by plunge into a cold stream or pond; a crude brush shelter was used when away from village during summer and fall food gathering; a balsa or tule canoe was used in most areas where there was calm fresh or salt water.

FOOD GATHERING, HUNTING, OR FISHING A seine net was used to surround fish, gill nets were stretched between two posts in shallow water to catch fish when they tried to penetrate the nets; poison from such plants as the soap root plant was used to stun fish for easy capture; oak acorns formed the primary food, generally some kind of mortar and pestle was used for grinding acorns and other seeds.

MISCELLANEOUS CULTURE ELEMENTS 2-piece skirts for women (usually made of plant material or cords in front and skin in back, the front part smaller and overlapped by the back part); men and small children were generally completely naked in good weather, or a man might wear a folded skin over the hips; in cold weather both sexes wore skin robes which were usually made of woven strips of rabbit fur; a crude loom of two upright poles was used to weave rabbit-skin blankets; a 4-holed flute was often made from a piece of elderberry branch; large clam shells were cut into disks or beads and used for money, usually well-polished; tobacco smoked everywhere in area, but not heavily, generally in tubular tobacco pipes; strings and rope commonly made of dogbane or milkweed fibers, but nettles might be used (in north iris fiber was used by Shasta, Coast Yuki, and Athapaskans); carrying net with a continuous headband used for large loads.

Material Culture Elements Common in Central California Area

SPECIAL TO THIS AREA   Sling, moccasin of single piece of soft deerskin without sole but two seams, men's head net mainly for holding items such as feathers or comb; harpoon with socket and detachable shaft, arrow straightener of 2-grooved slab of sandstone or hole in slab of wood; split clapping stick used in dances, cocoon rattle, deer hooves used for rattle mainly in adolescence ceremonies.

FOUND SOMEWHAT IN NORTHWESTERN CULTURE AREA   Dip net, sinew-backed bow.

FOUND IN SOMEWHAT LIMITED PARTS OF AREA   From San Francisco Bay Area north—pounding rock slab used for seeds, special separate hut for women during menses; from Pomo and Wintun south to Salinan and Yokut—acorns stored in large, outside, basketlike structures on four posts, but elsewhere, and sometimes in the same area, kept indoors in large storage baskets.

Middle Division

DISTINCTIVE CULTURE ELEMENTS   Large underground dance or ceremonial building, well constructed with heavy posts, wood slabs, and brush thatch, usually covered with dirt; large hollow log used as foot drum for dancing or beaten with end of wooden post; roasted, finely ground, and polished beads of magnesite rock used as most valuable money; some houses usually made of willow wood frames, covered with lashed-on brush or leafy branches, smoke hole in center (several smoke holes in large houses that sheltered several families).

Northern Border Division

DISTINCTIVE CULTURE ELEMENTS   (*as the Northwest Culture Area was approached, more of these people used varying parts of the following along with the general Central California Culture Area items*)   Houses with some split boards in their construction, dugout canoes on large rivers, cultivation of tobacco, basketry ornamentation using shining *Xerophyllum tenax* (bear grass) plant stems for designs, basketry cap worn by women, long narrow pole-paddle. (There culture was usually much simpler than the major area centers, either northwestern or central Californian, with less elaboration of utensils, houses usually for just one family, often just tipi-shaped bark shelters; men doing many different jobs without any specialization, and so on.)

Southern Border Division

DISTINCTIVE CULTURE ELEMENTS Stick loop for stirring mush (mainly Yokut), special type of basket of coiled ware with jarlike flat shoulder and slender neck with usually flaring, wider mouth; large baskets sometimes used to ferry children and women across large streams; ate dogs (mainly Yokut); used pottery (Yokut, Western Mono, and Tubatulabal).

CULTURE ELEMENTS BORROWED FROM SOUTHERN CALIFORNIA CULTURE AREA Cane smoking pipe; stone metate (southern type); coiled basketry cap worn by women, sandals (usually made of yucca fibers); steatite or soapstone arrow straightener; shallow steatite cook pots and dishes.

Material Culture Elements Common in Southern California Culture Area

(These elements could probably be considered an extension of the Southwest Culture Area, centering on the New Mexico and Arizona Pueblo peoples.)

DISTINCTIVE CULTURE ELEMENTS Sandals (usually made from yucca fibers), coiled basketry caps worn by women (specially used when carrying a back load with tumpline); long, narrow self bow (not sinew-backed), arrows generally of cane, arrow straightener of grooved piece of steatite (soapstone); moveable stone mortar, well-shaped and finished soapstone mortar used with toloache (jimsonweed) in youth initiation ceremony (rare or absent among the more interior tribes); board canoe found along coast; multiple-foundation coiled basketry; turtle shell or gourd rattle with cherry pits to make noise; cane smoking pipe; carrying net with 2 ends (one a straight cord, the other a loop); acorns stored in large nestlike structures woven of branches and twigs and usually set on large rocks.

Middle (Shoshone-Speaking) Division

DISTINCTIVE CULTURE ELEMENTS Pottery vessels (except Tongva); curved throwing stick (extends to Kamia); single-bladed paddle used along coast with board canoe and inland with balsa canoe.

Chumash Division

DISTINCTIVE CULTURE ELEMENTS Very large communal dwellings for many families, usually round (up to 60 feet in diameter); true beds on platforms, separate cubicles made with hanging mats; large earth-covered ceremonial building (unusual extension of similar type building from middle division of Central California Culture Area); much more frequent use of board canoes for adventurous voyages along coast and to outer islands; some canoes of large size (4 feet wide and 25 feet long, carrying up to 20 passengers), double-bladed paddle; whale rib wedge for splitting wood, harpoon with slender foreshaft, some use of sinew-backed bow; finely made wooden dishes and bowls, also dishes, bowls, and other items carved decoratively out of steatite (soapstone); large stone rings used as weights on digging sticks. (All these items show that the Chumash had a more complex material culture than most groups elsewhere in California.)

Kamia Division

DISTINCTIVE CULTURE ELEMENTS Dugout canoes used instead of plank canoes for the most part, canoes and double-bladed paddles cruder than those of the tribes immediately to the north; men wore braided girdle of agave fibers to support tools, weapons, etc.; women wore 2-piece skirt, usually of willow bark or with front part made of close-together strings; elliptically shaped brush house much more often covered with earth than among the tribes immediately to the north; soft textile fiber baskets of milkweed and similar soft plants used for sacks and wallets.

Appendix C. Definitive Social and Religious Culture Elements of the Pacific Coast

Elements Common to Whole Pacific Coast

SOCIAL ELEMENTS Largest political unit usually village or, at most, area with central permanent village, nearby subsidiary villages under sub-chiefs (exceptions among Yokut, Nootka, and Tsimshian who had something approaching true tribes); central-based foraging chief type of organization of life and economy with people spending part of year in a permanent village, but traveling and camping at good food spots during the more productive times of the year. Usually most influential families furnished council of elders under chief to help make decisions (exceptions among Coast Salish in Washington and Yurok and their neighbors in northwestern California). War is mainly small-scale feuds between enlarged families, clans, or villages with tribes practically never involved (exceptions among Yokut, Tsimshian, and Nootka). Chiefs were usually men, but some rare women chiefs (Tsimshian and Chumash); in most groups either revenge or an agreed-upon payment was demanded for any crime against an individual or family, but rich and influential families most likely to enforce this; courage and silence under pain was widely taught and admired among boys and men; trading was widespread and usually done by amateurs acting in groups, but some professional traders found (most likely among Tsimshian, Nootka, and Chinook, with the Pomo and Chumash a possibility in California). Marriage was usually by some form of formal or informal purchase (at least an exchange of gifts); crimes were usually held down to low limits by general disapproval of people, fear of revenge or heavy payments, and banishment from the group or death in extreme cases (see crimes of shamans under religious culture elements). There was no such thing as a police force among any of these peoples.

RELIGIOUS ELEMENTS Seclusion of girls at puberty under special taboos (usually watched and guided by older women), girls of wealthy or high-class families often guarded against loss of virginity. Shamans received power from dreams, sacred formulas, or rites (exception in Southern California Culture Area); shamans usually taught or helped by older shamans; pain object in body, theft of soul, witchcraft, or psychic poisoning by enemy shaman believed main causes of sickness; main crimes of shamans believed to be witchcraft or stealing of souls. Many taboos surrounded women at menses, at time of birth of child, around girl at puberty, and both men and women when men were preparing for or going on trips or hunts; in religion man and nature were generally believed to be intertwined spiritually so that special ceremonies, purification trials, and/or other observances were held to prepare for hunting, fishing, or trading trips, and the like; often ceremonies were observed at the end of such trips. Animals, birds, and plants were believed to have some kind of spiritual nature or souls; even rocks were thought to have spirits in them which could influence men favorably or unfavorably (recent scientific investigations have given some evidence of an aura or energy vibrations about plants). In the beginning ages of the earth, men and animals and birds were all believed to have had human form and communicated like men.

Elements Common to Southwest Alaska Culture Area (Aleut-Eskimo)

SOCIAL ELEMENTS Family alone usually managed revenge for crime, divorce frequent, no physical punishment of young child, women danced by swaying body while feet were held still; exchange of gifts at marriage; cleverly made masks, especially finger masks, used in dances and ceremonies; much humor and laughter, including jokes and tricks played at most social gatherings or wherever two come together; masks have lighter, more humorous touch than among Indians.

RELIGIOUS ELEMENTS Marine and land life believed hostile to each other so they are dealt with separately; sea mammal may be offered fresh water at death; elaborate ceremony for boy at first kill; religion based mainly on shamanism and animism (animal spirits); shamans had usually strong power over people; no secret religious societies; more emphasis than with other native Americans put on powers connected with amulets, charms, magic spells, and chants; demonic spirits of earth and sky and sea must be propitiated; each species of animal had a spirit person or head being whose aid was sought by the hunter; souls were believed to be perpetually reincarnated; a commonly-held sunrise ceremony; dead buried or put in caves and even mummified if highly respected.

Athapaskan (or Northern Interior Forest) Culture Area (mainly Tanaina)

DISTINCTIVE SOCIAL ELEMENTS   Inheritance by matrilineal (mother) descent; Tanaina divided into about 11 matrilineal clans, divided also between 2 moieties (subdivisions of the tribe in which marriages were allowed outside moiety only); boy's training usually by mother's brother; girl often tried out by boy's parents before marriage allowed; a wealthy man was generally considered to be a chief, being in charge of his relatives and slaves; chiefs generally chosen for wisdom, personality, and courage more than from inheritance; Tanaina had slaves and social ranks copied from the Tlingit; people very fond of singing and dancing.

DISTINCTIVE RELIGIOUS ELEMENTS   Boy sought guardian spirit more universally and steadfastly than with neighboring Eskimo or Tlingit; shamans usually had less power and influence, with individuals more likely to regard themselves as having shaman-like powers of healing; dead were usually cremated (as with Tlingit).

Elements Common to Northwest Culture Area in General (southeast Alaska to northwest California)

SOCIAL ELEMENTS   Strong emphasis on wealth to give power or prestige over others, a widespread system of money exchange mainly using dentalium as money; art with horn or wood carving and wood painting important in most of area; midwife helps with birth; slavery found in nearly every part of area (they were debt slaves in northwest California and southwest Oregon, but war slaves in rest of area).

RELIGIOUS ELEMENTS Most gods or other important spirits were generally of equal rank, unlike their human followers; morning prayer was common.

Elements Common to Northern Province and Wakashan Province

(These two provinces constituted the heart of the Northwest Culture Area as a whole, both very creative and inventive and both stimulating each other.)

SOCIAL ELEMENTS Because of living close to an often violent ocean environment, both the Nootka of Vancouver Island's frequently stormy west coast and the Haida of the storm-exposed Queen Charlotte Islands were outstanding canoe builders, mariners, and far sea voyagers, carrying elements of their culture with them both north and south. The long trading and slave-hunting expeditions of these people along the coast stimulated nearby peoples, such as the Kwakiutl, Tsimshian, and the Tlingit, to try the same. The warlike Haida, who were the feared "Vikings of the North Pacific," stimulated warlike reprisals from their neighbors, they therefore elaborately fortified villages and hill forts to resist attacks, and probably caused the gradual formation of village confederacies for mutual defense among the northern Nootka and by the Tsimshian along the Nass and Skeena rivers (see chapter 5 where a Nootka confederacy is described in defensive action against the Haida). By the time of the coming of the whites, these confederacies were well on their way to becoming true politically united tribes. War was much more organized and violent in these two provinces than to the north and south, and the common method of attack was to lead a war party by boat to a hidden landing near a village and then attack the village in the early dawn. Fortified villages were much harder to attack, but might be besieged by a large war party until they ran out of food and water. Fighting intensified after the arrival of the white traders with more dangerous weapons. As a last resort, people who were outfought and outnumbered fled into the woods in small parties and lived off the land. Chieftainship was hereditary. Slaves could be killed by whim of chief.

RELIGIOUS ELEMENTS   It is probable some of the more important secret societies, such as the Cannibal Dancers, the Shamans, the Nutlam, and "those descend from the heavens," originated with the Kwakiutl and spread to lesser or greater degrees to the Nootka in the south and the Bella Coola, Haisla, Tsimshian, and finally to the Haida in the north. Only the Tlingit apparently failed to take up these societies and dances, preferring their own.

NORTHERN PROVINCE

DISTINCTIVE SOCIAL ELEMENTS   Inheritance was through matrilineal (mother) descent, son often went to live with his mother's brother's family to inherit his powers; children usually went to the mother at time of divorce; chieftainship was usually hereditary, his power depending on force of character; a potlatch was generally given by one clan or moiety to enhance prestige (crests shown were clan-owned), potlatches also given for building a new house for a new chief by the house owner, an opposite clan of the moiety (division in tribe that determines whom one can marry) doing the building, and at the time of erecting a memorial to a dead chief; coppers were displayed as wealth and prestige items at potlatches, but their value remained the same; weregeld (blood payment) was given for murder to the offended family; slaves were captured in war and could be sold or given at will, having no rights.

DISTINCTIVE RELIGIOUS ELEMENTS   Songs for spirit of slain bear; inheritance of shamanistic powers by a relative, but heir not named by shaman, the inheritance decided by the person receiving a vision or a special feeling of power, etc.; shaman extracted dangerous object from sick person's body to heal him, then sent the bad object away.

Tlingit Division (includes Eyak)

DISTINCTIVE SOCIAL ELEMENTS   Seclusion of girl after puberty for 1 year; chief's daughter not called "princess"; marmot skins and caribou or moose hides were wealth items at potlatches.

DISTINCTIVE RELIGIOUS ELEMENTS   Ghost rites held for dead; no secret societies; some shaman's powers came from animal spirits; shaman's hair never combed; shaman performed sleight-of-hand tricks; shaman "sees" spirit world when dancing; clairvoyance by shamans.

Haida Division

DISTINCTIVE SOCIAL ELEMENTS Copper plaques were used as wealth displays at feasts and also given special names; seclusion of girl after puberty for 2 years; title for chief's daughter was "princess"; personal property of dead burned; masks used in society performances; berry and root grounds owned by families.

DISTINCTIVE RELIGIOUS ELEMENTS Shaman's hair never combed; magician cured by driving out mouse, also magician thrown in water; souls assumed animal forms; women clairvoyants; secret societies, including Cannibal Dancers present.

Tsimishian Division (includes also Haisla)

DISTINCTIVE SOCIAL ELEMENTS Seclusion of girl after puberty for 1 year; formal proposal party initiates marriage (also among Kwakiutl); title for chief's daughter was "princess"; eclipse meant a chief would die; personal property of dead burned; berry and root grounds owned by families also some hunting grounds; masks used in society performances; mormot skins as well as caribou and moose hides displayed as wealth at feasts and potlatches.

DISTINCTIVE RELIGIOUS ELEMENTS Winter ceremonials held by secret societies with ranked series of dances, including Cannibal Dancers; many shamans received power from animal spirits; shaman may wear coronet of claws or horn; shaman's hair may be combed; shaman captures soul in bone tube; clairvoyance by shamans.

WAKASHAN PROVINCE

DISTINCTIVE SOCIAL ELEMENTS Bilineal inheritance from either father or mother, with emphasis more often on father; children go to father at divorce; potlatch given by house group of village, but not by clan; games to capture bride; repayment of bride price in time by father of girl; laughing games played.

DISTINCTIVE RELIGIOUS ELEMENTS Female shaman hired at birth to help decide child's career in magic; special taboos with birth of twins; winter ceremonials given with many complicated and even fantastic performances and tricks to fool the audience, including some apparently violent deaths (this done to impress people with the power of the spirits that possess the dancers and performers); one source of disease was believed to be from evil spirit, also believed sent by evil shaman; black magic practice by some shamans; ghosts go to underworld; potlatch often used for performance of secret religious society.

Kwakiutl Division (Kwakiutl, Xaihais, Bella Coola, Comox, and Pentlatch)

DISTINCTIVE SOCIAL ELEMENTS   Copper plaques displayed as values and named at potlatches; value of copper doubles with each sale; ritual purchase of coppers; loans made to givers of potlatches and fixed rate of interest is paid; fictitious marriage of older man with small girl (usually to give status to the girl child); at funeral women scratch faces; personal property of dead burned.

DISTINCTIVE RELIGIOUS ELEMENTS   Novice shaman takes to woods to seek dreams; regular winter ceremonials put on by secret societies at which Cannibal Dancers and other special dancers act out legends of the people; ranked series of dances given on the basis of the importance of each secret society.

Nootka Division (Nootka, Makah, Quilleute, Hoh, and Quinault)

DISTINCTIVE SOCIAL ELEMENTS   Nootka were the premier fishers, makers, controllers, and distributors of dentalium money, special ceremonies related to the gathering of the dentalium shells; songs for slain bear; fixed order of potlatch seats by rank.

DISTINCTIVE RELIGIOUS ELEMENTS   Human remains used in purification rites for hunting; chief or leader who directs whale hunt goes through severe trials, fasts, etc., connected with bones of dead ancestors, to prepare for whale hunt, his assistants making lesser sacrifices; shaman's power often comes from animal spirits; supernatural experience of shaman makes him ill; wolf ceremonials, in which costumed "wolves" carry off boys to be initiated, were held at any time of the year, with unranked ceremonial performances of two distinct societies; initiation into society by abduction by supernatural wolves; bullroarer used in society performances; novice shaman stays away from his house.

PUGET SOUND-LOWER COLUMBIA PROVINCE

DISTINCTIVE SOCIAL ELEMENTS Paternal descent of inheritance; slaves captured in war, but rarely killed, could sometimes marry free person; chiefs generally had less power than in three northern provinces; often no true chiefs at all; upper-class girls and women were less severely restricted; children stayed with the father after a divorce.

DISTINCTIVE RELIGIOUS ELEMENTS Shamans were usually men; some non-shamans owned spirits; shamans killed if they lost too many cases or did evil; individual achieving spiritual power by vision-seeking and from guardian spirit more important than with tribes to the north; boys swam in fearsome spots to get help in courage and spirit, also initiated by ordeals of cold-water baths at dawn, lashing with nettles, etc.; guardian spirit songs were sung at the winter ceremonials.

(Border tribes of the Nootka division, such as the Quilleute, Hoh, and Quinault, and of the Kwakiutl division, such as the Comox and Pentlatch, mixed the lower Coast Salish elements to some extent with social elements borrowed from the Nootka and the Kwakiutl, as did other Coast Salish tribes near this northern border, but the further south the tribe, the lesser the extent the northern culture elements were used.)

Puget Sound-Southern British Columbia Division

DISTINCTIVE SOCIAL ELEMENTS Birth plus wealth gave social rank; burial in canoes or boxes, usually placed high; potlatch more important than in the division to the south, often given with "scramble" (throwing gifts to common people), usually had lots of fun and games, often held outside; slaves treated rather well, and slavery frowned on in back country where it was not well established; "wisher" sometimes employed by family to prevent divorce.

DISTINCTIVE RELIGIOUS ELEMENTS Vision seeking by children at early age, especially boys.

Lower Columbia and Northwest Oregon Division

DISTINCTIVE SOCIAL ELEMENTS Wealth gave social rank; potlatch unimportant, but sometimes held; first salmon rite to spiritually initiate beginning of salmon fishing season was important; burial in canoes on coast, but in boxes inland; singeing of hair by widow common at death of huband; modified version of dancing society; trading a way of life, particularly among the Chinook, with slaves brought to Chinook mainly from the south and west, then traded to the north; "Chinook jargon" widely used as a second language in this area to facilitate trading, but weaker farther away.

NORTHWESTERN CALIFORNIA AND SOUTHWESTERN OREGON PROVINCE

DISTINCTIVE SOCIAL ELEMENTS Wealth gave social rank; inheritance by paternal descent; no true chiefs, wealthy men acted as leaders; no potlatches; slaves obtained through debt instead of war, no slaves sacrificed, slaves could marry free person; war dance of incitement; burial in ground; no masks or secret societies; no clans or moieties (tribal divisions to determine who can marry who).

DISTINCTIVE RELIGIOUS ELEMENTS Shaman either man or woman; few non-shamans owned spirits; shamans rarely if ever killed, but had to repay money if they lost a case.

Southwestern Oregon Division (Siuslaw, Coos, Tututni, Takelma, and Upper Umqua)

DISTINCTIVE SOCIAL ELEMENTS Measurement of dentalium money was by tens; burial was made by sitting body in ground; no war dance of settlement; payments for injury or death less exactly specified than in northwestern California; the wealthy or "real men" were not so powerful in their control over others as in the northwestern California division.

DISTINCTIVE RELIGIOUS ELEMENTS Shamans about equally men or women; source of shaman's power was directly from spirits; no World Renewal dances.

Northwestern California Division (Yurok, Tolowa, Wiyot, Hupa, and Karok)

DISTINCTIVE SOCIAL ELEMENTS Measurement of dentalium money was by fives or by number counted on arm length; burial was made by laying body flat in grave; war dance of either incitement or settlement; payments for each kind of injury or death exactly specified in most instances; the wealthy or "real men" established

high standards of honor in morals and manners and exerted considerable control over relatives and hangers-on.

DISTINCTIVE RELIGIOUS ELEMENTS Shamans mainly women; shaman's power came from pain objects sent from spirits and these
objects must be mastered by the shaman; World Renewal dances
important, including famous White Deerskin Dance.

Elements Common to Central California Culture Area and Southern California Culture Area

SOCIAL ELEMENTS Large populous ethnic tribes of both central
and southern California culture areas had organized tribelets with
central permanent village with head chief and smaller, nearby set-
tlements in some river drainage system with sub-chiefs (except
for Yokut who had developed true tribal organizations for wider
dialect areas). Levirate or marriage of widow to dead husband's
brother was common, as was sororate or marriage of widower to
dead wife's sister; a semi-couvade saw both husband and wife
observe restrictions particularly for food and travel at time of
child's birth (not found among border tribes of the north). War
started mainly for revenge for injury or insult, sometimes on ac-
count of witchcraft, but rarely became more than a skirmish which
ended after a few were hurt or killed; tribelet chiefs often acted
as intermediaries or referees to prevent battles from starting or
to settle them quickly; scalps might be taken in war and danced
over in victory, but not preserved as trophies (Yokut, Valley
Maidu, and Pomo probably did not take scalps); bow and arrow
main battle weapon; no organized police or war forces; war leaders chosen at the time.

RELIGIOUS ELEMENTS Scratching head and abstention from eating flesh were taboos during girl's adolescence ceremony; initiation
of boys into religious secret societies happened in middle divisions
of both southern and central California areas. Primary function of
California shaman was to cure disease, mainly by removing foreign
object from body of patient, but cures were also effected by such
actions as singing, dancing, manipulation of body, and use of medi-
cinal herbs; all shamans were capable of either beneficial or
harmful acts, and many diseases were considered caused by bad
shamans; shamans who did not cure or used power for evil were

likely to be killed; some shamans specialized in healing people from rattlesnake bites; "bear doctors" were found in most areas and were believed to either turn into or get their powers from grizzly bears.

CENTRAL CALIFORNIA CULTURE AREA

SOCIAL ELEMENTS Widow singed hair after death of husband (not among most Yokut); mother-in-law taboo (no speaking to her except among some northern border tribes).

RELIGIOUS ELEMENTS Novice shaman seeks vision of guardian spirit, but little vision seeking among most of population; deer-hoof rattle used at girl's adolescence ceremony; either Kuksu religion (using complex colorful ceremonies with healing and moral rites coming from hero god) or old ghost-type religion (worship of ancestral ghosts) found over most of this area.

Middle Division

DISTINCTIVE SOCIAL ELEMENTS Highly developed use of counting money, sometimes in tens of thousands (especially among Pomo), counting mainly in 20s; chief in this division seemed to be more trained and ready to act as expert referee in family disputes or disputes and wars between tribelets than in southern California, hence this division was noted for general peacefulness of relationships between peoples.

DISTINCTIVE RELIGIOUS ELEMENTS Kuksu religion of spirit impersonation, with very colorful feather dance costumes and often initiation of youth by "ghosts"; old men of special knowledge and wisdom acted as directors of Kuksu cult ceremonies, which also included moral lessons and healing; 4 was a sacred number in this area; some special shamans to control weather found here, but not as common as farther south where weather was drier.

Northern Border Division (Shasta, Achomawi, Atsugewi, Yana, Wintu, and California Athapaskan)

DISTINCTIVE SOCIAL ELEMENTS Highest political unit often only band or enlarged family, or one village without subsidiary villages.

DISTINCTIVE RELIGIOUS ELEMENTS Old ghost-type religion and/or some religious elements from World Renewal ceremony of Yurok area; commonly used first-salmon ceremony; fewer ceremonies and dances than farther south or northwest, with most of them directed by shamans; more women shamans than men; shaman usually took pain object into his or her body to get power; more individuals sought for spirit power alone than happened to south or northwest.

Southern Border Division (Yokut, Esselen, Salinan, Western Mono, and Tubatulabal)

DISTINCTIVE SOCIAL ELEMENTS Yokut had stronger and widerspread tribal organization with special name, distinctive dialect, and head chief for each political unit; more use of war than to the north.

DISTINCTIVE RELIGIOUS ELEMENTS Some use of jimsonweed or toloache for dream stimulation, but with not much else of the Toloache religion of southern California; Kuksu religion weak or absent; some cave paintings in abstract polychrome used apparently in religious symbolism; rain-making shamans more prevalent than in north, but not as common or powerful as to south.

SOUTHERN CALIFORNIA CULTURE AREA

DISTINCTIVE SOCIAL ELEMENTS No parents-in-law taboos of avoidance.

DISTINCTIVE RELIGIOUS ELEMENTS Toloache or jimsonweed religion influenced most of area, at least to extent of the toloache drink being used to get visions; ground-painting religious ceremonies at *both* boys' and girls' initiations (except possibly with Chumash or Kamia); cave paintings with religious motifs widespread in area, but much simpler to south and in one color; shamans got spirit power from gods, monsters, or heavenly phenomena (such as a constellation in the sky); famous rain-making shamans known in the old days.

Middle Division

DISTINCTIVE RELIGIOUS ELEMENTS This was the division where Shoshone dialects prevailed, and these people seem to have had a more spiritual, philosophic, and esoteric view of religion than the peoples to the north or south, with belief in one god and an interest in the stars and the mysteries of the heavens; the assistant chief usually acted as the director of ceremonies in the religion; sand paintings used in religious ceremonies and were more symbolic and geometric than with the Kamia to the south; sand paintings used in *both* boys' and girls' initiation rites; older youth were put through a torture rite and initiation, using red ants to bite them; boys were given toloache to drink to give them visions (usually of guardian spirits) as part of special initiation into manhood; girls had initiation ceremony in which they swallowed balls of tobacco without throwing them up to prove their virginity, and they were kept for a few days in a pit with grass around them, warmed by heated stones; sermons were given to the youth of both sexes by the ceremonial chief on how to behave in an honorable way and avoid such things as being punished by avenging animals; legends of this area were sometimes rather chaotic, with people in them changing from bad to good and back again; dead were cremated (as also among Kamia).

Chumash Division

DISTINCTIVE SOCIAL ELEMENTS   Probably had the largest and most well-organized villages in southern California.

DISTINCTIVE RELIGIOUS ELEMENTS   Beautiful polychrome cave paintings were made, often in several colors, probably symbolic and spiritual in meaning; toloache probably used for individual vision seeking, but not with the elaborate ceremonies of the middle division; dead were put into graves in fetal position; no cremation.

Kamia Division

DISTINCTIVE SOCIAL ELEMENTS   Cave paintings quite simple and made with red paint; more stubborn and warlike in their resistance to foreign encroachment than other southwestern California tribes; many small clans, but individual could not marry into either father's or mother's clan.

DISTINCTIVE RELIGIOUS ELEMENTS   Sand paintings used at ceremonies for boys but not for girls; sand paintings show circles of heavenly bodies and realistic animals instead of geometric figures (Kamia were more interested in world as it is, not mystic meanings); girl's adolescence ceremony of old type (immolation in a special hut), without Toloache cult ceremony or use of sand paintings; eagle dance and toloache ceremonies of Toloache religion were used, but were only recently acquired and so were sung in foreign language of the Tongva.

Appendix D. Native Languages of the Pacific Coast

The following outline of the languages found in the areas described in this book follows more or less closely the ideas of the following anthropologists: R. B. Dixon, Philip Drucker, Jack D. Forbes, Alfred L. Kroeber, Marshall Newman, and Morriss Swadesh. The outline tries to show, in as clear a way as possible, how the tribes described or mapped in the book are related to each other linguistically. From this we can draw the conclusion that at some time the different groups had common centers of origin. Often their legends give hints as to where they came from, as when the Kwakiutl and Nootka tell of long-ago journeys out of the southwest, and the Tlingit and the Haida tell of the coming of some of their ancestors from the east. Most of the language families listed are fairly definite in showing relationships of the tribes named, but two, the Penutian and the Algonquin, have tribes mentioned that are much more difficult to relate to each other. Only time and much more research will determine how true the pictures of these two families given here can be.

Classification of Native Languages of the Pacific Coast (see also maps for names and locations of tribes)

ALEUT-ESKIMO LANGUAGE FAMILY
    A. Eskimo sub-family
        1. Southwestern Alaskan Eskimo division (Sugpiaq)
    B. Aleut sub-family
        1. Unalaskan division (Eastern Aleut)
        2. Atkan division (Western Aleut)

ATHAPASKAN LANGUAGE FAMILY

A. Northern Athapaskan sub-family
    1. Tanaina-Ingalik division
    2. Tahltan-Kaska division
    3. Tutchone-Ahtena-Tagish division
B. Divergent Athapaskan sub-family
    1. Tlingit division
    2. Haida division
    3. Eyak division
C. Pacific Coast Athapaskan sub-family
    1. Washington Athapaskan division (Tlatskanie, Kwalhiokwa)
    2. Oregon Athapaskan division (Tututni, Chetco, Tolowa)
    3. California Athapaskan division (Hupa-Whilkut branch: Hupa, Whilkut, Chilula; Nung-gahl branch: Kato, Mattole, Sinkyone, Nongatl, Wailaki, Lassik)

PENUTIAN LANGUAGE FAMILY

A. Tsimshian sub-family
    1. Tsimshian division
    2. Coast Tsimshian division
    3. Niska division
    4. Gitskan division
B. Chinook sub-family
    1. Chinook division
    2. Clatsop division
    3. Cowlitz division
    4. Wishram division
C. Oregon Penutian sub-family
    1. Alsea division
    2. Coos division
    3. Siuslaw division
    4. Umpqua division
D. Kalapuyan sub-family
    1. Kalapuya division (Willamette Valley)
E. Takelma sub-family (language isolate)
F. California Penutian sub-family
    1. Maidu division (Maidu, Konkow, Nisenan)

2. Mewan-Wintu division (Wintu-Nomlaki branch: Wintu, Wintun [Nomlaki]; Patwin branch: Patwin, Suisun; Mewan branch: Miwok, Plains Miwok, Saklan, Coast Miwok, Lake Miwok)
3. Ohlonean (Costanoan) division
4. Yokut division

MOSAN LANGUAGE FAMILY

A. Wakashan sub-family
  1. Kwakiutl division (Southern Kwakiutl, Xaihais, Northern Heiltsuk, Haisla, Wikeno, Southern Heiltsuk)
  2. Nootka division (Nootka, Makah)
B. Salishan sub-family
  1. Bella Coola division
  2. Coast Salish division (British Columbia branch: Comox, Pentlatch, Setchelt, Squamish, Nanaimo, Cowichan, Strait Salish, Halkomelem; Washington branch: Lummi, Nooksak, Skagit, Klallam, Quinault, Chehalis, Twana, Duwamish, Snoqualmi, Puyallup; Oregon branch: Tillamook)
C. Chemakum sub-family
  1. Quileute division
  2. Hoh division
  3. Chemakum division

ALGONQUIN LANGUAGE FAMILY

A. Ritwan sub-family
  1. Yurok division
  2. Wiyot division (Sulatelak)

YUKIAN LANGUAGE FAMILY

A. Yuki sub-family
  1. Coast Yuki division
  2. Huchnom division
  3. Yuki division
B. Miyakma sub-family
  1. Miyakma division (Wappo)

HOKAN LANGUAGE FAMILY

A. Northern California sub-family
   1. Palaihnihan division (Achomawi, Atsugewi)
   2. Shastan division (Shasta, Kahutineruk [New River Shasta], Okwanuchu)
   3. Karok division (Karok)
B. Yana sub-family
   1. Yana division
   2. Yahi division
C. Pomoan sub-family
   1. Pomo division
D. Esselen sub-family
   1. Esselen division
E. Iskoman sub-family
   1. Salinan division
   2. Stishini division (Obispeno)
   3. Chumash division
F. Yuman sub-family
   1. Kamia division (including Ipai and Tipai, also called Diegueño)
   2. Paipai division

UTO-AZTECAN LANGUAGE FAMILY

A. Shoshonean sub-family
   1. Tubatulabal division (Tubatulabal)
   2. Vitamic division (Tongva [Gabrieliño, Fernandeño], Maringayam [Serrano], Atahum [Luiseño, Juaneño], Cahuila [Iviatim], Kupangakitom [Cupeno])
   3. Nemeh division (Western Mono)

Bibliography

BAGLEY, CLARENCE B. *Indian Myths of the Northwest*. Seattle: Lawman and Hanford Co. Reproduction by Shorey Bookstore, 1971.

BECKHAM, STEPHEN DOW. *Requiem for a People; the Rogue Indians and the Frontiersmen*. Norman, Okla.; University of Oklahoma Press, 1971.

BOAS, FRANZ. *Tsimshian Texts*. Bureau of American Ethnology, Bulletin 27 (1902). Washington, D.C.: Smithsonian Institution.

———. *Kwakiutl Ethnography*. Edited and abridged, with an introduction by Helen Codrie. Chicago: University of Chicago Press, 1966.

COLLINS, JUNE MCCORMICK. *The Upper Skagit Indians of Western Washington*. Seattle: University of Washington Press, 1974.

CONROTTO, EUGENE L. *Miwok Means People*. Fresno, Calif.: Valley Publishers, 1973.

CRESSMAN, L. S. *The Sandal and the Cave—The Indians of Oregon*. Portland: Beaver Books, 1944.

DAVIS, JAMES T.; KROEBER, A. L.; HEIZER, ROBERT F.; AND ELSASSER, ALBERT B. *Aboriginal California—Three Studies in Culture History*. University of California Archaeological Research Facility. Berkeley: University of California Press, 1963.

DENSMORE, FRANCIS. *Music of the Maidu Indians*. Los Angeles: Southwest Museum, 1958.

DRIVER, HAROLD E. *Wappo Ethnography*. University of California Publications in American Archaeology and Ethnology 36 (1940): 179–220. Berkeley: University of California Press.

DRUCKER, PHILIP. *Contributions to Alsea Ethnography*. University of California Publications in American Archaeology and Ethnology 35 (1943):81–102. Berkeley: University of California Press.

———. *The Tolowa and their Southwestern Oregon Kin*. University of California Publications in American Archaeology and Ethnology 36 (1940):221–300. Berkeley: University of California Press.

———. *A Karok World-Renewal Ceremony at Panaminik*. University of California Publications in American Archaeology and Ethnology 35 (1943):23–28. Berkeley: University of California Press.

————. *Cultures of the North Pacific Coast.* New York: Chandler Publishing Co., 1965.

DU BOIS, CORA. *Wintu Ethnography.* University of California Publications in American Archaeology and Ethnology 36 (1935–1939): 1–148. Berkeley: University of California Press, 1940.

ERIKSON, ERIK H. *Observations on the Yurok: Childhood and World Image.* University of California Publications in American Archaeology and Ethnology 35 (1934–1943):257–301. Berkeley: University of California Press, 1943.

FORBES, JACK D.; GORMAN, CARL N.; MARTIN, KENNETH R.; AND RISLING, DAVID, JR. *Handbook for the Development of Native American Studies.* Davis, Calif.: Native American Studies, Tecumseh Center, University of California, 1970.

GARFIELD, VIOLA E., AND WINGERT, PAUL S. *The Tsimshian Indians and Their Arts.* Publication XVIII of the American Ethnological Society. Seattle: University of Washington Press.

GIBBS, GEORGE. *A Dictionary of the Chinook Jargon, or Trade Language of Oregon.* New York: Cramoisy Press, 1863. Reprinted, New York: Amspress, 1970.

GODDARD, PLINY EARL. *Indians of the Northwest Coast.* New York: Cooper Square Publishers, 1972.

GODDARD, PLINY L. *Life and Culture of the Hupa.* University of California Publications in American Archaeology and Ethnology Vol. 1, No. 1. Berkeley: University of California Press, 1903.

GOLDSCHMIDT, WALTER R., AND DRIVER, HAROLD E. *The Hupa White Deerskin Dance.* University of California Publications in American Archaeology and Ethnology, 35 (1934–1943):103–142. Berkeley: University of California Press, 1943.

HEIZER, ROBERT F. *Languages, Territories and Names of California Indian Tribes.* Berkeley: University of California Press, 1966.

HEIZER, ROBERT F.; DAVIS, JAMES T.; AND KROEBER, A. L. *Aboriginal California—Three Studies in Culture History.* University of California Archaeological Research Facility. Berkeley: University of California Press, 1963.

JACOBS, MELVILLE. *Coos Myth Texts.* University of Washington Publications in Anthropology. Vol. 8, No. 2, Pp. 127–260. Seattle: University of Washington Press, 1940.

JOHNSTON, BERNICE E. *California's Gabrieleno Indians.* Los Angeles: Southwest Museum, 1962.

KIRK, RUTH, AND DAUGHERTY, RICHARD P. *Hunters of the Whale, An Adventure in Northwest Coast Archaeology.* New York: William Morrow, 1974.

KNIFFER, FRED B. *Pomo Geography.* University of California Publications in American Archaeology and Ethnology 36 (1940):353–400. Berkeley: University of California Press.

KRAUSE, AUREL. *The Tlingit Indians, Results of a Trip to the Northwest Coast of America and the Bering Straits.* Seattle: University of Washington Press, 1956.

KROEBER, A. L. *Yurok and Neighboring Kin Term Systems.* University of California Publications in American Archaeology and Ethnology 35 (1934–1943):15–22. Berkeley: University of California Press, 1943.

———. *Handbook of the Indians of California.* Berkeley: California Book Co., 1953.

KROEBER, THEODORA. *The Inland Whale, Nine Stories Retold from California Indian Legends.* Berkeley: University of California Press, 1959.

KROEBER, THEODORA, AND HEIZER, ROBERT F. *Almost Ancestors.* San Francisco: Sierra Club, 1968.

LANTIS, MARGARET. *Alaskan Eskimo Ceremonialism.* Seattle: University of Washington Press, 1947.

MCFEAT, TOM, ed. *Indians of the North Pacific Coast.* Seattle: University of Washington Press, 1966.

MCREAVY, JOHN MORGAN. *Makah Indian Whale Hunters.* Healdsburg, Calif.: Naturegraph Publishers, 1973.

MERRIAM, HART C. *Studies of California Indians.* Berkeley: University of California Press, 1962.

MOCHAN, MARIAN JOHNSON. *Masks of the Northwest Coast.* Milwaukee Public Museum, 1966.

NELSON, EDWARD W. *The Eskimo About Bering Strait.* 18th Annual Report of the Bureau of American Ethnology, 1596–97.

NIBLACK, ALBERT P. *The Coast Indians of Southern Alaska and Northern British Columbia.* Originally published 1890. Reprinted, New York: Johnson Reprint Corporation, 1971.

NORNLAND, GLADYS AYER. *Sinkyone Note.* University of California Publications in American Archaeology and Ethnology 36 (1940):149–178. Berkeley: University of California Press.

OBERG, KALAVERO. *The Social Economy of the Tlingit Indians.* Seattle: University of Washington Press, 1973.

OSWALT, WENDELL H. *Alaskan Eskimos.* New York: Chandler Publishing Co., 1967.

OWEN, ROGER C.; DEETZ, JAMES F.; AND FISHER, ANTHONY D., eds. *The North American Indians, A Source Book.* New York: Macmillan, 1967.

SMYLY, JOHN, AND SMYLY, CAROLYN. *Those Born at Koona.* Saonichton, British Columbia: Hancock House Publishers, 1973.

SPOTT, ROBERT, AND KROEBER, A. L. *Yurok Narratives.* University of California Publications in American Archaeology and Ethnology 35 (1934–1943):143–256. Berkeley: University of California Press, 1943.

POWERS, STEPHEN. *Tribes of California.* Contributions to North American Ethnology, Vol. 3. Washington, D.C.: Smithsonian Institution.

PREBLE, DONALD. *Yamino—Kwaiti.* Caldwell, Idaho: Caxton Printers, 1948.

RICH, JOHN M. *Chief Seattle's Unanswered Challenge.* Privately published, 1932.

ROSMAN, ABRAHAM, AND RUBEL, PARLA G. *Feasting with Mine Enemy!* New York: Columbia University Press, 1971.

SAUTER, JOHN, AND JOHNSON, BRUCE. *Tillamook Indians of the Oregon Coast.* Portland: Binfords and Mart Publishers, 1974.

SWANTON, JOHN P. *Haida Texts and Myths.* Bureau of American Ethnology, Bulletin 29. Washington, D.C.: Smithsonian Institution, 1905.

SWANTON, JOHN R. *Indian Tribes of Washington, Oregon and Idaho.* Fairfield, Washington: Ye Galleon Press, 1968.

WARBURTON, AUSTEN D., AND ERDERT, JOSEPH F. *Indian Lore of the North California Coast.* Santa Clara, Calif.: Pacific Pueblo Press, 1966.

WATERMAN, T. T., AND KROEBER, A. L. *Yurok Marriages.* University of California Publications in American Archaeology and Ethnology 35 (1934–1943):1–14. Berkeley: University of California Press, 1943.

———. *The Kepel Fish Dam.* University of California Publications in American Archaeology and Ethnology 35 (1934–1943):49–80. Berkeley: University of California Press, 1943.

Index